Wilkinson
Granite Dells Ranch
Prescott, Arizona

Fire and Movement

Fire and Movement:

Bargain-Basement Warfare in the Far East

by JAC WELLER

THOMAS Y. CROWELL COMPANY
Established 1834 New York

Designed by Edwin H. Kaplin

Manufactured in the United States of America
by Vail-Ballou Press, Inc., Binghamton, N.Y.

L.C. Card 67-18528

FIRST PRINTING

Acknowledgment is made to Newsweek, Inc., for permission to reprint material from "The Bloody Checkerboard," which appeared in *Newsweek* on May 23, 1966, copyright, Newsweek, Inc., May 1966.

To the fighting men of the Free World
in Vietnam and Malaysia

Preface

⁣llllllllllllllllllllllllllllllllllllllllllllllllllllllllllllllllllllllllllllll

The major purpose of this book is to describe the weapons and tactics of all forces in the Far East, whether presently engaged or not, with emphasis on small units, particularly those which fight mostly on foot. In order to present a meaningful picture, I have touched on some other aspects of the situation including the historical evolution of bargain-basement war, the socioeconomic status of the Far Eastern nations and, occasionally, have included details of civil and political actions.

Some parts of the manuscript originally were dictated in the humid heat of the U.S. Marine base at Danang; other portions in a military barracks in the snowy New Zealand hills while wearing every stitch of clothing I possessed at the time—including my rainhood. I enjoyed good fortune in big and small things and had unusual privileges for a civilian.

Many officers in the U.S., British, and allied armed forces contributed to this effort. They were almost always efficient and considerate, whether or not public information was one of their responsibilities. I want to thank particularly those men who had most to do with arranging my military visits: Lt. Col. Chuck Burtyk at the Pentagon, Col. Don Derryberry at USMC headquarters, and Lt. Col. David Rooke of the British Ministry of Defence. Their efforts both before and after my Far East travel are truly appreciated.

Many individuals aided me in my on-the-spot research. To name a few only is always unfair, but there is no other choice. Among the Marines I want to thank are Lt. Gen. Lew Walt and many in his efficient III Marine Amphibious Force in Vietnam, Col. Tom Greene in Japan, and Maj. Bill McMillan on Okinawa.

I appreciate the assistance of the U.S. Army. Lt. Col. Bob Nelson, Maj. Jack Baker, Lt. Col. John Houghen, Maj. A. S. Strange, and Maj. Frank Laroux, all in Vietnam; Col. Stacy Capers, U.S. Army and United Nations Command Public Information Officer in South Korea; and Col. Neil Groves, U.S. Military Attaché at Wellington, New Zealand, were extremely helpful.

Col. Charles Laughton's British Public Information organization for the Far East was magnificent. Special thanks are due to Maj. Terry Compton-Bishop in Hong Kong, Maj. Sherry Sherbrooke in Singapore, and Lt. Col. John Woodhouse and Capt. Mike Day in Borneo. Col. Peter Andrews and Col. Peter Hall showed me the outstanding British Jungle Warfare School in Jahore; Col. Andrews gave me extremely valuable help with baffling ambiguities later.

Australia was a revelation. I appreciate particularly the remarkable knowledge of weapons which Col. R. S. Garland and Maj. Peter Badcoe made available to me at their School of Infantry and the time and clear presentation of Australian jungle warfare aims of Col. K. A. Peddle of Canungra. The Aussies are fine people; they even managed to get me a shot at a kangaroo.

New Zealanders were equally helpful, efficient, and kind, particularly Maj. Jim Brown and Capt. David Walton. I also am indebted to Capt. Camilinio Curaming for more than he realizes. He not only showed me the Republic of the Philippines Army and Constabulary, but also made clear so much that I did not understand about Southeast Asia.

Closer to home, the generosity of Bill Davis in sharing his superb knowledge of small arms is truly and deeply appreciated. Jerry Stowe, Curator at West Point, helped with weapons and gave his personal time for experiments and photographs. Mrs. Martha Holler, in charge of Pentagon Accreditation, also helped—often in a remarkably short time.

Again I thank my small staff headed by my wife. She made arrangements for travel, inoculations, and dozens of other things; she also kept track of appointments and collected material from those visited throughout a hectic fourteen weeks. My secretaries transcribed disks that many people would have found unintelligible due to physical damage or improper dictating habits and rewrote from notes that even I could not read a few days after writing them.

I apologize for errors that will undoubtedly creep into this manuscript, even if they are not present initially. East Asia will change during the time the book is in production. I hope, however, that future developments will not interfere too greatly with the subject matter itself. The original idea was not to write an article of current interest, but rather to describe a situation that has come about over the years with emphasis on low-level weapons and tactics. Fortunately, these change slowly. But the present war in Vietnam, which has been my major source for tactical examples, could cease, get bigger, or evolve in some other way. Similar combat in other areas appears, however, to be the curse of evolving nations and may be sporadically alive in the world for the rest of the century.

Jac Weller

Princeton, New Jersey

Contents

|||||||||||||||||||||||||||||||||||||||||||||||||||||||||||||||||||||||||||||||||

Illustrations

‖‖‖

Soldiers in star fortification bunker with U.S. 1919 medium machine gun

Typical delta country seen from helicopter

U.S. infantryman with 3.5-inch rocket launcher

81-mm mortar on Bien Hoa perimeter

Jeep with U.S. M60 medium machine gun on swivel mount

UH1B U.S. Army helicopter

U.S. 4.2-inch mortar and crew

Two Air Force F-100's

Generals Lew Walt and Thi, U.S. and ARVN I Corps CG's

Following page 174:

General Walt, USMC Ontos, and crew

General Walt addressing newly arrived Marines

USMC self-propelled 155-mm howitzer

M48M2 tank in support of a Marine rifle battalion

Joint maneuvers by USMC and Royal Thai Marines in Thailand

Thai infantrymen supported by M41 light tank

U.S.-South Korean army position just south of demilitarized zone in South Korea

ROK infantrymen with 60-mm mortar

Japanese soldiers with a Type 62 general purpose machine gun

Japanese officer firing a Type 64 infantry rifle

Australian soldiers on 6 X 6 truck

Energa antitank rifle grenade and the self-loading rifle

Tables

‖‖‖

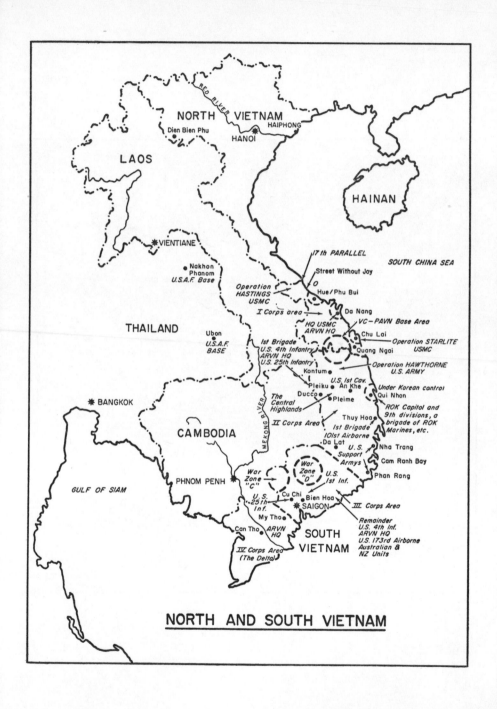

NORTH AND SOUTH VIETNAM

1: Starlite

||||||||||||||||||||||||||||||||||||||||||||||||||||||||||||||||||||||||||||||||||||||||||||||||

U.S. Marines won a three-day battle south of Chu Lai which began on 18 August 1965. There will probably be larger U.S. victories in South Vietnam before the war is over, but not one so important. This action known as Operation Starlite was the first significant American victory. The Viet Cong suffered their first serious defeat.

For many months Vietnamese Government forces with more than 500,000 troops in various battle zones had accomplished little. They were often defeated; when they claimed to have won, the operations were usually small or indecisive. Advice from thousands of Americans at many levels was not enough. Combat support from the U.S. Navy and Air Force was insufficient for the Vietnamese armed forces to win decisively in the field.

The VC attacked Government units where and when they liked; these Communists did not always win, but almost never lost. If they had no hope of a victory, they would just disappear for the time being. They had never suffered severe casualties; probably no more than two hundred were lost in any one action. In spite of U.S. combat troops being committed in March 1965, the VC were still usually able to choose the time, place, and manner of their fighting. They managed to keep intact the most important ingredient of all guerrilla propaganda, the inevitability of their own final victory based on their avoidance of serious defeat. The U.S. Marines changed this in Starlite. They caught the First VC Regulars, perhaps the best regiment in the Communist army, made it fight at a time and place not of its own choosing, and destroyed it as a combat force for several months.

1

Early in 1965 the VC were particularly strong in the I Corps Area, which is the quarter of the country closest to North Vietnam and Communist China. The South Vietnamese armed forces held only the ground within their fortifications; they had lost most of the roads and many towns and villages. ARVN, the Army of South Vietnam, controlled perhaps as little as 5 per cent of the I Corps Area. U.S. Marines had to be brought in quickly to prevent the capture of the important Danang air base. Maj. Gen. Lewis W. Walt, Jr., took over the Third Marine Division, the First Marine Air Wing, and all other U.S. forces in the I Corps Area on June 4. But the VC were still powerful and active, and they managed to keep the initiative. They were still threatening all installations held by U.S. and ARVN forces in this territory as late as mid-August.

Marines defended and flew from the major airfield at Danang and a minor one to the north at Hue/Phu Bai during the spring of 1965. There was a long strip of relatively unprotected I Corps territory to the south. Another air base like that at Danang was needed quickly. Its construction was begun at Chu Lai some sixty miles to the south by Seabees and Marines who not only did the work, but were ready to protect themselves against the enemy. Planes were using the field long before it was finished. Stepped-up air strikes by fighter-bombers called in by forward observers operating with rifle units and by light reconnaissance fixed-wing aircraft began to hurt the VC not only in casualties, but in morale. The three Marine tactical bases for operations—Hue/Phu Bai, Danang, and Chu Lai—soon became targets for suicide demolition attacks and sudden concentrations of VC mortar fire. The enemy could see a pattern emerging as these three equidistant centers of power started to expand and began offensive operations against them. The VC had some success in small attacks because it was impossible to maintain airtight perimeter defenses which could hold them out of all areas from which their mortars could reach profitable targets in the bases. There were not enough Marines available.

RVNAF troops which had to be used to supplement Walt's own units were not always reliable. The VC could learn their exact dispositions and defense plans, probably from ARVN personnel, then push a small ARVN unit back suddenly, and attack grounded U.S. aircraft with mortar fire, or even destroy them with packages of high explosives carried on to the airfield by individual soldiers. This happened on a small scale at all three places. Marine and ARVN units executed sweeps, numerous patrols, and similar offensive ground operations near these bases with inconclusive results. The VC appeared to have prior information about the time and place of these attacks and shifted their positions accordingly.

On 16 August 1965, however, General Walt's expanding intelligence system came up with a report that the Chu Lai airfield was about to be attacked by a large VC force from the south. This was not another raid or even a hit-and-run operation, but something bigger. There had been rumors about this for several days, but nothing definite. The new information gave the area to be used by the VC for their preoperation concentration and the probable time of the attack. Special U.S. reconnaissance flights by light planes flying low and jets at high altitude for photography were ordered immediately. They confirmed both the concentration and its location. A VC force larger than a battalion was assembling in the Van Thuong Peninsula, a rugged rectangle with the sea on two sides located southeast of the Chu Lai airfield perimeter. Most of this area was out of range of artillery then at Chu Lai, but close enough for the VC to attack the new Marine base in heavy strength efficiently.

General Walt reviewed all intelligence gathered and decided within minutes to beat the VC to the punch. The Van Thuong concentration occupied territory about four and a half miles long by two and a half miles wide. The South China Sea stretched along one long and one short side; the Chu Lai perimeter occupied the northwest end. If the last was beefed up and the long inland side closed suddenly, the whole area would be sealed off. Since Korea Marines have been practicing envelopment maneuvers in which a portion of the total assault force comes across beaches and the rest lands well inland from helicopters. This new procedure was now to be used for the first time against real opposition.

Companies E, G, and H of the Fourth Marine Infantry Regiment were to come in by air and form the northern half of the long land side of the rectangle. Companies I, K, and L of the Third Regiment were to come in by sea; they were to be supported by two platoons of tanks—a total of nine regular M48A2 tanks and two flame throwers—and eight Ontos, light armored vehicles mounting six 106-mm recoilless rifles each. A total of fifteen heavy amphibious armored vehicles, often used in Marine operations on shore as armored personnel carriers, were to help carry Companies I, K, and L into position. The initial attack was made by a total of slightly fewer than 1800 Marines.

Artillery support was to be provided by two 155-mm howitzers located at the southern end of the Chu Lai enclave—the 105-mm howitzers there would not reach far enough—the 6-inch dual purpose guns of the cruiser U.S.S. *Galveston,* and similar 5-inch weapons of the destroyers *Orleck* and *Prichard.* Five 155-mm self-propelled howitzers were to move south within the Chu Lai perimeter after the action started and be ready to add their fire, if it was required. These armored vehicles look like big tanks, but do not have as much protection.

The first attacking Marines came from the Chu Lai enclave, but temporary replacements had to be brought in from Danang and Hue/Phu Bai. The Third Battalion, Seventh Regiment, newly assigned to the Third Marine Division, was loaded into an assault carrier so as to be ready to support this operation as necessary. The whole division was stretched thin. There were not enough Marines in I Corps Area at that time to provide a strike force of this size without dislocations. Cooks were in defensive perimeters around the Marine enclaves; everybody ate canned rations.

Starlite was, as finally conceived, a joint operation involving Marine air and ground forces, Marine helicopters, units of the U.S. Air Force, and the U.S. Navy. Tactical over-all control was to be established ashore as soon as possible by Seventh Marine headquarters, but General Walt was planning to be on hand personally. Certain other Marine units were available for use, including a helicopter mobile Howtar battery of six special light airborne cannon capable of firing powerful 107-mm shells precisely. No ARVN units were to be used in the initial attack; information in connection with the assault was not sent to ARVN until shortly before it started, too late for a leak to the VC to do any harm.

On the morning of August 18 at 0630 hours three helicopter landing zones were attacked suddenly and in heavy strength with bombs, shells, bullets, and napalm from fixed-wing aircraft and by naval gunfire to clear them of VC. A few minutes later Marine transport helicopters escorted by armed helicopters landed the three rifle companies of the Second Battalion, Fourth Regiment, one in each zone. Meanwhile, the heavily reinforced Third Battalion, Third Regiment crossed the beach and moved inland, dividing into three columns. The two which had farthest to go had five or six tanks each plus several of the great lumbering troop-landing vehicles.

The operation began well: all helicopters and landing vessels hit their targets on time and discharged their assault forces without mishap. The airborne Marines did run into some medium machine-gun fire as they came down in their zones, but it was nothing serious at first. The seaborne landing met no enemy opposition at all crossing the beach. The tanks and landing vehicles could negotiate the low cliff between beach and jungle because of their climbing ability and sharp, heavy steel blades installed on the front of the leading vehicles. The eight Ontos had trouble; the banks at the inshore edge of the beach were too high, but they finally got up where tanks had cleared the way.

One seaborne company came quickly to its starting position; the other two had farther to go, but arrived satisfactorily. All six companies, three airborne and three seaborne, were roughly in line and began their sweep across the rectangle by 0800 hours. Each company spread out so that the six formed almost a continuous line. For a few minutes, the operation went off with astonishing ease; opposition was mainly small-arms fire. Some Marines feared that this would be another "walk in the sun" across territory recently evacuated by the VC.

Suddenly the whole complexion of the operation changed. VC materialized almost underfoot and in hedgerows. There were more than just a battalion of them. Actually all three battalions of the First VC Regiment plus some irregular elements were caught in the rectangle. The enemy fought back with the courage of desperation and the efficiency of fine combat troops. For a period of several hours Marines had all the VC they wanted and more besides. The Communists were firing automatic weapons from various types of concealed fortifications which appeared at first to withstand even the high velocity 90-mm guns of the tanks. The Marine helicopters which were returning with logistic support and to evacuate wounded were particularly hard hit; nearly all were damaged, some seriously.

In spite of heavy casualties the VC held what appears to have been almost a line to oppose the Marines, supported it with mortars throughout its length, and brought quite a number of recoilless rifles into action. For the first time in the Vietnam war Marine rifle battalions were locked on nearly even terms with the VC in bloody fighting.

Even the tanks were having a tough time. One was hit by four enemy 57-mm recoilless rifle rounds and so badly damaged by anti-tank grenades—probably Chinese-made copies of the Russian and German weapons—that the driver's periscopes were useless. The crew reacted characteristically for their corps; hatches were thrown open and heads thrust out. The tank commander began to fire his outside-mounted .50-cal. heavy machine gun at the concealed earthworks around him. The main gun pumped high explosive rounds accurately through meters of dense jungle and into possible bunkers. Even more important, the tank itself began to move against the enemy and crush him with its tracks.

Some personnel carriers helped with .50-cal. machine-gun fire; the Ontos' 106-mm recoilless rifles were all in action. The six rifle companies were temporarily at a disadvantage, however, because their battalion heavy weapons were not yet all in action. They were not as well supported by mortars and recoilless rifles as the enemy. Counting guerrillas as well as hard-core troops, the VC outnumbered the Marines by probably 2 to 1.

General Walt took personal command. A VC counterattack was stopped in its tracks. Discipline and weapons efficiency of the Marines began to assert itself. Walt was either on the ground or flying his own helicopter just overhead to get a better perspective of the whole battle area. He brought to bear quickly and efficiently his entire fighting potential. Fighter-bombers plastered the VC with bombs, rockets, and automatic cannon fire. Naval guns from the light cruiser and two destroyers of the U.S. Seventh Fleet registered accurately on special targets by means of spotting from observation aircraft. The seven 155-mm howitzers in the Chu Lai perimeter were similarly employed. The unique Marine light Howtars were carried in by helicopter and began to fire their powerful shells.

General Walt diverted all helicopters throughout the rest of his corps area to Chu Lai. Only one Marine whirlybird had actually been destroyed, but several had been damaged and put out of operation. These losses were quickly replaced. Vitally needed materiel and support arms arrived by air; wounded Marines were evacuated. Two companies of Seventh Regiment Marines were ordered to come ashore by air; they would be available for a combat assignment well before nightfall.

The VC lost more men during the morning of the eighteenth than they ever had before in any single action in the war. They fought hard and effectively, but the pressure on them began to tell. Toward midafternoon U.S. Marines swept forward throughout two-thirds of their line and captured or destroyed many of the VC fortifications. In the very center, however, where the two Marine rifle battalions joined, the VC still held. Their defenses in this area were extremely strong. Earth and concrete fortifications were cleverly concealed in hedgerows and connected by tunnels with bombproof supply chambers as much as forty feet below ground. This central fortified mass also contained heavier than ordinary recoilless rifles. A flame-throwing tank was destroyed; another standard model was put out of action temporarily by a direct hit on its turret, probably by a 75-mm recoilless rifle. The VC were now occupying an area roughly triangular in shape, with the northeast coast the only open side.

Late in the afternoon the first two companies of the Seventh Regiment Marines to get ashore attacked the central VC position. The rest of their battalion was now coming across the beach. There was not enough daylight for the amphibious portion of this battalion to be effective during the fighting on the first day, but it was available to stop VC counterattacks that night. There were several of these, two delivered viciously and in heavy strength. But the Marines were ready; they now had an abundance of support weapons, from tripod machine guns to Howtars. Illumination from artillery and mortar shells fired high in the air and parachute flares kicked from C-123 aircraft turned night into day. The Marines won all these actions, big and small, but some VC slipped between Marine units and made their escape into the jungle to the west.

Meanwhile other VC were attempting to get away in seagoing boats from the north face of the triangle. The searchlights of the U.S. Seventh Fleet picked up the enemy vessels; gunners resorted to fire techniques they had learned in basic school, but rarely practiced. They were hitting surface targets which they actually saw through their sights.

On the second day the three Marine battalions and their support elements delivered an assault soon after daylight. The central VC fortification was subjected to bombardments from naval guns, airplanes, mortars, and Howtars. It was carried by a combined assault made by Marine infantry, tanks, and Ontos.

Stiff fighting still remained. The area of combat appeared on the map to be all coastal plain, but actually contained some extremely irregular jungle with steep hills and deep small valleys. There were villages, hamlets, and hedgerows with fortifications only slightly weaker than the central strong point taken in the morning. There were many caves, fortified trenches, concrete bunkers, and spider holes. The latter were covered foxholes that could not be detected even when stepped on until the VC inside removed the cover and opened fire. These were deadly when passed over; a VC rifleman could suddenly push off the cover and shoot a Marine in the back.

Organized VC resistance had begun to crumble; individuals were still fighting hard, but not so effectively. Their casualties on land and sea during the night had been heavy, and a decision was probably made by the VC commander before daylight to pull out small units with their mortars, recoilless rifles, and medium machine guns. Individuals, particularly the wounded, merged into the local civilian population, or went into hiding in carefully concealed caves.

Another reason why the VC were not so effective was that they were up against Marines who were now veterans of this type of fighting. Marine units had learned fast that first day and were using the enormous firepower of U.S. M14 rifles and M60 machine guns tested in almost equal combat on a large scale for the first time during this operation. They were also taking full advantage of their battalion support weapons plus Ontos, tanks, artillery, and air power. Their informal but efficient combat teamwork was paying big dividends. Rifle platoons moved under cover of their own direct fire in spite of the nearly impenetrable jungle, the VC, and superhothouse weather.

The sweep to the seashore was completed soon after midday. Another strong VC fortification was discovered in the middle of the line near the coast. But it fell much more quickly than the first because the Marines now had their own blasting power zeroed in and controlled. High-angle naval gunfire joined with the 155 howitzers, air bombing, mortars, and Howtars. Marine riflemen, tanks, and demolition teams captured it easily. The entire original rectangle had been taken.

But Marines had not been combing an area like a big wheatfield in Kansas. Even though relatively small, the peninsula was full of places for the VC to hide. There were not enough Marines to advance shoulder to shoulder. General Walt, after a personal on-the-ground reconnaissance, realized that his first sweep to the sea against heavy opposition had not destroyed all the enemy troops in the area. He ordered a sweep back across the same territory. More VC were discovered. They would shoot from their previously undetected spider holes; groups occasionally opened fire from bunkers not found the first time over. Again some of these defensive positions were connected with others and with deep caves by a system of tunnels. Fighting was intense in small areas. Howtars, Ontos, and tanks once more contributed their fire to support rifle units.

In this second sweep the fighting was not so severe because the VC were now using only rifles and light automatics. VC support weapons appeared to have been withdrawn or buried. At least one new system of tunnels was discovered, but it was not defended efficiently. Marine demolition teams closed all entrances with explosives; its garrison was presumably wiped out.

Darkness came before the second sweep was completed; all three rifle battalions formed perimeters for defense and sent out patrols. There was some short violent fighting, apparently against VC guerrillas not previously engaged. These appear to have been sent in to aid the remnants of VC hard-core units to escape. The third day was spent in searches and mop-up operations of no great significance.

The First Battalion, Seventh Regiment came ashore in the afternoon of the third day. ARVN units were brought in also. The two original battalions of the operation returned to their regular jobs around Chu Lai. Marines borrowed from Danang and Hue/Phu Bai went back to their normal duties. Total Marine casualties amounted to 45 killed and 203 wounded. Some of the latter were at Danang hospitals within an hour after being hit and in the continental U.S. three days later, having received all necessary medical attention including operations at hospitals along the way. The number of Marines killed was less than the death toll of 58 when a transport plane crashed about this time while taking men to Hong Kong for rest and recreation.

VC casualties were not determined precisely, but they probably suffered more than 1600. Marines recovered 641 VC bodies; ARVN units found 380 more in fresh graves. There were about 200 prisoners. Wounded who managed to hide and get away, men blown to bits by 750-pound bombs and 100-pound artillery shells, and those VC dead whose bodies were not recovered from caves, tunnels, and jungle would have surely increased the count considerably. Not many of the VC aboard the 39 vessels blown up by the guns of the U.S. Seventh Fleet escaped, but only a few of these seaborne casualties were ever counted.

Throughout Starlite Vietnamese civilians who gathered in their villages, beside the sea, and in other sheltered places received food, medical attention, and some clothing. Everything possible was done to show them that the Marines were not fighting against them, but only against the VC. On the other hand, many male civilians between the ages of about fifteen and thirty-five were taken into custody as VC suspects. They might have been innocent, but were more probably enemy soldiers who tried to disappear into the civilian population. They were questioned by Marine intelligence units and then turned over to ARVN who flew them to Saigon for further interrogation.

A few days after Starlite, General Walt and his Marines conducted a similar operation which appeared at first to have a chance to succeed even more dramatically. It was known as Piranha and took place only a few miles farther down the coast. But most of the surrounded area had been evacuated by the VC only hours before, perhaps because of a security leak. ARVN units took part in this assault from the start and furnished half the troops taken in by air and across the beaches. If Starlite had not preceded Piranha, the latter would have been called a great victory. Another VC attack on Chu Lai in strength was foiled; an enemy battalion was destroyed as a combat unit for some months. The body count revealed 198 VC dead; known VC prisoners and suspects taken into custody totaled about 300 more.

A careful study of Starlite and Piranha indicates that these victories were not due to luck. General Walt, his staff, and his fighting Marines used a sound system of intelligence, standard operational procedures based on Marine concepts of offensive war, fine equipment, and a facility for changing plans as necessary in order to win. The whole team in each action was professionally competent and delivered 100 per cent when the chips were down.

Operations like these are the high points of successful counterinsurgency. The proper use of intelligence, mobility, and power to surprise, surround, and destroy enemy units as General Walt and his Marines have done erases the image of VC invincibility. If the VC can be made to fight at a time, place, and under conditions not of their choice, the U.S. and its allies will almost invariably win the ensuing action. News of victories of this magnitude spreads fast. If the villagers decide that the U.S. and RVNAF are going to win, they won't help the VC regardless of how much terror is employed. If Communists persist with their coercive policies after they lose their popular support, they become little better than local bandits. Actions like Starlite can be of great importance in guerrilla war. Sometimes what people think is more important than the total number of casualties. Vietnamese civilians were smiling more easily at U.S. military personnel and even at middle-aged U.S. writers in the I Corps Area than anywhere else in their unfortunate country.

Months after these two operations their favorable effect was still felt. The three Marine Corps operating areas sometimes called enclaves are still the most pro-Government spots in South Vietnam. The VC have been unable to concentrate for significant offensive action within them, or even close to them. VC battalions or larger units operating where Marines can employ their amphibious and heliborne landing capabilities and their armor, artillery, and tactical air support are at a great disadvantage. When the VC fight by squads and platoons only, they don't accomplish much. Besides, U.S. Marines are learning to fight effectively at that level, too.

2: Bargain-Basement War

The Marine Corps victories in Starlite, even though of extreme importance, are not typical of counterinsurgency war. Tanks, naval guns, and big self-propelled howitzers cannot often be used against Communist guerrillas. The VC were caught twice in quick succession in areas not well adapted to their greatest relative strengths. They are not likely often to repeat this mistake. The real struggle in Vietnam now and in other similar combat areas of Southeast Asia in the future will be mainly at lower levels. Rifle companies and platoons far less heavily supported than in Starlite and Piranha must do a lot of the fighting.

Starlite may have hurt the U.S. in one respect. Too much effort has gone into trying to repeat operations of this size. The West cannot regularly take such dramatic advantage of its enormous firepower, coordination between separate arms, and superior logistics. If this were possible, Americans would have an easy time in counterguerrilla operations. Insurgents are difficult to defeat with conventional weapons because they avoid contact. They use simple, cheap arms, available everywhere, and employ them in combination with political effort and terror. These conflicts are not unique in military history, but have come to the fore dramatically since 1945.

Conventional war fought by armies operating openly with full support of their nations along regular systems of transportation reached a level of bigness in the twentieth century never approached before. The fighting during World War I soon became essentially vast siege operations in which artillery pieces in unprecedented numbers fired thousands of tons of ammunition mainly to destroy enemy medium machine guns that would otherwise control battlefields. Relatively primitive aircraft, unreliable and slow-moving tanks, and motor transport were all used, but the war was ultimately won and lost by infantry and artillery. Industry and transportation were also important. The side that could produce more war materiel, take it to combat areas, and use it effectively won. But organized armies numbering in the millions were locked in bloody battles which lasted for weeks. Casualties exceeded those of any other war, before or since. Spiritual, moral, and industrial fatigue may also have contributed to the final defeat of the Central Powers.

Astonishing developments in weapons preceded and accompanied World War II. Strategic air raids involving a thousand or more planes became common. The belligerents managed to avoid much of the trench warfare of World War I. Even though both sides on occasion paid some frightful "butcher bills" for small territorial gains, mobility, both strategic and tactical, usually prevented protracted trench battles. Strategic mobility was based on railroads, thousands of ships, tens of thousands of motor vehicles, and even transport aircraft. The blitzkrieg tactics used by both sides depended upon internal combustion engines in aircraft, trucks, and tanks. New types of weapons developed rapidly and in almost unbelievable quantities. Efficient logistic support across thousands of miles of ocean became commonplace; more successful major amphibious assaults were made on enemy-held fortified positions during World War II than in all the rest of military history. Airborne landings were also frequent, but probably not so efficient as amphibious assaults in terms of effort expended.

Firepower on land, water, and in the air reached unbelievable heights. Small-arms bullets by the billions were manufactured by the U.S. alone, incorporated in cartridges, transported to combat areas throughout the world, and fired in the direction of the enemy. Other things were in proportion. Some U.S. offensive operations in the Pacific saw a weight of projectiles in excess of the total combined body weight of all defending forces thrown into enemy positions every few minutes. The U.S. battleship *South Dakota* and her sister ships were said to have been able to throw into the sky a weight of antiaircraft projectiles equal to the take-off weight of a Japanese dive bomber every nine seconds.

The articulation of many different types of weapons in the hands of different services on land and sea and in the air into a single combined operation reached a stage that would have been inconceivable to anyone who had not seen it develop. The efficiency of these efforts depended in part on tons upon tons of paper work and communications equipment. Planning and organizing as well as the relatively short-term research and development of wartime harnessed the efforts of enormous military staffs, huge teams of scientists, and thousands of engineers. The cost of the two atomic bombs used against Japan has been computed at more than a billion dollars each.

Total war, World War II style, became so costly that only a few countries could possibly wage it. In addition, the total military potential of nations in this category appears to vary at about the second power of the simple arithmetic sum of all their resources. Wealth, financial and commercial organization, and scientific and industrial production appeared to give one modern nation an enormous ultimate advantage over another with even slightly less of these. Primitive, agrarian countries were simply outclassed. Improvements in transportation and communications have made the world smaller. For a time, the U.S. and Russia appeared to control it completely. Britain and the Anglo-Saxon Commonwealth countries came third, but they were allies of America.

It must be borne in mind that land battles, such as those in World War II, as well as all other battles in the clearly foreseeable future, are won in the final analysis by infantrymen. Although no atomic bomb, aircraft, or tank can hold ground, a rifleman can. But infantry in conventional war—a conflict between world powers who attack each other openly and at maximum outlay of power—must be recruited, trained, equipped, organized, and transported to battlefields. It must also now be supported by other forces of enormous size and complexity, sometimes operating hundreds of miles from ground battlefields. Logistics and other services have almost eliminated hunger, disease, and even boredom. A division in combat consumes hundreds of tons of supplies each day. All this must be based on a powerful, integrated economy. Military spirit, individual bravery and training, and depth of desire will always be important, but so are science, industry, experience, and money.

A countertrend has developed, however, particularly in the Far East. The non-Communist powers, because of their wealth and other assets, tended to dominate much of the world. Russia and her satellites reacted strongly against this situation by giving moral support as well as material aid to people in other countries who would become Communists. The idea from the beginning was violent revolution. But the form that these insurrections took and the manner in which they developed was dependent upon guerrilla rather than conventional strategy and tactics. A few efficient individual arms, medicines, and political techniques supplied from an outside sponsor made mid-twentieth-century guerrillas even more formidable than their predecessors. These wars are cheap to wage, save for human life and misery; they have been called bargain-basement wars.

These new conflicts have assumed great importance since 1945. They are both military and political. On a military plane they are local in scope, but the insurgents take full advantage of world opinion. Improvements in communications and education have created an informed and articulate international population extremely liberal in its collective views. A century ago European gunpower and military discipline could be used when needed to dominate native populations. Colonialism in all forms is not now fashionable, while nationalism usually has an immediate appeal. The insurgents also are aided by the poverty that exists in many parts of the world. There are nations which have little more than a desire for independence. Some are too small and poor in resources to support in the foreseeable future a reasonably modern standard of living. This and their political incapacity doom them to turbulence.

The most active and dangerous bargain-basement war area in the world is now Southeast Asia. Prior to World War II virtually all of this enormous territory was controlled by Western colonial nations, who ran local governments with varying degrees of enlightenment.

The Philippines had already achieved a commonwealth status and were scheduled for complete independence. In Australia and New Zealand British colonists so outnumbered the natives that these two were essentially Western nations. But the Dutch in what is now Indonesia, the French in Indochina, the British in Malaya, Burma, parts of Borneo, and other smaller places, and the Portuguese in their limited holdings all governed numerically much larger native populations. The only exception to this general pattern was Thailand, which had managed to preserve a precarious independence in a reduced area by playing Britain and France against each other.

World War II brought drastic changes in thought patterns of the people of Southeast Asia. The colonial nations were not able to protect their areas of responsibility from Japanese conquest. Oriental soldiers not only defeated those from Europe, but encouraged local nationalism and hatred for white men in most areas. The intellectual climate under which colonialism was accepted, or at least tolerated, in the colonies themselves suddenly disappeared. Even in the Philippines and in British colonies which had enjoyed relative peace, stability, economic progress, and a fair rate of social and educational advancement, control of any type from abroad became unpalatable after the war.

A Filipino whose friendship I value and whose intelligence and good will are beyond question brought this forcibly home to me. He said it would have been impossible, even had the United States wished, to have extended the commonwealth status of the Philippines beyond 1946. "It was better for us to make mistakes than have even Americans, no matter how friendly and unselfish, do jobs right."

Where European nations did attempt to restore colonial governments, strife broke out as a result of the new sense of nationalism. There were also other tensions created by the dislocations and damage of World War II. Communism was already strong in some places, particularly where great poverty and great wealth existed side by side. Local Communists were quick to try to associate themselves with the nationalist movements against the colonial powers. The U.S. did not delay Philippine independence; Britain had the good sense to let India, Pakistan, Ceylon, and Burma go without serious fighting involving British forces. The French in Indochina were not so fortunate; a long bloody war resulted. The Dutch had similar trouble in their Indies. Due to a number of factors, Britain was almost innocently involved in Communist guerrilla war in Malaya. Even though entirely independent, the Philippines were also cursed with Communist-backed insurgents.

On a purely military basis the U.S. and its allies have discovered that big-war combat power cannot be divided and applied in small amounts efficiently against a primitive, resourceful enemy who knows how to use terrain, propaganda, and terror. Some guerrilla techniques have been known since biblical times, but others have been developed in this century. A regular conventional army and air force do not operate well against skillful guerrillas in difficult terrain. Bargain-basement wars are ideal for Communist aggression because they are both cheap and effective.

Groups of individuals have waged war at the cheapest possible levels for thousands of years. Judas Maccabaeus of biblical fame began as a guerrilla in 168 B.C.; his family using essentially guerrilla tactics finally won independence for Judaea in 142 B.C. This was the first time since 586 B.C. that the Jews had ruled themselves. There have been many other instances of similar successes achieved at low cost in money. Francis Marion's guerrilla operations in the southern theatre of the American Revolution were of great value in determining the final extent of the American revolutionary victory. Wellington used Portuguese and Spanish insurgents against the French in the Peninsula between 1808 and 1814. The word "guerrilla" dates from these campaigns.

Communism and world revolution as proposed by Marx, Lenin, and others became associated with guerrilla warfare in the vast land mass of Russia after the Bolshevik revolution in November 1917, but the extensive operations in European Russia and Siberia were not really much like guerrilla wars today. The Communist revolution in China has had far more to do with modern Communist strategy and Southeast Asia's bargain-basement tactics.

A new China appeared to emerge from the old after the revolution of 1911. But the new republic was almost as incapable of dealing with internal and foreign problems as the emperors had been. Foreign troops still remained on Chinese soil in 1941; Britain, Japan, Russia, and the U.S. had exerted undue influence in different areas for long periods.

During the early years after World War I, both nationalism and Communism developed within China. At first these two movements were more or less amalgamated under the Kuomintang party and the Chinese patriot Sun Yat-sen. After Sun Yat-sen's death (12 March 1925), Chiang Kai-shek dominated the Kuomintang. He controlled much of China, but was not powerful enough to maintain Chinese sovereignty. U.S. and British gunboats in the Yangtze protected foreign lives by firing on Nanking, the future Nationalist capital.

On 12 April 1927 Chiang instituted a purge to eliminate Communist and other left-wing elements from his combined party. This led, of course, to a break between Nationalist and Communist forces even before the Kuomintang had won all China. A rival government to that of Chiang in Nanking already existed at Hankow. A kind of three-cornered war ensued; actually it became four-cornered, for the Japanese began to take part in it on a limited basis from Manchuria. For a while Chiang appeared to be winning, against his Chinese enemies at least. He took over areas which he had not formerly governed, in part because of fear of the Communists, or the Japanese, or both. He drove the Communists out of northeastern China; they took temporary refuge far to the south.

Chiang launched five large attacks against Mao Tse-tung and his comrades between December 1930 and October 1933. Finally, in October 1934, the Communists were driven out of southeastern China, but they managed a fighting retreat of several thousand miles—the Long March—to the west and then to the north. After a whole year they arrived in northern Shensi, just south of the Great Wall and far inland.

Meanwhile, Japan had been taking more and more territory from China. Manchuria became the Japanese puppet state of Manchukuo in 1933. Further penetration south across the Great Wall continued;

the provinces of Hopeh and Chahar passed partly into Japanese control in 1935. On 7 July 1937, a general war grew out of a minor clash between the Japanese and Chiang's Kuomintang Nationalists near Peking. The Chinese Communists and Nationalists nominally joined forces against the common enemy. But the Japanese soon beat both in the field and forced Chiang's government to move almost a thousand miles inland to Chungking. The Japanese controlled all the important ports and most of the railroads.

During the six-year period between 1939 and 1944 the Japanese ruled most of eastern China. There was a great deal of bloody fighting between them and both the Nationalists and the Communists, but the foreign invaders were finally able to move their heavy columns hundreds of miles without serious opposition. They could not, however, set up an effective puppet government. The Chinese forces of both Mao and Chiang used guerrilla tactics successfully. The Communists were able to control their areas more effectively because they won the minds and hearts of the people; their rule was based only partly on terror. The Communist Fourth Army composed of several divisions operated on the lower Yangtze entirely behind Japanese lines. The Communist Eighth Route Army did practically the same thing in the mountainous northeast.

The collapse of Japan in August 1945 did not lead to a lasting peace in China. The advantages the Nationalists had over the Communists in 1937 were greatly reduced. While pretending to negotiate, Mao continued to improve his position and made a determined effort to win over Chiang's soldiers. Throughout a large portion of China the Communists already controlled enough people to dominate or kill the rest. Semipermanent guerrilla organizations existed; hard-core Communist armies were more powerful than ever before. The fighting between the forces of Chiang and Mao was at this time mostly on a guerrilla basis, but the latter was building for the day when his armies would be strong enough to fight a conventional war against the Kuomintang. Neither Chinese leader had any real faith in negotiations, which were under the direction of U.S. General George C. Marshall, World War II Chief of Staff of the Army and later Secretary of State and Secretary of Defense.

The Nationalists appeared at first to have the upper hand. They had used U.S. naval and air transport to take over eastern Chinese cities and railroads from the Japanese in the autumn of 1945. They were also able to do the same thing in the north in 1946 and 1947 when the Russians pulled back from Manchuria. But Chiang's forces were overextended. The Communists isolated their enemies in cities cut off from each other by a vast sea of peasant guerrillas reinforced by hard-core or regular, full-time units at unpredictable but usually decisive points.

Mao was able to change from guerrilla tactics to mobile war in Manchuria in 1947; his formations increased in size rapidly. The Nationalist armies in Manchuria were finally destroyed in 1948 by conventional war against an enemy already weakened by political action. Mao moved south and used similar tactics; the Communists took Nanking on 24 April 1949. The Nationalists moved their capital to Canton a thousand miles southwest, but lost this also on 15 October of the same year. Chiang was driven from the mainland and established a third capital at Taipei on Formosa (Taiwan) on 8 December 1949.

This Chinese Revolution established a standard pattern for other Communist insurgency movements. This was true even before it was over. Russia was then more or less directing similar Communist efforts in Southeast Asia, but the influence of Mao grew increasingly important. By 1949 there was already bloody fighting in Indochina, Indonesia, Malaya, the Philippines, and Burma. These wars, always of the bargain-basement type, did not require heavy artillery, tanks, aircraft, and mountains of munitions. Many Communists were already veterans of guerrilla opposition to the Japanese; they not only knew how to wage guerrilla war, but also fully appreciated its effectiveness. The fighting and the political maneuvering were far more carefully planned and scientifically carried out than many people realize. The amount of force is relatively small, but it must be precisely applied for maximum effect.

Before any of these guerrilla conflicts were concluded, the Far East was suddenly jolted to its foundations on 25 June 1950 by the outbreak of what was by comparison a conventional war. Communist North Korea's armed forces attacked across the Thirty-eighth Parallel. The South Korean Government was firmly supported by the U.S. and the United Nations, but it took time before military force—always mainly U.S. units—arrived in sufficient quantity to stop the assault. The United Nations Command, including, of course, units from the Republic of South Korea, held only the Pusan beachhead in heavy fighting during August and early September. But U.S. General Douglas MacArthur, in over-all U.N. command, counterattacked on September 15 both from Pusan and by an amphibious landing at Inchon. The victorious non-Communist forces almost completely overran North Korea, but the Chinese Communists were drawn in "unofficially" by the end of the year. The conflict waxed and waned; MacArthur was not allowed to bomb China. Even though the Chinese did not have modern weapons in adequate quantity, they made up for this lack with more numerous and more experienced soldiers and various expedients learned in part in guerrilla war. The conflict lasted until July 1953 and then subsided into an uneasy armistice almost where it started three years before.

The Chinese Communists found themselves a world power in 1953. But they were probably closer to defeat than the world realized. Their industrial capacity, systems of transportation, and gross national product did not allow them to wage even their modification of modern conventional war without severe damage to their economy. They did not want any more battles in the open where U.S. air power, heavy artillery, and massive logistic support could be brought into full operation. Mao, no less militant than before, was convinced that bargain-basement wars were the best means for China to achieve Asiatic and eventually world domination.

Communist China has begun to advance in scientific and industrial capacity. Her accomplishments are not as startling as those of Russia, but progress is being made. The two great Communist powers now see the future differently. The Russian standard of living has risen higher than the Chinese. Russia is no longer a vast agrarian nation without suitable targets for nuclear weapons, but rather a modern, extensively integrated society that could be irreparably damaged in a nuclear war. There were signs of friction even before the leaders of the two nations became openly critical of each other in 1960. With small, temporary reversals this trend has continued. One of the most important questions of our time is the extent of this cleavage.

After Korea the Chinese rather than the Russians became the foremost world exporters of new Communist insurgency war. Mao did not even attempt to capture the offshore islands still held by Chiang's Nationalists; these are within medium artillery range of the Chinese mainland. But Chinese Communists sponsored guerrilla fighting thousands of miles away. China obviously supported the Viet Minh against the French, and now does the same for the VC through North Vietnam.

The Chinese have become proficient, however, in supplying more than ideology and weapons. They have tied together almost in a single package a lot of their own experience and know-how. Mao himself is important in this. He was born in east central China in 1893 of peasant stock, but acquired an unusually good education. After graduating from a school for teachers he served as a librarian in Peking University. He was one of the early Chinese Communists and was fortunate to survive Chiang's purge of 1927. Mao was an early organizer of the Communist resistance in South Central China and directed the Long March in 1934–35. He was one of the important thinkers of the guerrilla period and by far the most articulate of them; he has written voluminously and well.

The first and foremost principle of guerrilla war, according to Mao, is the paramount and permanent importance of civil action. The minds of the people are where the war is won and lost. Mao insisted on strict discipline, honesty, and helpfulness in the actions of his guerrillas toward the people. All military operations had to further political objectives, or they were not to be undertaken. Every period of military inactivity is to be utilized to promote further Communist indoctrination both within the guerrilla units themselves and among the people. Self-criticism—the time-honored human need in the form of confession—was introduced and is used to the full for control, as well as for its beneficial effect on most individuals.

Mao at first had to use inferior forces, both in number and in the quality of their training, discipline, and weapons. But the Communists fought only when they had an advantage. In Mao's theory of war there was disgrace not in running away, but only in fighting at a time and place favoring the enemy. Mobility and surprise were the major ingredients in thousands of small Communist victories. Intelligence was important and came principally from the people. Mao realized that inherently guerrillas would be less well armed and equipped than their enemies, but he saw no great disadvantage in this. If guerrilla arms had only short effective ranges, combat was begun at close quarters. Mao wrote in 1938:

The equipment of guerrillas cannot be based on what the guerrillas want, or even what they need, but must be based on what is available for their use. Equipment cannot be furnished immediately, but must be acquired gradually. Each combat soldier should be armed with a rifle. If there are not enough rifles, each squad should have two or three. Shotguns, lances, and big swords can also be furnished. The distribution of rifles does not have to be equalized in platoons. As different missions are assigned to platoons, it may be necessary to give one platoon more rifles than another.

Mao also realized the importance of home or village manufacture of materiel. Chinese craftsmen copied not only rifles and pistols designed elsewhere, but also produced land mines, mortars, and automatic small arms. Repairs, reloading of cartridges, and simple manufacture of hand grenades and edged weapons went on in each guerrilla district. Mao may not have invented primitive booby traps, but he fully endorsed their employment not only because of their effect on the enemy, but because they were good for the morale of friendly civilians who made most of them.

Unlike some guerrilla leaders that have come after him, Mao did not pretend that guerrilla war was inherently strong, but acknowledged its weaknesses. Strong conventional operations conducted by healthy, disciplined, and well-organized troops provided with modern weapons and ammunition and supported along secure regular lines of transportation are obviously more desirable. Permanent orderly control of areas based upon obvious government is superior to clandestine domination in part by terror. But bargain-basement war is used because nothing better is possible. Guerrilla activity is cheap for an outside sponsor and can sometimes be started with an astonishingly small number of friendly civilians. This type of conflict is all that is available to the politically dissatisfied and the have-nots in many areas.

Mao also formalized three stages in guerrilla war in his writings. First comes organization and the establishment of bases within the civilian population, including what is now called infrastructure. In this stage fighting is kept to a minimum in order to win as many people as possible without alerting the enemy, but terror is used against unpopular people of importance. The second stage includes most of what we now think of as typical guerrilla war. There are ambushes and surprise attacks on defended positions, terror in much larger doses against common people who refuse to join, assassinations of government soldiers, and some operations by battalion- and company-sized units from controlled bases in inaccessible areas. For a complete victory Mao believed that a third stage of almost conventional war was necessary. His own operations against Chiang in 1947–49 were of this type.

The Communists were able to pass on to new guerrillas a number of techniques which they either developed themselves in their own revolution, or witnessed as advisers in other guerrilla struggles. These have become standard for use by guerrillas throughout Southeast Asia and elsewhere. Properly applied, these enable rudely armed and poorly equipped peasants to win against superior weapons, technology, and logistics. But the techniques are often diabolically clever and require careful training, planning, and first-rate leadership. Further, they are usually practical only where the guerrillas have a cause which appears to them to be worth their extreme sacrifices, even to life itself.

Perhaps the most important of Mao's teachings are in connection with camouflage, darkness, and difficult terrain. Men moving at night on foot are difficult to detect or attack by regular troops who do not know the area well. Supplies which are carried by humans or animals, or pushed or pulled on some primitive wheeled cart—even on an ordinary bicycle—along jungle trails are nearly impervious to interruption by air power. Camouflage at all levels from an individual rifleman to a battery of heavy mortars can be extremely effective, particularly against enemies from more urbanized nations who generally do not observe closely.

The Chinese Communists also stressed the usefulness of earth and concrete fortifications connected by tunnels to each other and to chambers deep in the ground. These can neutralize high-explosive firepower from artillery or bombers. Since these can be built with little besides human labor—the work itself is good for morale —and can be camouflaged quickly and almost perfectly in growing vegetation, they are extremely valuable. The rifleman inside may be undersized, undertrained, underfed, and armed with an inferior weapon, but he has obvious advantages. Even if only one fortification in a hundred is ever used, the guerrillas are ahead.

The Chinese also have exported some do-it-yourself materiel expedients. Mortars and ammunition for them are cheaper and more easily transported than artillery. They can be produced by village artisans who receive proper instruction. Even high-explosive bursting charges can be manufactured simply. Mines of large size and power—those used for antitank missions—are still relatively cheap. Electric circuits to control them can also be rigged with simple equipment. Enthusiasm for self-produced makeshifts, however, has not prevented Chinese advisers from pointing out to their protégés the great value of some light, modern weapons either supplied by China or taken from opposing government forces. Rocket launchers, recoilless rifles, and similar devices don't weigh too much and can knock out tanks. Machine guns firing .50- and .30-cal. rounds are capable of bringing down hostile aircraft, if skillfully and courageously operated. These weapons also aid the insurgents psychologically.

The Chinese realize that to encourage local Communists to fight governments aligned with the Free World was to steer a collision course. They probably know that the U.S. has the power to defeat them quickly and completely in nuclear war. But can this power be used? Mao and his associates obviously believe that it cannot be. One reason is retaliation by Russia against America directly. The efficiency of this deterrent is now suspect, but world opinion probably precludes the use of nuclear explosives against targets which contain vast numbers of people.

China, in spite of its enormous size and ultimate military potential, does not appear to want to fight the U.S., at least not until it has developed reasonably effective nuclear weapons. This appears to be at least a generation away. At the present time, the U.S. could not conceivably defeat Red China on the Asian continent in a land war without nuclear force. The Chinese armed forces at present are extremely powerful and integrated with the civilian population to an extent not approached in any other nation. Their organization, training, and indoctrination are all difficult for Westerners to understand, but may be efficient. They have more than 130 combat divisions supported by a trained, armed, and organized militia which is said to exceed 30 million. Ultraheavy and complicated weapons appear to be lacking; air power is limited. But these deficiencies might be compensated for by an extreme national patriotism and an enormous population. There are already more than 700 million mainland Chinese; most of those who might have favored living peacefully with the West have been liquidated.

The succeeding chapters will be devoted to national situations and the armed forces of the Far East. Before embarking upon this, however, a few words should be said about three countries which will not be treated individually—Burma, Indonesia, and Nationalist China.

Burma was the scene of some of the bloodiest fighting of World War II. Much of what the British had done for the Burmese materially during a relatively short colonial period was destroyed. In 1945–46 the old ways were gone both in government and in life. The new spirit of Asia and anticolonialism was being expressed loudly by the more vocal sections of the people. Britain withdrew gracefully; the final separation took place on 4 January 1948. The Burmese governments since that time have struggled against local insurgents of several types, including both nationalist minorities and groups of the extreme left. The country has remained neutral; U Thant, Secretary-General of the United Nations, is a Burmese.

The Dutch East Indies became Indonesia after some bloody fighting following World War II. The anticolonial forces might not have been able to win the war on a purely military basis, particularly in New Guinea. But the Dutch certainly lost in world opinion. They were forced to withdraw more by what others thought, said, and wrote than by the armed might of their enemies.

The Communists in Indonesia were one of the two major anticolonial elements; the Nationalists were the other. In Indonesia, however, the two did not mix. The dynamic, powerful, dictatorlike Sukarno dominated both during the early years of the new country. But he found himself riding two most incompatibly gaited horses. The Indonesian Communists wanted a close alliance with Communist China and to copy that enormous nation in practically everything. The Nationalists were relatively conservative and controlled the Indonesian Army.

Sukarno personally became an enigma. Under his guidance Indonesia was, during the late 1950s and early 1960s, close enough to the West to send young officers to military academies in both Britain and the U.S. Later he struck out verbally and to some extent with force against these two nations and moved closer to the Chinese Communists. The abortive Communist revolution in Indonesia which failed quickly and completely in October 1965 has reversed this trend. Recent developments in this connection will be discussed in the section on Britain and Malaysia.

Nationalist China under Chiang has continued to exist on Formosa, or Taiwan, as it is often called. The island is less than a third the size of New York State or North Carolina, but contains more than 12 million people. It lies about 110 miles off the Chinese mainland and was Japanese from 1894 to 1945. Chiang and his associates still run things there autocratically and cherish the thought of returning to the mainland. The Chinese Nationalist armed forces are relatively strong, supported in part by U.S. aid. The country has made advances economically and industrially, but is too small to be of real importance. It depends upon the U.S. Seventh Fleet to protect it against being completely overrun by the Communists.

3: France in Indochina

War makes strange bedfellows. Perhaps the strangest misalliance of the twentieth century was between France and Japan during World War II. Even though Japan encouraged nationalism throughout much of Southeast Asia, the French colonial government, which was loyal to the Vichy government, was allowed to continue limited rule in Indochina until near the end of World War II. One cause of the present coolness between the French and the U.S. and Britain is that Frenchmen important in the present government were treated as enemies in Indochina in 1945.

With the fall of France in the summer of 1940 the Japanese put extreme pressure on the French commanders in Indochina. President Roosevelt refused them support and even held up delivery of planes already paid for by France. The Japanese came in and occupied bases in Indochina after a short but bloody war. It lasted two days and cost the lives of about eight hundred Frenchmen. The torpedo planes that sank the two great British capital ships, the *George V* and the *Repulse,* took off from Vietnamese bases. Their loss sealed the fate of Singapore. After the Japanese invasion the French cooperated against their will with the enemy until a sudden, carefully planned Japanese attack throughout the country swept them into prison camps on 17 May 1945.

Even though some Frenchmen in Indochina wanted to resist the Japanese throughout the war, the Allies gave them no support or promises of it. The main reason for this appears to have been Roosevelt's belief that France had exploited the local people. The French appear not to have done so. Their control of Indochina lasted only about half a century and did not produce any profits, either financial or military.

Roosevelt's death disrupted whatever plans he may have had for Indochina. U.S. and British theatre commanders were absorbed in more important tasks where actual invasions were being made of Japanese-held territory. Indochina was not to be invaded; nobody outside gave its future much thought. But within the country there was a lot of political maneuvering and some fighting. While the French were collaborating with the Japanese, a nationalist resistance movement eventually dominated completely by a man known to the world as Ho Chi Minh began to oppose them both. Ho had been a Communist, but temporarily played down this association. He appealed to all nationalists throughout Indochina—the countries now known as North and South Vietnam, Laos, and Cambodia—but patterned his movement on what the Chinese Communists were doing under Mao. Even though Ho's Viet Minh did not often fight the Japanese, they consolidated their political strength among the people. They took full advantage of aroused patriotism and the natural desires of the peasants for land. Unpopular local officials, landowners, and their representatives were sometimes murdered along with people likely to remain enemies of Communism.

After the collapse of Japan—the war came to an end on 14 August 1945—British and Dutch forces quickly reoccupied with token force at least their former territories. In most cases they received the surrender of the Japanese in these areas. The French were not allowed, and perhaps also not able, to do this in Indochina. Ho's Viet Minh and, three months later, Chiang's Nationalist forces from China took over in the north. A British force occupied Saigon on 12 September 1945 and controlled for a time what is now South Vietnam.

The French were not reinstated in their former position in Indochina. Some French officers, imprisoned since May 17, remained in stockades in North Vietnam for weeks after the Japanese surrendered. U.S. officers were present, but made no effective efforts to free the French. This is still bitterly resented by de Gaulle and his older associates. They feel that they did all that was possible with the means they had against the common enemy, the Japanese, and deserved immediate liberation and appropriate treatment as allies of the U.S. and Britain.

Meanwhile, Ho took full advantage of his temporary supremacy in what is now North Vietnam. He proclaimed the Democratic Republic of Vietnam on 2 September 1945 and began to run the country. The Chinese Nationalists did not arrive until November. British soldiers never came north at all and were soon gone, even from Saigon; they had enough to do in other areas. The French finally returned on 6 March 1946, but had been forced to recognize Ho's government as a "free state within the French Union."

The aims of Ho and the French were probably irreconcilable; war may have been inevitable. For eight months there was an uneasy peace while Ho ran his "democratic" country. His party wanted complete independence for all Indochina. On 23 November 1946 the French opened fire on rioting civilians in Haiphong and killed about six thousand. Ho's Viet Minh attacked French troops at several places on 19 December 1946. The first Indochinese war had begun.

This war was a strange one for the U.S. In its early stages Ho and his forces received some logistic support from commercial interests originating in America. The Viet Minh had a record of fighting against the Japanese while the French were collaborating. At that time many Americans thought of the Viet Minh as more nationalist than Communist. Besides, only recently the U.S. had been the ally of Russia.

But political change was in the air; new international alignments were beginning to take shape. As the Communist world began to support wars of national liberation—their term for bargain-basement war—the Western democracies were led by the U.S. to support local established governments. The U.S. and Britain became, whether they liked it or not, the allies of the French and the enemies of Ho.

With the outbreak of the Korean War in July 1950 the U.S. became convinced that United Nations interests would suffer if the French did not continue to hold out against Ho's Viet Minh. The French military effort in Indochina was supported diplomatically, financially, and with American military materiel and advisers. Even when the Korean War came to an uneasy end, the French fought on, although many in the army and the government wanted to get out. The U.S. continued to support France, but to an extent less than necessary for victory over the Viet Minh. When the French were faced with defeat at Dien Bien Phu, they appealed directly to Washington for emergency U.S. military assistance. A U.S. Air Force relief operation was considered and even planned. But U.S. military leaders realized that ground support would also be necessary. The Korean conflict was only just over; Americans did not want another war. Direct participation by U.S. forces was ruled out.

Dien Bien Phu fell to the Viet Minh on 8 May 1954; this and the U.S. decision not to participate actively decided the war against France. After eight years of fighting which cost 95,000 French and French-commanded lives, the tricolor was forced out of all Indochina at the Geneva Conference. This international meeting at Geneva under the co-chairmanship of Britain and Russia set up the two Vietnams, Laos, and Cambodia. The announced intention of the agreement was that North and South Vietnam would be reunited after free elections to be held by 20 July 1956. Ho remained in control in the north; his portion of the country became Communist. But South Vietnam was to be closer to France, the U.S., and the West. Laos and Cambodia were to remain neutral. The French position even in South Vietnam deteriorated rapidly after 1954; all Indochina became hostile in 1955 so that they were unable to continue their military presence allowed under the Geneva agreements.

This Indochinese War—often now called by the French the First Indochinese War—is still extremely important in regard to strategy, weapons, and tactics in the Far East. So much of what was used in 1946–54 is being employed by both sides in South Vietnam today that a brief military review of the eight years of war is in order.

The fighting can be divided chronologically into three parts. The period from December 1946 to December 1949 was characterized by French action, both military and civil, which was "too little and too late." France was not at first willing to give Indochina any real independence, but continued to negotiate with the Viet Minh until

March 1947. Then the French set up a puppet government under Bao Dai, a prince of the old Vietnamese ruling house. In order to end the war, the French gradually offered even greater concessions than Ho had demanded at first, but to no avail. Ho and his associates now wanted only complete independence and a free hand in making the entire combination of countries Communist.

The French did well militarily during this first period. Ho and his able military lieutenant, Giap, were thrown out of the larger towns. The Communists were beaten in numerous actions, but the hardened guerrillas among them took to inaccessible base areas, or disappeared into the civilian population. They continued their resistance in much the same way the VC do today.

The French tried to control the entire country from a few static fortifications and used tactics based on conventional warfare in World War II. Relatively powerful forces, including armor and artillery and supported by aircraft, advanced against supposed enemy concentrations which disappeared. The Viet Minh won small victories at platoon, company, and occasionally battalion level. They expanded the use of terror against French sympathizers, unpopular landlords, and informers. In addition, they were able to maintain and secure some large base areas in inaccessible places.

This phase of the war came to an end in December 1949 when the Chinese Communists, after defeating the Nationalists under Chiang Kai-shek, arrived on the border between China and North Vietnam. Ho could now receive logistic support including heavy mortars and ammunition for them from the Communist world by normal means of transportation in that area. The Viet Minh improved considerably not only because of better arms, but also because they were now able to get more advisers, better training material, and encouragement based on the recent Communist victory in China.

On 1 October 1950, Giap launched an all-out attack against a series of French fortifications along the border with China. These stretched from the coast to Cao Bang, 140 miles inland. Individual posts were surrounded, subjected to concentrated mortar and sometimes artillery fire, and taken by greatly superior forces. Full advantage was taken by the Communists of surprise and their ability to concentrate the same soldiers for use in successive operations. The French were not able to organize and move a rescue column into the area in time to avoid disaster. Airborne support was not enough. All posts were taken; the French forces suffered about ten thousand casualties and lost heavily in weapons, equipment, and prestige.

The fall of the Cao Bang forts brought to an end the first period of the war. The second began with the appointment of Marshal de Lattre de Tassigny to supreme French command on 17 December 1950. He was given more support from France, and he revived morale in his entire command. More troops were brought in, especially African colonials and Foreign Legion units. Armored vehicles, artillery, trucks, and aircraft were all reinforced, in many instances with U.S. materiel.

De Lattre came too late to save the northeast border posts, but he had a plan for winning in spite of their loss. The French were to hold the Red River or Tonkin delta in North Vietnam. This area included both Hanoi and Haiphong and was roughly a triangle about 120 miles on a side; 90 per cent of the people in North Vietnam resided in this area which also included about 75 per cent of the fighting area of the entire war.

De Lattre's plan also called for control of the rest of the country by means of heavy mobile columns which would have powerful artillery and armor components. The idea was to hold the northern delta and draw the Viet Minh into set-piece battles outside it. The new French commander had a great reputation and a lot of personal ability and energy; he breathed new life into the French armed forces.

Ho and Giap, though operating outside the delta, drew most of their political support from within it. If the de Lattre line of fortification could deny the Viet Minh access to the area, the war would probably end in a French victory. But holding this line of large and small posts created a problem. Would there be enough French soldiers to do this and still furnish the mobile power which the de Lattre plan required? Bao Dai's government could supply a considerable number of Indochinese units, some of surprisingly good quality.

All went fairly well at first; 51 million cubic yards of concrete were poured into forms for 2200 bunkers and similar fortifications according to the latest French designs. Within a month after de Lattre took command, one of his mobile forces, a large one, fought a chance engagement at Vinh-Yen against Viet Minh using medium machine guns and 120-mm mortars. The French Union Forces were outnumbered by a considerable margin, but de Lattre used his well organized and well led infantry, artillery, and tactical air power to win the two-day battle. Viet Minh casualties included 6000 dead and 500 prisoners.

Another somewhat similar major action was fought at Ninh-Binh between 29 May and 18 June 1951. Giap attacked the southern corner of the delta and was repulsed with heavy loss by French armored and partially armored river boats, tanks, and mobile reserves. De Lattre was taking full advantage of his superior long distance mobility, materiel, logistics, and tactical air power. The French were less successful, however, in holding the de Lattre line. Since many of the posts were at least a kilometer apart and separated by jungle, they could not really block small units of Viet Minh even during the daytime. Hard-core Viet Minh battalions were operating inside the delta area permanently.

The French began an operation on 14 November 1951 which was to develop into the meat-grinder battle of Hoa Binh. This lasted for more than three months. The French endeavored to penetrate west of the delta, to cut Communist supply lines which were beginning to extend south. Instead of opposing the enemy in front, Giap gave way there, but ambushed reinforcements and supply columns by land and river. He also attacked French forces assigned to cover critical points along these routes and in the Hoa Binh area. The French finally pulled back to the delta.

The main area of combat now shifted to the west. The French held a series of posts south of the Red River which to some extent protected not only Laos and Cambodia, but also South Vietnam. Giap started to attack these from the north on 11 October 1952.

The actions which followed were in many ways similar to those in connection with the border posts of Cao Bang. The Viet Minh were using three divisions—Giap had organized his hard-core army into five in 1950—and overpowered in turn French posts as well as light reinforcing columns of paratroopers.

To remedy this situation, de Lattre undertook Operation Lorraine on 29 October 1952. A powerful French force penetrated a hundred miles northwest from the corner of the fortified delta triangle at Viet Tri. This command fought its way beyond Phu Hien against varying opposition. De Lattre's forces captured a lot of Russian-made materiel, including heavy trucks, but did not stop Giap's offensive plans farther west. One of the principal objectives of the Red River offensive, a fortified post at Moung Khua, fell after a dramatic resistance on 18 May 1953. Even de Lattre must have realized that he was not winning. The French were losing both in the delta and to the west and south of it. The health of the gallant commander was also failing; he was relieved in December 1953.

The third and last period of the French Indochinese war began when General Henri Navarre became commander in chief. He continued with the de Lattre plan, but was even more anxious than his predecessor to draw the enemy into battles where France could use her materiel advantages. This desire led ultimately to the tragedy of Dien Bien Phu. This village is in North Vietnam almost on the border with Laos. It had fallen to the Viet Minh in the spring of 1953 during Giap's push across the upper Red River, but had then been retaken by the French and heavily fortified.

When Navarre assumed command he appears to have thought of Dien Bien Phu as bait for a trap. He wanted to give Giap a target sufficiently favorable for him to attack in heavy strength, but the idea was, of course, to have it resist successfully. Navarre thought that French artillery, discipline, coordinated leadership, and air power could be decisive. The result is well known. Giap concentrated more infantry and artillery than Navarre thought possible and employed them better. The Viet Minh actually used 40,000 men, three full infantry divisions and one heavy (artillery) division. Human labor brought in 300 guns, 350 tons of ammunition, and hundreds of additional tons of other Communist munitions. French air power could not perform the tasks that were required because of 80 Russian 37-mm antiaircraft guns and 100 .50-cal antiaircraft machine guns. The active siege lasted from 12 March 1954 to 8 May 1954 and ended with a complete victory for the Viet Minh.

Another series of operations should be mentioned. These occurred far from the delta, in the central highlands of South Vietnam. With the conclusion of the fighting in Korea, the French force there was transferred to Indochina and became the nucleus of Group Mobile 100 which operated between Pleiku and the coast. Activated on 15 November 1953, it included not only Frenchmen, Legionnaires, and Africans, but also Vietnamese, Cambodians, and a company of Montagnard scouts. This fine unit was of regimental size, about 3500 men initially, and contained artillery, tanks, and armored personnel carriers. It moved long distances and fought gallantly, but, weakened greatly by ambushes and by attacks on the fortified posts it occupied, was finally destroyed on 24 June 1954. The First Korean Battalion lost more men in five days on Route 19 in Indochina than in its two years in Korea. This series of actions is particularly pertinent to present operations in South Vietnam because the U.S. First Cavalry Division, Airmobile, is operating in this same general area today.

Americans often look for lessons in the wars of the recent past. What happened in Indochina between 1946 and 1954 is full of these. The most serious error made by the French was not to appreciate the significance of the end of the colonial era. Extreme nationalism made the old types of government impossible in all large areas. The mere fact that personal freedom, personal dignity, and standards of living may be better under a colonial government is not important. The French efforts to channel nationalistic feelings into a commonwealth arrangement known as the French Union probably never had a chance.

Perhaps the second most serious military mistake of the French was to build steel and concrete defenses and to make them too important in their over-all strategy. Reminders of the Gallic love for fortification are apparent all over South Vietnam today. The French surrounded even small areas that they thought important with barbed wire, mines, trenches, and concrete blockhouses. They also put up small castles, sometimes of the Beau Geste type. In theory, these were interdependent and joined together by radio and mobile reserves. They were to be used as bases for offensive action. In actual practice, however, it seems fair to say that most French garrisons usually retired into their defenses at the approach of darkness and remained inside until daybreak. They relied on their superior firepower to offset the advantages of mobility, surprise, and ability to concentrate superior force which obviously lay with the Viet Minh. When Giap thought that one of these small fortified places was worth the effort, he could generally destroy it in a single night.

Another apparently poor decision made by the French was to try to use armored vehicles in areas not suitable for them. Since the enemy had little mobile artillery and no armor, it would be logical to suppose that tanks, self-propelled howitzers, and armored personnel carriers would give the French a considerable advantage. This often was just not true. The presence of these vehicles made the word "mobile" a mockery in the title of a task force. Such a force was not mobile in Indochina. Save in a few areas, it could move only on roads. Although the Viet Minh actually had sufficient antitank weapons to crucify road-bound armored vehicles which endeavored to function as bunkers, they preferred to use mines. Concealed explosives accounted for some 84 per cent of the 398 vehicles the Viet Minh destroyed between 1 January 1952 and the end of the war.

The French tankers appear to have lacked a proper appreciation of shock tactics, usually relying on fire power alone. Tanks lose at least half their effectiveness when stationary. If unfriendly infantry can approach in jungle surroundings, they are likely to become incinerators for their crews. Even in Group Mobile 100, French Union riflemen were not able to keep the enemy at a safe distance. Hard-core Viet Minh units lost all fear of armor because they rarely saw it employed properly.

Mobile groups were evolved to eliminate the disadvantages of static defenses, but they often became little better than temporary immobile fortifications at night, and sometimes for longer periods. They were forced to expose themselves frequently to ambush in a long slender formation only one vehicle wide with no flank guards at all. In much of the Indochinese countryside they could be stopped by the Viet Minh at any desired point by mines, recoilless rifles, or mortars.

The French appear also to have made a mistake in regard to tactical air support. Many French officers and NCO's remembered vividly the German Stuka dive bombers in the Battle of France. They tried to adapt more powerful aircraft to produce the same results in the jungle. This was not possible. A village could be destroyed fairly easily, but Viet Minh soldiers could not often be seen from the air, even when fighting against French ground forces.

At Dien Bien Phu both tactical air support and supply by air failed in part because of insufficient planes. The Viet Minh were able, however, to contribute to this result by camouflage and firepower. When French planes attempted to bomb enemy artillery that successfully used camouflaged forward slope positions, heavy volumes of antiaircraft fire came out of the green jungle.

The French endeavored to gain mobility with helicopters, but these were in their infancy. There were never as many as twenty in all Indochina. Paratroop drops were not outstandingly successful because of the terrain into which these often had to descend. Resupply either by free fall or parachutes was inefficient. During the later stages of the siege of Dien Bien Phu supply drops had to be made from above effective antiaircraft range. Fully three-quarters of all bundles wound up in the hands of the enemy.

The French also tried to channel the war into conventional battles in which they thought their firepower, tactical air support, communications, and discipline would bring them victory. Occasionally they were successful; more often they failed. Giap and his subordinates learned early to avoid set-piece battles in territory close to French bases. Later on, in order to get one of these, Navarre had to risk too much.

The French often attempted search and destroy missions of various sizes. When these were based on accurate and current intelligence, they were sometimes successful. More often, however, large French Union commands complete with artillery, vehicles, and air support would surround an area and find few identifiable Viet Minh. Occasionally they would run into prepared defensive positions of strength and lose heavily for a short time only to have the enemy disappear later. The main episode of Bernard Fall's book *Street Without Joy* is one of these large-scale missions. It took place in July and August 1953 in the coastal area between Highway 1 and Tonkin Bay in what is now I Corps Area of South Vietnam. This unhappy combination of amphibious landings and a paratroop drop occurred about 140 miles north of the scene of Starlite, the U.S. Marine Corps operation, just below the Seventeenth Parallel or more precisely the Song Ben Hai, a small river which is the real border between the two Vietnams today.

The French armed forces appear to have lacked a real desire to make friends with the people. In a way, this is understandable, for efforts in this direction sometimes led to their own murder. The high command, however, was not able to maintain tight discipline among different units of the French Army, which included Legionnaires, Arabs, and Senegalese. Robbery, rape, and murder were not uncommon. Indochinese thought to be friendly with the Viet Minh suffered especially. This misbehavior plus the antiwhite, anticolonial feelings fostered by the Viet Minh helped create extreme hatred.

Despite this, the French succeeded in enlisting a large local army in their service; it numbered by 1954 more than 330,000. Some of these troops fought gallantly and efficiently. Volunteers from the units parachuted into Dien Bien Phu along with Frenchmen, Africans, and Foreign Legionnaires even after the place was doomed. As far as a large part of the local population was concerned, however, the Indochinese who fought for France became despised foreigners.

Another weakness of the French in Indochina was poor support at home. France did not recover completely industrially and economically from World War II until long after the Indochinese war was over. French Union forces were not supplied with all that they needed to fight at top efficiency. But more important, Communists and other left-wing groups in Metropolitan France practically backed the Viet Minh. It was hard for soldiers to do their best in a vicious, bloody, uncomfortable war when they felt that their efforts were not widely appreciated at home.

This attitude of mind may have contributed to the most serious handicap the French had at battalion level and below. In spite of the extreme bravery of young French officers and NCO's—more than 3000 were killed including 21 sons of general officers and marshals —many units lacked the skill and morale necessary to go out and meet the enemy face-to-face in the jungle at night. French rifle battalions and even companies appear to have relied too heavily on fortifications, armor, artillery, and aircraft.

Another French handicap was in connection with intelligence. The French made the mistake of underestimating their opponents, but were frequently unable to find out anything about them. In spite of air and armored infantry reconnaissance, French commanders at all levels frequently operated in an intelligence vacuum.

The Viet Minh, on the other hand, were superb at gathering information. Their organization for this purpose included not only crippled old men, children, and women, but also Indochinese throughout the French-sponsored Bao Dai government and even trusted employees of the French. Giap could base his plans on accurate intelligence; the French never could in large operations and were seldom able to do it even at company level.

No discussion of the French in Indochina would be complete without a brief outline of French efforts to induce the local tribesmen to take a hand in the conflict. French cadres were introduced among the primitive Meo tribes in northwestern Vietnam and appeared to have been successful. Some logistic support was supplied to them, mostly by air drop. Navarre based his plan for Dien Bien Phu in part on the ability of these units to disrupt Viet Minh lines of communications which were eight hundred kilometers long extending back into Red China. But the French-led Meos were unable to accomplish this mission. Tragically, some of these commands did succeed in fighting efficiently, but were abandoned after July 1954 to fight on unsupported to a slow and terrible extinction stretched out over months, even years.

The French used a variety of arms at company level and below. At that time the Foreign Legion had German World War II weapons complete with the original manuals in German. There were also many pre-World-War-II French arms and some from the U.S. The three most popular individual weapons appear to have been the French bolt-action Model 1936, which fired the 7.5-mm French cartridge; the MAT 1949 French 9-mm submachine gun, and the U.S. M1 carbine. The Viet Minh used anything that would shoot, including many U.S., Japanese, British, and French arms, some made before World War I. But they had some efficient materiel as well, particularly modern U.S. infantry support weapons captured by the Chinese Communists in Korea.

The French did not perform at their best, but they appear to have been opposed by a good commander and fine troops for the war that was actually fought. They did not have either the superlative logistic and materiel support that U.S. units now have, or the air mobility. They probably lacked both adequate training and desire in many individuals. Many Americans in important jobs in Vietnam are well acquainted with French mistakes and are trying not to duplicate them. Sometimes this is more difficult than might be expected.

Both the French and the Viet Minh used battalions of 750–800 men organized into three rifle companies, a heavy weapons company, and headquarters. French tables of organization and equipment called for 624 rifles, 133 submachine guns, and 41 BAR's (Browning automatic rifles); the Viet Minh had about 500 rifles, 200 submachine guns, and 20 BAR's. A French rifle battalion had four 81-mm and eight 60-mm mortars, but normally lacked both rocket launchers and recoilless rifles. The Viet Minh matched the French in mortars and usually had three U.S. 57-mm or 75-mm recoilless rifles and three 3.5-inch rocket launchers.

Small-unit tactics employed by the French tended to be based upon conventional war with supporting fire from heavier weapons, either an organic part of their organization or temporarily assigned to it. Giap's men fought as guerrillas; squads were armed with rifles and grenades only. Where there were heavy support weapons at platoon level—there frequently were not—two light machine guns would be in a separate squad; medium machine guns and 60-mm mortars, when available, were attached to company headquarters. The Viet Minh specialized in ambushes and surprise night assaults.

At Dien Bien Phu, Giap used the tactics of siege warfare brought to perfection in the eighteenth century. The French fortifications were surrounded by a formal system of Viet Minh trenches, at first quite far away. These trenches were pushed closer and closer, however, as local attacks gained ground. Severe bombardments by Viet Minh mortars and artillery followed by infantry assaults chewed away at French defenses and morale.

The classical answer to Giap's siege approach was the sortie, or surprise counterattack, on the trenches of the enemy. French Union soldiers cut off from all real hope of relief delivered dozens of these with extreme bravery. They took the works of the enemy, but were unable to hold them because the fighting which ensued was just man-to-man in tunnels, caves, and bunkers, mostly with grenades, submachine guns, and knives. The French were not able to establish and hold boundary defenses. The Communists were willing to absorb a two-for-one casualty ratio; they had many more men. Slowly the area within the French perimeter shrank. Finally their forces were so congested that efficient use of even the support weapons that remained operable became difficult. As in all war, fortifications can be taken if the attackers are willing to pay the price.

4: Britain in Malaya and Malaysia

Britain lost her colonies and protectorates in Malaya and North Borneo to the Japanese early in World War II. Singapore was Britain's great naval bastion in the Far East, but the Japanese took it by an attack from the land side on 15 February 1945. Active operations between Britain and Japan moved many hundreds of miles south and west, but there was also some local guerrilla opposition to the invaders. When the war was over, British forces were welcomed back throughout the entire area.

Britain had been remarkably unselfish in these colonies. The governments established before 1942 were autocratic but benevolent. By and large, the people had been unusually contented politically. But nationalism was on the march here as elsewhere. Colonialism was doomed. Even though individual Malay states had considerable independence and were almost completely in charge of their own local governments, the majority of the people wanted essentially to run their own country at all levels.

After one brief effort at a union arrangement Britain agreed to give up all rights. Plans were made for complete freedom for Malaya in an orderly manner. A federation of all Malaya—never achieved before—came about in 1948. Free elections were held in 1955 for virtually all legislative and many executive jobs. Complete independence was granted on 31 August 1957.

A Communist guerrilla war began in 1948, however, on orders from Moscow. It had no great popular backing, but dragged on long past the final establishment of the new government. In order to understand this situation, it is necessary to look back into history.

Malaya and North Borneo were populated predominantly in 1840 by Malays. These people were still in charge of the various local governments in 1941 and again after 1945. They were the hereditary sultans, judges, civil servants, teachers, and police.

By World War II, however, much of the population—nearly 50 per cent in some political subdivisions—was Chinese. Most of them had come in the preceding hundred years either as traders and store-keepers, or as laborers. Malays, even when poor, will not normally do hard physical work; mines and rubber plantations required a lot of this kind of labor. But the Chinese who were brought in to do these jobs did not take much interest in government or other local activities. They remained Chinese even after several generations; intermarriage with Malays was rare. Culture, language, and ways of thought were still essentially Chinese, even in the laboring classes.

To oversimplify somewhat, the Malays ruled, and the Chinese worked. There were many wealthy educated Chinese, but they usually spent their time and energy in commerce and professional pursuits. Hours were long and hard in the mines and on the rubber plantations; wages were low. Living conditions and social services were below world standards. Communism had a following in the mass of underprivileged Chinese long before 1941. During World War II more Chinese than Malays fought as guerrillas against the Japanese. Chin Peng, a young man of rare courage and determination, emerged as the most important local leader and worked closely with a British underground detachment for the last two years of the war. He received the Order of the British Empire and marched in the victory parade in London.

An orderly movement toward independence for Malaya was not, however, what the predominantly Chinese Malayan Communists wanted. An exchange of Malay rule for that of the British might not be an improvement. Chin Peng was still in charge. He appears to have been delighted in June 1948 to execute his orders and begin the same sort of fight he had conducted in 1943, 1944, and 1945 with excellent arms saved from the earlier war. Mao and his Chinese Communists helped with new techniques, particularly in connection with civil and political activities. Terror was important in Peng's new strategy. The Communists became known as CT's—Communist terrorists.

The British conclusively won this thirteen-year war. It did not end finally until 1960, although the severe fighting was over by the end of 1954. This victory over Communism in a bargain-basement war was really important for the Free World. There have been only two other Free World victories since World War II, one in the Greek Bandit War (1946–49), the other in the Philippines, against the Communist Hukbalahaps (1948–54).

The British anti-Communist war in Malaya was more like the present war in Vietnam than any other guerrilla conflict, save for the French Indochinese struggle. The British effort there was big in several ways. Close to 100,000 British troops were involved at one time. More than 600,000 villagers were relocated in strategic hamlets, won away from Communism, and taught to protect themselves.

Less than three years after the official end of the CT emergency, Britain had another bargain-basement war on her hands. The new country of Malaysia, which included Malaya, Singapore, and most of North Borneo, became totally independent in 1963 with British Army, Navy, and Air Force protection. But President Sukarno of Indonesia launched an open, blatant guerrilla effort against Malaysia. He wanted to force the individual parts of the new country to join his nation.

Indonesia is an enormous group of islands containing 735,000 square miles and about 100 million people. Malaysia is small in comparison, with 130,000 square miles, although considerably larger than Britain (including all of Ireland). There are only about 10 million Malaysians, but they have a good deal of industry, mineral wealth including mines in operation, and agricultural production especially of rubber. Their commerce is strong but located principally in Singapore. If Sukarno could have added Malaysia to Indonesia and assimilated it all, he would have dominated Southeast Asia.

The Indonesian dictator attacked Malaysia in his public exhibitions of rage and hate in a manner similar to Castro's attacks on the U.S. in Cuba. Sukarno swore to crush the new country and violently attacked both Britain and the U.S. His opposition was not confined to words. He sent Indonesians to assault a police station north of the border in Borneo on 12 April 1963, five months before Malaysia officially became independent. This aggression was unprovoked and unannounced. It accomplished nothing, but lives were lost on both sides. Obviously British forces had to be ready to fulfill their pledges to Malaysia; the new country would have only a limited capacity for defending itself.

At first sight, the strategic problem of protecting Malaysia from Indonesia appears insurmountable. The border, land and water, extends from the Strait of Malacca in the west to the Phillippines in the east, a distance of more than 1600 miles. Most of the Malayan peninsula can be reached from Sumatra by canoe. The Borneo border stretches for more than 900 miles mostly through a wilderness of mountains and jungle.

The Indonesian border intrusions of 1963 and the first half of 1964 were mainly to set up pockets of guerrilla resistance inside Malaysian Borneo. Sukarno's idea appears to have been to penetrate with cadres and have them recruit local inhabitants to fill out guerrilla units of the Viet Minh and Viet Cong type. This did not succeed because the people would not join these foreigners, or even foreign-trained locals. They reported the cadres to the British and their Malaysian allies. When Indonesian units concealed themselves for a time, they were reported when hunger forced them into the open. During the second half of 1964 Sukarno endeavored to use the same tactics against Malaya and came by sea and air. In September 1964 the Indonesians attempted three simultaneous parachute drops of forty-eight men each into Johore. Every man in all three units was killed or captured. At first, the forces infiltrated were about half Indonesian regular soldiers and half guerrilla-trained "civilians," but with the passage of time the percentage of regulars rose to over seventy-five.

The Indonesian dictator had sworn that the sun would not rise on Malaysia on 1 January 1965. When the date arrived, the new country was prospering politically, economically, and militarily. Casualty figures stood at about 1200 to 245 in favor of the British and their allies. But the Indonesians were not through; they shifted their tactics. Instead of trying to set up pockets of Communist resistance, they concentrated on sabotage and small attacks on police and military units. Forces of from three men to as many as a hundred came across the land border in Borneo and by sea into both Malaya and Borneo. These attacks continued throughout 1965.

The Indonesians were also engaged in what they called confrontation. Sukarno deployed several full brigades, perhaps 40,000 troops in all, along portions of the Borneo border. But violation of Malaysian air space by Indonesian bombers and fighters ceased, following establishment of the British Air Defense Identification Zone. Aircraft that attempted to intrude were quickly destroyed. Small-scale fighting continued on the ground and at sea throughout 1965 and into 1966, even though Sukarno's internal troubles, particularly in connection with the attempted Communist coup of 30 September 1965, were considerable.

In this uprising the Indonesian Communists made a coordinated effort to take over the government by violence. They were successful at first in some local operations; high-ranking military officers and their families were murdered. But the Army reacted efficiently and won quickly. Scores of thousands of Communists—according to a British source, more than 300,000—were executed by the military governments established in most areas to deal semi-independently with the problem. Sukarno remained nominally in power for a time, but then lost power completely. The Indonesian Army under its Chief of Staff, General Suharto, appears to be firmly in power and running the country on non-Communist principles. Malaysia and Indonesia may be approaching a peaceful settlement of their difficulties. They are operating jointly against border Communists.

During 1965 and early 1966 British-directed forces defeated more than two hundred separate, identifiable enemy operations with surprising ease; other infiltrators were caught individually and in small groups. Indonesian attacks on Malaysian border installations always failed; only four Indonesian units penetrated to within mortar range of their objectives. Security forces under British command have done an efficient, professional job in this area for almost twenty years. What are the technical reasons for their success?

Perhaps the greatest single advantage the British have had is experience. They have more than two centuries of political and military successes in the Far East. They had the sense to perceive the end of colonialism and to give up India, Burma, Pakistan, and Ceylon gracefully. They were obviously sincere in their willingness to give up Malaya and their holding in Borneo, too, as soon as the local populations could cope with the problems of independence and demonstrate conclusively that a majority wanted it.

More important militarily, Britain had and continues to have a skillful professional army which includes about 14,000 Gurkhas (mercenary soldiers from the small independent country of Nepal who have served in the British Army for 150 years). The British fought successfully in Malaya and later in Borneo and Malaya because their weapons and tactics were adapted to the type of war they were fighting and to the terrain and climate where they were fighting it. The British Jungle Warfare School in Johore helped enormously; its faculty worked out combat procedures that appeared effective in theory, tested them, and then improved them by more study based on experience. It also trained officers and enlisted men fresh from Western Europe to use the jungle environment to their advantage.

The essential ingredient for the British victories over their native and Indonesian enemies was the individual rifleman and his weapon. Riflemen, supported only by the fine British light machine guns, learned to operate in small patrols everywhere in the jungle, at night as well as during the day. They were better trained, better disciplined, better organized, better fed, better armed, and—most important of all—better led. Britain realized that if guerrillas could not be met man-to-man in the jungle at night and beaten, all other efforts by more elaborately organized and equipped armed forces would probably fail.

With astonishing speed, British soldiers acclimatized themselves to the jungle environment and the conditions of war in Malaya.

They learned to patrol and ambush; they were as able as the guerrillas to disappear into the jungle. The Gurkhas were an enormous help in these operations because of their capacity for individual combat and also because of their continuous availability in the theatre for many years. They are small men, but incredibly strong for their size. They are also tough, brave, and skillful in all forms of war. They have proven themselves particularly effective in the jungle. Even when ambushed, their reactions are so quick and vicious that they can frequently win the ensuing fight. They suffer casualties, but will pursue an enemy force until every single man in it has either been killed or captured.

The Gurkhas make highly favorable impressions on outsiders who have the privilege of visiting them in their barracks, schools, and training activities. Those who go on patrol with them and remain for a time in their forward areas become confirmed Gurkhaphiles for life. But a very special soldier, even by Gurkha standards, is Lance Corporal Rambahadur Limbu, V.C., the only man to win the Victoria Cross since Korea.

On 21 November 1965 a Gurkha platoon on patrol encountered an Indonesian force dug in on Malaysian soil in Borneo. Rambahadur, leading a three-man fire-support team, discovered them first and attacked along a knife-edged ridge, still ignorant of the extent of the enemy's strength and position. The gallant Gurkha killed a sentry and took a portion of an enemy trench. He and his team held it for a time, but both his men were seriously wounded. He carried them back through enemy fire, one at a time. This took about twenty minutes. According to his citation: "For all but a few seconds of this time the young NCO had been moving in view of the enemy and under continuous aimed fire from their automatic weapons. His escape from injury or death was miraculous."

His two men taken care of, Rambahadur rejoined his squad, took over its Bren light machine gun, and contributed supporting fire in the initial stages of the ultimately successful Gurkha assault. When this was finally delivered, Rambahadur was with the van and was credited with killing four more of the enemy. The hour-long battle ended with the Indonesian company retreating across the border leaving twenty-four dead and many weapons. The Gurkha platoon's losses were three dead and four wounded.

The complete success of this action against heavy odds and Rambahadur's own heroic contributions are unusual in any war. But the ratio of Indonesian to Gurkha casualties is about normal for clashes between them. The extreme personal ambition and valor of these adopted British soldiers seem somehow to protect them. Audacity when accompanied by professional competence can surmount numerical and terrain obstacles.

Even though the individual and small-unit effectiveness of the British and their allies operating in the jungle has been great, these men have not been asked to endure unnecessary hardships. Careful study at the Jungle School and in the field indicates that British, Gurkha, and the new Malaysian soldiers function better in the jungle environment when provided with a kit that allows comfort. Mosquitoes, leeches, wet feet, and uncomfortable sleeping arrangements do not do anyone any good, not even CT's. Both health and morale suffer from poor food and exposure. On the other hand, a soldier must not have so much equipment that he becomes immobile. Each man must be prepared to carry his kit in the jungle for several days. Bivouac living must not be so complicated that a combat turnout cannot be made within sixty seconds.

Individual equipment in Malaysia presently weighs slightly more than fifty pounds, including the rifle and 180 rounds of ammunition in magazines. There is one standard jungle uniform plus boots—a black nylon coverall and a pair of sneakers for emergency night combat. Bedding arrangements vary with the previous life of the soldier, but are all adequate to give protection from jungle insects and leeches. Soldiers are kept as dry as is possible under jungle conditions. Adequate individual medical supplies, drinking water, and necessary tools are all carried in a comfortable harness. One of the hardest decisions was to substitute a machete, or *golok,* for the traditional Gurkha *kukri.* The new weapon is not only more effective for jungle cutting, but also easier to keep usefully sharp and less likely to be broken.

One result which emerged from the studies at Johore was the importance of food to individual morale. A real effort is now made to provide the best food obtainable because it becomes almost the only pleasure that a patrolling soldier has for days on end. Individual taste plays a large part not only in choosing the food before a patrol starts, but also in planning and preparing each meal. The limiting factor is weight; whatever a soldier wants, he must carry himself.

Even though the British continuously emphasize the individual soldier, his personal equipment, and his operation in the jungle on foot with a rifle, they are not averse to taking advantage of more complicated equipment. They have usually been successful in adapting electronic communications to jungle conditions. Radio reception in rain forest is notoriously poor, but British and Gurkha experiments indicate that special techniques with minor redesign can restore full range and clarity of reception. Lightly armored vehicles are extremely useful where they can operate. The Saladin armored car was as effective as a tank against irregulars and required less maintenance. The smaller Ferrets could do a first-rate job at present in reasonably open areas.

Various landing craft and other small vessels have been utilized in Malaysia, particularly in Borneo. Where water transport was possible, the British took maximum advantage of it. One of the anomalies of this war is that the British Army has operated its own "navy," entirely independent of the Royal Navy, in Borneo for several years. Flat-bottomed vessels sufficiently large to take several armored cars, trucks, and the like not only perform regular supply runs, but also are useful operationally. They are sufficiently sturdy to be driven ashore in favorable places, to allow disembarkation of men and materiel, and to back off again. Hover craft have also been used successfully, but have disadvantages. The jungle sometimes hems them in almost as completely as if they were waterborne. They make so much noise that tactical surprise is impossible.

Malaya did not have a good system of roads; Borneo has practically none. Rivers often do not run in the right direction and are not always navigable. Air transport was and is important. Britain has managed to integrate helicopters, small fixed-wing aircraft, and much larger planes which drop heavy equipment by parachutes in effective logistic support for a combat force of approximately

20,000 in Borneo. Fewer than 100 helicopters and approximately 100 other transport aircraft not only brought everything that was needed, but also multiplied effective strength on the border by aiding strategic mobility and giving all personnel periods of rest and recreation in base areas along the north coast. Sometimes men flew in an hour over a route that would take six weeks by river craft and jungle trails.

Britain has realized from the beginning of the Malayan emergency the extreme value of intelligence in all counterguerrilla activities. By 1948 several British officers already knew much about Chin Peng and the way he conducted guerrilla war because they had fought with him against the Japanese. General Sir Gerald Templer made special use of this as well as his own great energy and military ability during the time he was British commander in chief, in the crucial period between 1952 and 1954.

But more lasting effectiveness comes from a continuous supply of small bits of information on a day-to-day basis. This depends mainly on friendship with the local people. Templer and his successors took full advantage of the enviable British record for fair dealing, decent government, and honest economic and social progress during the colonial period. British exploitation, if it ever existed, is gone save from Sukarno's fevered mind. Britain backed Malaysia to the limit. It decided in February 1966 to remain in a protective capacity for as long as a majority of the population of Malaysia, Singapore, and Brunei really want British help. British economic aid and advice probably will continue, too.

British civil action, particularly in the portions of Malaysia where the Government composed mostly of Malays is weakest, also is important. The "hearts and minds" program is most effective in border areas where the people are predominantly Dyak or Ibans. Free medical treatment and modern miracle drugs have been given away in large quantities; wells have been dug and public buildings erected. British, Gurkha, and Commonwealth soldiers have shown a personal interest in the people. This extends down to squad level. The soldiers under British command have been good advertisements for the democratic way of life.

The standard British infantry rifle, used also in the armies of the wealthier members of the Commonwealth, is a semiautomatic called the SLR (self-loading rifle). This fine weapon fires 7.62 NATO ammo, twenty rounds in each detachable box magazine. As presently issued, this weapon does not fire full-automatic, but can deliver rapid single shots with astonishing accuracy. It was entirely satisfactory during the last stages of Malay emergency.

Jungle Warfare School experiments indicate, however, that the NATO-round SLR is inferior in several respects to the U.S. M16 (or AR-15) which fires the 5.56-mm cartridge. The high-velocity 55-grain bullet from this new light round has been found satisfactory for killing at all jungle ranges. The M16, with 180 cartridges in magazines, weighs 13.8 pounds compared to 23.5 for the SLR with the same number of rounds. The M16 is 38.6 inches long as opposed to 41.0 for the SLR and is appreciably lighter, 7.4 pounds to 10.7 when both are fully loaded. The M16 is said to be quicker for handling in an emergency and it has full-automatic capability. For use in the jungle the British Army feels that the M16 is superior and has begun to arm whole rifle battalions with them.

Britain has recently adopted a new general-purpose machine gun, which also fires 7.62 NATO ammo. It uses the same disintegrating link belts as the U.S. M60 machine gun. The GPMG in its light role has a bipod mount and buttstock similar to most modern LMG's. It can also be equipped with a heavy barrel and mounted on a tripod for MMG operation. The British GPMG is one of the best and most reliable in the world today when used in conventional warfare situations as either a squad legal machine gun or as a company MMG. It had competition, however, in both of these roles in Malaysia.

The weapon in its light role weighs more than twenty-six pounds with a canvas pouch containing a belt of fifty rounds attached to its side to form a kind of magazine. Once this ammo is fired, reloading is a problem. But firing belts either loose, or from a container, requires a second man in constant attendance. Even then a belt-fed LMG in the jungle has several disadvantages. The redesigned 7.62 NATO Bren weighs only seventeen pounds and uses thirty-round magazines; these are more convenient than belts amid creepers and vines. The new Bren is shorter, handier, and considerably lighter. A second man is not necessary. Currently British jungle patrols who have a chance to take Brens usually choose them over the bipod GPMG.

The new GPMG when fitted with a special recoil-absorbing tripod of British design and two sighting systems is efficient, accurate, reliable, and much lighter than the old 1.303 Cal. water-cooled Vickers. When it has to be moved, the new weapon wins hands down. In the jungle, however, the British have recently made considerable use of company bases in which gun weight is of little importance because MMG's are generally installed in bunkers and remain there until the entire fortified area is moved. The old Vickers fires slower and more accurately; it can be kept in action indefinitely with no barrel changing.

The air-cooled GPMG has to have its barrel replaced, if it is to fire several long bursts. A skillful crew can change a barrel in seconds and be back in action. But even seconds may be too long in a jungle bunker, if an enemy only a few yards away chooses the barrel-changing time to run forward and bowl a grenade through the embrasure. In some base camps today, the new weapons are in cosmoline in boxes while the old water-cooled Vickers are in the bunkers ready to fire.

There is considerable difference of opinion among British officers on the importance of submachine guns in the jungle. Some feel that rifles are superior, even though the 9-mm Parabellum cartridge of the submachine gun has been satisfactory in many actions. Some submachine guns are currently being carried in the jungle by soldiers whose primary responsibility is directing others or carrying ammo, or operating communications equipment. The current British submachine gun, the L2A3, also known as the Patchett or the Sterling, is an efficient weapon. But the heavier Australian Owen, one of the clumsiest in appearance, is highly regarded in combat. The two-pistol-grip arrangement in the Owen is said to aid in delivering accurate fire at close range in emergencies. With its vertical magazine, feeding failures are rare.

The British have a new 84-mm recoilless rifle known as the Carl Gustav; it is of Swedish origin and will knock out any tank. The weapon is lighter and shorter than any other comparable arm, including the new U.S. 90-mm recoilless rifle. But antitank weapons are not required against guerrillas. Medium recoilless rifles do have an antipersonnel capability, but the British usually rely on the 3.5-inch rocket launcher against personnel—it is simpler to carry and operate, lighter, and equally effective.

The only other support arms organic to British rifle battalions and smaller units in Malaysia are the 81-mm mortars used throughout the world and the unique British 2-inch mortar. The 81's cannot be carried by soldiers on jungle patrols save at a sacrifice of mobility, but the small 2-inch pieces are popular, particularly with the Royal Marines and Gurkhas. These weapons are supposed to be obsolete, but they are light and can effectively deliver both direct and high-angle high-explosive fire. I saw a Gurkha sergeant fire accurately at a range of seventy-five yards with one of these mortars, which he held unsupported. It spun him around on firing, but he and his assistant—who feeds in the shells but does not help support the mortar—delivered a second round quickly.

Combat tactics in Malaya and Malaysia have emphasized company strength and smaller units because Communist guerrillas and more recently the Indonesians have rarely used more than 150 men at a time. British and Commonwealth battalions and even brigades sometimes maneuver together, but platoons usually did the fighting. A British, Gurkha, or Royal Marine rifle platoon varies considerably in accordance with available personnel and mission although the official strength is the same in all three services (1 officer and 31 men). Each platoon is divided into a headquarters (1 and 7) and three rifle squads, called sections (0 and 8 each). Each platoon in theory has twenty-nine rifles, a 3.5-inch rocket launcher, a 2-inch mortar, and three light machine guns, one in each section. An authorized local variation dispenses with the two headquarters weapons and distributes six men from this unit to the rifle squads, two to each. Each squad is then more capable of independent action and is composed of a leader, plus usually a local Iban guide, and three groups of three men each. Although the entire section is interdependent and is the smallest regular operational unit, it is composed of a reconnaissance team often armed with three submachine guns, a rifle team always with three SLR's or AR-15's, and a Bren fire-support group. These three teams can be used ideally to find and fix the enemy, gain fire superiority over him by all firing together, and then maintaining this with the Bren group alone. The other two teams under the section leader move so as to kill or capture their opponents. All these jungle patrols carry sufficient ammunition even on foot to engage in a fairly extensive action without resupply.

Perhaps the most important reason that British platoons and even squads are able to operate independently far from support has been that they are the hunters, not the hunted. They know how to take advantage of the jungle while denying its full use to their enemies. They have confidence in their weapons and fire discipline; they do not fire away blindly all their ammunition and then wait for more to be brought to them. They have been safe in the jungle on long patrols because they change their bivouac area every night and establish a secure perimeter at dusk. But they can move out of it quickly and efficiently if necessary. These soldiers have a lot of actual combat experience and much more jungle practice. They could patrol and ambush more deftly and with greater effect than either the CT or Indonesian enemies.

In order to make their small-unit offensive maneuvers more efficient, the British have adopted a system of company bases; these earth, timber, and sometimes concrete fortifications are surrounded by barbed wire, *pungis* (sharpened bamboo stakes), and mines. They usually contain one 105-mm pack howitzer and two 81-mm mortars. One of these bases will rely heavily on medium machine guns in bunkers, usually the water-cooled Vickers. But the basic idea of a defense of this type is to support offensive patrolling. A British rifle company contains four platoons. One of these plus headquarters and assigned troops can hold a base camp while as many as three are patrolling outside it, perhaps aided by friendly aircraft. They have used heliborne forces effectively.

In some situations, the British have preferred a large number of small patrols—even single rifle squads—to a smaller number of larger patrols. The idea is to confuse an enemy; it also has secondary advantages of covering a larger amount of ground and impressing more civilians. If small patrols are coordinated but irregular in time and path, they support each other. So long as British and Malaysian intelligence continues to be superior to that of their enemies, their better radio and transportation equipment will allow them to disperse to protect a lot of border, but concentrate for effective action when necessary.

The British have used dogs with considerable success over an extended period, actually units composed of a man and a dog in each. For offensive operations, they have developed a tracker team which usually consists of two man-dog units and two human trackers from the inland North Borneo tribes often called head-hunters. Each dog handler and each Iban has a rifleman for close-in protection; they can devote their full attention to tracking. The tracker team also has an NCO with a radio and a commanding officer in good physical condition for a total strength of ten. The animals used in these units are chosen for their sensitive noses rather than their viciousness; they are usually Labradors. One of these teams is able to move fast, far, and accurately. They can catch one or a few infiltrators without augmentation; where necessary, they can be suitably reinforced.

The British also use dogs for security around their bases and for alerting patrols to danger at night. These animals are different from those on tracker teams; they are chosen for their over-all alertness, viciousness, and sense of hearing. German Shepherds are usually best for this duty.

Partly as a result of friendship and civil action already discussed, British and Malaysian forces have maintained a real superiority in intelligence. This has been of extreme value to them in their tactics. Indonesian forces which tried to hit British and Malaysian bases with mortars, rocket launchers, and medium machine guns were usually reported ahead of time. They were frequently under Iban surveillance while they were still on their own side of the border. Most of them were ambushed before they reached their objectives; none had succeeded in taking one. Casualties were overwhelmingly in favor of the British and their allies.

The Gurkhas deserve a lot of credit both for the military record of the British Army in this conflict and for their civil-action accomplishments. They are superb jungle fighters and also good at selling the British way of doing things. These little brown men can steal shoelaces from war-game opponents or cut the throats of real enemies without giving away their presence. In half an hour after halting in the jungle, they build comfortable bivouacs. They are intensely ambitious militarily, but can have a good time anywhere. Their ability to move in jungle terrain day or night is remarkable.

The future is, of course, in doubt. At present (February 1967), the Indonesians seem to be moving toward peace. Sukarno appears to have lost power; he may be tried for treason soon. Indonesian Communists are finished for some time to come. Suharto and his generals could still want to conquer Malaysia and add its resources to their own, but they would be fighting essentially for the Chinese Communists. They certainly don't want to do this.

The Indonesian nation, in spite of internal problems, is powerful militarily. The armed forces number at least 415,000 in the Army, 35,000 in the Navy, and 30,000 in the Air Force. Equipment is spotty, but includes high-performance aircraft and modern guided-missile naval vessels from Russia. The Indonesian Army is predominantly an infantry force, but has a number of armored vehicles of various types. It presently uses the most comprehensive collection of small arms ever assembled by one nation, including complete assortments of Dutch, British, Japanese, and U.S. weapons from World War II plus some not usually encountered even in those armies. They still have German, Swedish, and Russian weapons and were buying arms in Western Europe and America in the early 1960s, including Armalite rifles and FN machine guns. They are now manufacturing some weapons for themselves.

Malaysia without Commonwealth help cannot stand against Indonesia. The native Malaysian army numbers only about 20,000 men. These units are under British guidance and are improving in discipline, efficiency, and experience, but the defense of the new country is still dependent upon British, Australian, and New Zealand troops and equipment. A considerable collection of essentially light vessels is needed to protect Malaysia against seaborne infiltrators and saboteurs. Navies take even longer to build than armies. If Britain should withdraw her naval support before friendly relations are assured between Indonesia and Malaysia, the latter could not survive.

Mention should be made of the situation in Singapore and the independent Sultanate of Brunei. Both planned originally to be part of Malaysia. Singapore was for a time and then withdrew; Brunei never formally joined. They are both independent countries at present, but joined to Britain by treaties. They were militarily a part of the solid resistance to Indonesia. Singapore's public announcements should not be taken out of context; capitalism appears firmly established there essentially because it has done an astonishing job for most of the people. Brunei has a very large income from its oil compared with its population of only 80,000; the Sultan has spent this money lavishly on his people.

The possibility of a Southeast Asia federation of Thailand, Malaysia, Indonesia, the Philippines, and perhaps some smaller countries is encouraging but not imminent. The Malaysians have seen how their British and Commonwealth protectors learned to live and fight in the jungle. In countless instances, they have cooperated with their white and Gurkha allies in making friends with the people the Indonesians have tried to subvert. The enemy may have accomplished nothing except to draw the Malaysians closer together. Because of Indonesian ultimate military strength and the economic condition of some Malaysian minorities, however, the situation is still potentially dangerous. There are local areas where Chinese, Indonesians, and Ibans outnumber the Malays, but are governed by the latter. Chin Peng and 300–500 CT's are said to survive in the tropical rain forest on the Malay-Thai border.

The future security of many nations is subject to question, but presently the British and their allies have Malaysia on the road to meaningful independence. These Commonwealth forces are valuable beyond their numerical strength to the Malaysians and to the non-Communist world not only because of their fighting efficiency, but also because of their example. They have won militarily and have proven that Communism does not always appeal to relatively primitive people like the Ibans, or to similar ethnic minorities with low standards of living.

5: The Philippines

|||||||||||||||||||||||||||||||||||||||||||||||||||||||||||||||||||||||||||||||||||||||||||||||||||

The Japanese launched a surprise attack on Clark Field in the Philippines coincident with their Pearl Harbor assault in December 1941. U.S. air power in the Far East was crippled. Two days later the Japanese began their invasion of the Philippines by land, sea, and air. General MacArthur, who commanded both the U.S. forces and those of the Philippine Commonwealth, was forced to retreat into the Bataan Peninsula and Corregidor Island. The defense was heroic and well managed, but the Japanese were far too strong. The end of organized resistance came in April and May 1942 after Mac-Arthur had been transferred to a higher command.

The Filipinos continued to fight the Japanese with a whole-hearted hatred and effectiveness unique among colonial peoples. They remained intensely loyal to the U.S., having enjoyed a commonwealth type of government which gave them progressively greater self-rule from 1934 on. This was to culminate in complete independence in 1946.

The extent and depth of the Philippine World War II effort is astonishing. MacArthur commanded more than 80,000 Philippine soldiers in his ill-fated but heroic campaign of 1941–42. More than 250,000 Filipinos, regulars and guerrillas, aided in the final recovery of the islands from Japanese control in 1945. Tens of thousands more worked and fought as irregulars. The few Filipinos who collaborated with the Japanese have not been heard of since.

The Republic of the Philippines became independent on schedule. The new country was soon beset, however, by internal troubles. The Hukbalahap movement—the Huks—began during World War II as a resistance organization against the Japanese. It was effective and contributed along with other guerrilla groups to the final Allied victory. The Huks appear to have had from their beginning strong Communist intentions. Following full independence, they became increasingly harsh toward landowners and local officials in the less well-developed areas where they were strong. Finally, in 1948, they set out to overthrow the Government by force. Though they could receive little help from other Communist countries in the form of military supplies because the U.S. and Philippine navies and air forces controlled the South China, Sulu, and Celebes seas, they needed outside assistance less than other revolutionary movements. There were plenty of weapons left over from World War II and food is abundant in these fortunate islands.

The Huks under an able leader, Luis Taruc, increased in strength quickly. They fought initially against the then generally corrupt local police and inept politicians who failed to appreciate the importance of civil action. Government military forces, in spite of fine weapons and veteran leaders, were avoided or actually beaten in small actions typical of Mao's Phase Two. The Huks were assembling in semipermanent battalions and operating from some reasonably secure base areas in Luzon and Panay; Taruc seemed to be winning and was planning even larger operations.

All this came to an abrupt halt. The gifted and dynamic Ramon Magsaysay became Secretary of Defense in 1950. He commanded troops in the U.S. Army in 1941–42, but was not captured in the Bataan Corregidor disaster. He became an extremely successful guerrilla leader and aided the final Allied victory. In his new job he linked the Constabulary with the Army and improved both. Even more important, he knew the problems of the village people because he was one with them. He had grown up in a hamlet, but worked his way through college. He understood the basis of Huk power and was able to counteract it. Communism had been on the ascendancy but it soon declined.

Magsaysay's policy was simple, but efficiently and dynamically carried out. He offered the Huks and their sympathizers "total friendship or total force." To those who surrendered he gave land, seeds, tools, and a water buffalo, but on an island not infected with

Communism. To those who continued to resist he gave only violence and war. He would not see his beloved new nation spoiled by a relatively small group of malcontents before it got a good start.

Magsaysay profited from his own guerrilla experience. He soon had a system of intelligence that was at least equal to that of his enemies and formed counterguerrilla units which matched Huk terror, secrecy, and mobility. The Government armed forces adopted Huk tactics including civilian clothes and a wide variety of weapons. Government agents melted into the civilian population; small groups of soldiers disguised as peasants penetrated Huk areas to ambush and execute. Guerrilla base camps were located and attacked at dead of night; all men found there were killed. Magsaysay sometimes personally commanded small units of his forces; he was fearless and made the right command decisions quickly.

While ruthlessly exterminating Huk fighters, Magsaysay was also cutting away their political base by improving the life of the portion of the people from which the guerrillas came. The Army and the Constabulary were now kind, fair, and generous to noncombatants. Civil servants were compelled to do their jobs efficiently and honestly. Medical facilities and schools improved. A system of land reform was begun, not just discussed. The Army ran the first truly honest national election in Philippine history.

In his drive for large reforms Magsaysay did not neglect small things. He was personally always on the go, talking man-to-man, praising, and punishing. He was a real leader, always ready to go first into combat. He instituted a new procedure under which any Filipino who thought any department of the Government had treated him unfairly could send Magsaysay a telegram stating the circumstances; total cost of the message to the sender was five cents. A preliminary reply was sent back within twenty-four hours; every complaint was fully investigated. Many people received full justice for the first time in their lives. Magsaysay even reviewed elections personally at village level.

In less than four years the Huks were beaten completely in both military and civil action, with Taruc surrendering personally in 1954. Magsaysay kept his word; to all those who came in voluntarily, he gave even more than he promised. Most became useful and loyal citizens. Those who continued to fight were almost completely exterminated. The final and complete defeat of the Huks in the Philippines proved that a nation courageously led can defeat Communism in bargain-basement war in spite of conditions usually considered favorable to insurgents.

Magsaysay was a true patriot, a dynamic leader, a gifted general, and a really good man. His personal contribution to this victory was enormous, and was made possible by his knowledge of and his love for his people. He was fearless personally, inspired others with his own drive, and made shrewd decisions in regard to his senior military commanders. Even more important, his soldiers helped the villagers repair their roads and bridges and build schoolhouses and playgrounds. They mingled with these rural people as friends.

Magsaysay was elected President in 1954, but did not give up his job as Secretary of Defense until all Huk leaders surrendered later that year. He continued in complete control of his country until his tragic death in an air crash in 1957. Had he lived, Southeast Asia would be a better, happier place today.

There is still a Huk problem in the Philippines, but the guerrillas who now use the Huk name probably do not have any close relationship to those Magsaysay either killed or made into good citizens. For centuries there have been local bandit groups on Luzon and other large islands. Sometimes they had political and religious causes, but plunder has always been an important motive force of these groups. The current level of fighting, mostly by a few squad-sized units, appears to be no more than normal, but the Communists could be waiting for better opportunities.

Meanwhile, Government armed forces are doing their best to guard against this possibility. Their basic concept of their military mission is different from most Western armies, which are concerned primarily with military efficiency and combat accomplishments. This is not true in the Philippines. Mostly due to Magsaysay, the Army and Constabulary have another type of mission fully as important as fighting. They must not only protect in war, but also help during peacetime. There is a remarkable monument of this great

Filipino in front of the principal Army headquarters, one of the most moving pieces of stone I have ever seen. But I found a simple printed statement tacked up in a barracks which might have pleased him more. It does not bear his name, but embodies what he wanted and so largely achieved:

While the basic mission of the Philippine Army is preparation for eventual employment in war, in land operations, the exigencies of the times demand its participation in the socio-economic development and in the growth of the country. The last war ended 20 years ago, but our country's economic and social development has not yet overcome the aftermath of that war. In this field, our organization has been doing a magnificent job. But we must not rest on past laurels. More roads have to be constructed; more jungles must be cleared. Our people need our willing hands. It has become our manifest destiny to blaze the trail to progress. They look up to us. We cannot afford to fail them and the country. In times of peace we prepare for war. But in addition also, we labor for the peaceful pursuits of everyday life.

Magsaysay guided the Army and Constabulary into paths that have brought them close to the people, especially those in the countryside and villages. A program of this type is unusual for military forces, but if it is willingly and efficiently carried out, it makes Communist insurgency nearly impossible. I saw Filipino soldiers working on roads and irrigation projects, sometimes with big modern equipment. I also saw them among the civilian population functioning as family relations counselors and Boy Scout masters. Some men actually teach in schools where there are not enough qualified civilians. They do all these jobs well.

Since 1946 the Philippines and the U.S. have worked out a most advantageous mutual defense arrangement. Philippine armed forces protect U.S. bases in the islands. Clark Field, Cavite Naval Base, and some other installations are of enormous strategic importance in the joint fight of the two nations against Communism. Without them the U.S. position in Vietnam would be impossible, but there are no U.S. combat forces stationed in the islands. Philippine forces take care of local security for all. The U.S. Navy and Air Force, cooperating with smaller similar Philippine units, protect the islands from seaborne and perhaps airborne aggression. Essentially the Philippine Government provides territory and an army while the U.S. contributes a navy and an air force.

The closeness of the two nations is based on more than treaties and military need. English is not only the official language in the Philippines, but also the one most frequently spoken by all Filipinos. It unites a nation of 32 million people who would otherwise be speaking more than seventy different languages. Systems of law, government, and commerce similar to those of the U.S. unite 7100 islands totaling more than 115,000 square miles. The Philippines are roughly 80 per cent larger than all the New England states combined.

The armed forces include an air force of 5000 men and 200 planes and a navy of 4000 men and about 70 small vessels. Ground forces are more important and consist of Magsaysay's two interdependent elements, the Army and the Constabulary. The latter is far more like regular infantry than it is like the national police of other countries. It is trained, uniformed, equipped, and organized like a regular army complete with mortars, medium machine guns, and other infantry support weapons. It does not perform normal local police functions.

These two together now number more than 50,000 men; both units are still composed of a higher ratio of veteran soldiers to recruits than normal. All are well trained and organized for the type of combat they are most likely to see, but are predominantly an infantry force. Larger units have artillery and armor commensurate with probable needs for these in the country, but geography limits drastically what would be required. There are no land bridges from potentially unfriendly areas across which an enemy could bring armored divisions. An invading force could not in the foreseeable future carry much heavy equipment. Besides, the Philippines are composed of many separate islands—few of which have good tank country. The countryside is predominantly rice paddies, or rugged mountains and thick tropical jungle full of deep streams. Rifle units with organic support weapons are more important than armor.

There is one combat-ready infantry division with a near normal amount of artillery and tanks, but semi-independent reinforced rifle battalions, which are called battalion combat teams, are more important. The division is triangular: it contains three rifle regiments with three battalion combat teams each. It can be said to be motorized and has U.S. tanks, mostly M41's, and 105- and 155-mm howitzers.

A battalion combat team (51 officers and 812 men) has more men and heavier weapons than normal for a rifle battalion. It consists of a battalion headquarters and headquarters company (24 and 167), a combat support company (9 and 147), and three rifle companies (6 and 166 each). Battalion heavy weapons are supposed to include four 4.2-inch and ten 81-mm mortars, three 106-mm recoilless rifles, and three 50-cal. machine guns. There are also twenty-two medium machine guns, thirty-five 3.5-inch rocket launchers, and sixty BAR's.

Each rifle company contains a headquarters (2 and 17), a heavy weapons platoon (1 and 35) with three 81-mm mortars, two 75-mm recoilless rifles, and two 3.5-inch rocket launchers, and three rifle platoons (1 and 38 each). A rifle platoon consists of a headquarters (1 and 2), a heavy weapons squad (0 and 9) with two medium machine guns and one 3.5-inch rocket launcher, and three rifle squads (0 and 9 each). Each rifle squad has two BAR's, two M1 rifles with grenade-launching attachments, and five standard M1 rifles. The Philippine rifle squad is the only one in Southeast Asia outside those of the U.S. Army and Marines with more than one automatic rifle.

Philippine infantry small arms are now completely of the U.S. World War II and Korean types. All personal weapons fire one of three cartridges, the .30-'06, the .30 carbine, and the Cal .45 ACP (used in the U.S. semiautomatic pistol). The rifle round is used in the U.S. M1 rifle and the BAR, as well as in three models of Browning .30-cal. machine guns.

The M1 rifle was the finest individual shoulder arm of World War II. It was the first militarily successful semiautomatic and has functioned from the Arctic to the Equator. The only close rival to the BAR as a squad-level light machine gun is the British Bren. Both are fairly heavy, but slow-firing, accurate, and reliable. They use magazines rather than belts and are gas operated. But the Philippine infantry, like all others in the Far East today, has an abundance of an inferior arm, the U.S. M1 carbine. This weapon is light, short, easy to carry, and recoils less than a rifle, but it fires ammo that has essentially pistol power. Philippine officers claim that they do not place much tactical reliance on the carbine. There are not supposed to be any carbines in rifle squads and only a few at higher level, but you see too many of them to be used only by members of support weapons crews and in headquarters at various levels. Magsaysay's counterguerrillas used a lot of carbines.

The Cal .45 ACP ammunition weapons are the U.S. Model 1911A1 pistol and the U.S. M1 Thompson submachine gun. Pistols are sparingly issued in the Army, but fairly common in the Constabulary. Submachine guns are not official arms at any level within Army battalion combat teams, but they are in evidence when troops go on maneuvers, or even on guard details. The Constabulary seems to have more submachine guns than the Army. They are popular with police in many countries, perhaps because of a reputation gained from American movies. Civilians tend to exaggerate their effectiveness.

The most important of the crew-served weapons are the Browning machine guns. These consist of the two air-cooled types, the tripod-mounted Model 1919A4, usually referred to as the A4, and the bipod and buttstock Model 1919A6 called the A6. There are two A6's in the weapons squad of each rifle platoon. A4's are used at all higher levels, particularly in the combat-support company of each battalion combat team, where there are normally four. The heavier water-cooled Model 1917A1 is still used by the Constabulary. Like the British water-cooled Vickers medium machine guns in Malaysia, these old weapons are particularly valuable in counterinsurgency defensive operations. Lonely police headquarters feel more secure with three or four water-cooled Brownings in their corner bunkers than with any more modern MMG's.

Mortars are also important. Four big 4.2-inch mortars are unusual at battalion level in Southeast Asia. Ten 81-mm mortars are also more than are normally provided. But when these mortars limit mobility, they can be left behind. Infantry units also have the U.S. 60-mm mortar. This fine light piece was abandoned in all U.S. forces, but was then reintroduced in the Marine Corps and the Army perhaps because of Vietnam. In many Philippines operations the 60's were more effective than the larger mortars against the Huks because of their weight. The piece plus ammunition does not weigh so much that a small Constabulary patrol which carries one becomes immobile. There were instances in the Huk war, however, when even 4.2's could be used effectively. They are much lighter and almost as powerful as 105-mm howitzers.

Philippine soldiers realize, of course, that their weapons are old, but do not consider this a handicap. Many who have fired both the M1 and the M14 prefer the M1. They all prefer the BAR to M14 Modifieds and are highly pleased with their Browning medium machine guns. Comparative tests with similar, more modern mediums, including the U.S. M60, have only confirmed their opinions. They feel that all 7.62 NATO cartridge arms are only marginally better than those chambering the .30-'06. Their principal advantage, lightness, is offset by inaccuracy and some loss of reliability. They are currently aware of the 5.56-mm ammunition rifles, automatic rifles, and medium machine guns. If these are successful, the RP Army may be able to bypass the interim 7.62 NATO round entirely.

The one RP conventional division is ready to repel an invasion, or possibly to fight overseas. The other units are more directly concerned with maintaining order at home. Because of the large number of islands, battalion combat teams and even companies frequently operate independently. Military leaders do not really expect a full-scale invasion or an overseas war that would require more than one division. But they realize the imperative need for forces like their battalion combat teams, which are kept deployed not only for internal security, but also to enable the populace and the armed forces to get to know one another.

Deployment in small comfortable semipermanent bases does not mean there is a defensive attitude however. The Huks were defeated by an imaginative use of the most aggressive ideas. The Filipino soldier has a natural tendency to attack, even if he has only a bolo. But bravery without thought and system leads to defeat sometimes, and nearly always to unnecessary casualties. Where possible, attacks were launched in secret to gain the advantage of maximum surprise. Sometimes the Huks were surrounded at night and destroyed.

Normally offensive infantry tactics were based on what worked well in World War II, when units of any size would advance in various formations in accordance with terrain and training and take maximum advantage of cover to contact. Once under fire, the RP infantry would gain fire supremacy with their amply supplied support and personal weapons and then move in accordance with previously conceived and announced plans, or improvised orders.

This attaining of fire superiority followed by movement is common in almost all armies. Regular Philippines units have good firepower to aid them, but the principal aim is to cover an attack, not win a fire fight. In the last year of World War II U.S. and Philippines forces were able to smother the Japanese in fire, using not only their own organic weapons, but other assigned arms, including artillery and tanks. They maintained this superiority for short periods with a less powerful base of fire while riflemen and perhaps light support weapons moved forward or to a flank, to either form a closer firing line or actually go into the enemy with shock-action fire, grenades, bayonets, and, in some instances, knives.

Philippines companies and battalions still use this general system of fire and movement, but a final assault can now be delivered with marching fire from all rifle company weapons save the 81-mm mortars. Although this is inconvenient for 3.5-inch rocket launchers, 75-mm recoilless rifles, and medium machine guns, it can be done. This final attack by all friendly forces present is more difficult to direct, but places men where they are most useful. Sudden counterguerrilla attacks delivered in this manner against the Huks were particularly effective, in part because support arms were light. Where necessary, crew-served arms could "go to ground" in advantageous spots to continue their covering fire while riflemen finished the assault.

Defensively, against a conventional enemy, the Philippine Army at battalion level would take full advantage of its heavy weapons. But if a foreign invader should deliver a heavily supported seaborne assault, as the Japanese did in World War II, the Philippine Army would probably be outnumbered and surely overmatched in heavy artillery, armor, and air power. The Army and the Constabulary would use extreme fluidity, concealment, ambushes, and counter-attacks. So long as they had some tactical air support, they could maintain a line defensively. In the absence of tactical air power, however, they would not try to occupy obvious positions, but would defend their population centers with dispersed independent units operating at a distance. These would attack the rear of enemy columns advancing toward important sectors and use all the other devices dear to the heart of irregular forces. They would avoid formal battles and conceal their regular defensive systems based on firepower while relying on hit-and-run surprise. The home forces would benefit particularly from their greater than average age, experience, and knowledge of the country. Many NCO's and even junior officers fought both the Japanese and the Huks. Sixty percent of one battalion team I visited in October 1965 were Korean veterans. What men remember from actual combat is more important than what they learn in even the best training exercises.

At a lower level and against a conventional enemy the infantry would use the normal interdependent defensive firepower. Against revived Huk forces, however, the Constabulary, at least, would use fortified bases. Units would be able to offer resistance at a few moments' notice, but would endeavor to learn of contemplated attacks against them beforehand so that the enemy could be ambushed on the way, or suitably received by a fully alerted garrison upon arrival.

Even though the new Huks do not presently constitute a serious problem, their strength could revive. Communism has shown astonishing ability to take advantage of even small amounts of injustice and economic troubles. The Philippines are still a young country with problems. Dishonest officials exist there as in most democracies; unemployment is too high. In the villages land reform has not always worked out satisfactorily. There are still deficiencies in education, medical facilities, and hygiene. But the future is bright.

A new president, Ferdinand E. Marcos, was elected in November 1965. He had a brilliant record as student, young soldier in World

War II, lawyer, and politician. He received the highest grades ever given in a bar examination and won more combat decorations than any other Filipino. One of his first acts as President was to raise the number of men inducted into the army from 3500 per year to 20,000. He plans to increase the number of Philippines troops in Vietnam several times, and to include combat units. He is also fighting customs corruption, a severe economic evil. Like Magsaysay, Marcos is also Secretary of Defense and has brought back to active duty as his Chief of Staff a lifelong friend and classmate, politically retired Brig. Gen. Ernesto S. Mata. Both men are under fifty, but know conventional and guerrilla war well. They were close to their idol, Ramon Magsaysay, and remember how to give total friendship or total force.

The armed forces are trained for both heavy conventional war and counterinsurgency. They appear remarkably efficient for their size and cost. No nation, not even the very largest, could invade Philippines territory, save with an enormous superiority and at heavy cost. The Army and Constabulary have to spend some of their time building roads and canals and helping the people in other ways. But they have managed to gain through these activities an unusually close relationship with the civilian population.

The Philippines people, including their leaders and the armed forces, realize that they stand in the path of possible Communist expansion in Southeast Asia. They appreciate what the U.S. has done for them in the past and is still doing both in Vietnam and in and around the Philippines. They will help all they can. They are especially prepared to defend themselves internally. Marcos, like Magsaysay, will not allow a minority even with heavy Chinese Communist backing to spoil the land he loves. The Filipinos don't want to fight anyone, but they will if war is forced on them. The U.S. and Free World are fortunate in having such allies.

6: The Enemy in Vietnam

The development of bargain-basement war in Southeast Asia discussed in the preceding chapters would be of relatively little importance to the English-speaking world if it were not for Vietnam. But the U.S. is now deeply committed to this bargain-basement war. American casualties already exceed those of the Revolutionary War of 1776–82 and are rising. The local enemy, the Viet Cong, or VC, deserves a close look.

When the French left Indochina, Ho had complete control of North Vietnam. South Vietnam, separated from the north by a demilitarized border along the Song Ben Hai River near the Seventeenth Parallel, was briefly controlled by Bao Dai, but was soon taken over with some semblance of a popular election by Ngo Dinh Diem. The scheduled elections for the unification of North and South Vietnam were not held before July 1956, the time specified in the Geneva Agreements.

The VC, whose close association with the old Viet Minh and Ho's government in North Vietnam appears undeniable, began to develop all through South Vietnam soon after the partition in 1954. Although VC leaders refrained from most forms of violence, they began to use terror against local officials of Diem's government late in 1957. They secured base areas, won over sections of the population to Communism, and trained for the war they obviously planned.

One often hears that the VC are the Viet Minh who fought the French through 1954. This is not strictly true; the VC are, like other good troops, predominantly young men: 90 per cent are under twenty-eight, and not old enough to have been soldiers in 1954.

74

But all bear certain similarities to the Viet Minh. Many VC NCO's and officers, or those who occupy positions of similar authority in their forces, are veterans of the earlier war. When the Communist Viet Minh were supposed to leave South Vietnam, many of them just buried their weapons and mingled with the villagers.

The VC have the enormous advantage of an integrated Communist organization many years old, which is controlled from relatively secure headquarters almost certainly located in North Vietnam. This structure extends right down into many villages and hamlets of South Vietnam. Further, there are some secure Communist base areas which have been functioning for more than twenty-five years. All this has been improved through trial and error as well as Chinese Communist advice. The VC know-how in both civil and military action is based not only on the principles and tactics of Mao, Ho, and Giap, but on their own continuous experience. They have found out what will work and what is dangerous.

Equally important, they have found out what will be believed. South Vietnam is not a country with a high level of education. News travels slowly; truth is almost impossible for most of the people to determine. There are no unbiased newspapers, no periodicals at all with even moderate circulation outside the cities. Communal radios often blare forth programs chosen by the VC commissars which originate either in VC stations within the country or in North Vietnam. Travel is limited; face-to-face conversations are unreliable.

There are many Vietnamese who do have education, read newspapers, and have access to private radios, but most of them live in the cities. The VC are interested mainly in the villagers and the have-nots in the big towns. They have already done a remarkable job of making these elements anti-American in many areas. One of the strangest VC advantages is that many of their rank and file and most of the people they dominate really think that U.S. forces are the same as the French. In addition, some of them even think that U.S. Marines eat human liver for breakfast.

Americans generally have heard too much of the faults of their enemies and too little of their virtues. In World War II it was said that German junior officers and NCO's could not make combat decisions. The Japanese were said to be impossibly handicapped by inferior equipment and minds incapable of independent thought. These things were just not true. The U.S. won World War II in Europe and in the Pacific not because of the weakness of the enemy, but because Americans and their allies finally learned to fight better and use more efficiently the vast production of American industry.

During the Korean War the successes of the Communists were sometimes attributed entirely to numbers. Statements such as "There were more of them than we had bullets!" were obviously false. Human-wave attacks were used occasionally, but the enemy also employed other tactics. They were brave men with fairly good weapons; in spite of their materiel handicaps, they fought effectively.

Why fool ourselves in regard to the VC? The truth would certainly be more useful to Americans who may have to fight them in their own territory, or make over-all plans for that fighting. It is too early to write history, but we do know a lot about the VC, how they operate, and the arms they use.

Compared with American fighting men, most Vietnamese are short and slender. A physically powerful Vietnamese is unusual. A 220-pound U.S. athlete could probably break the necks of several 100-pound VC in unarmed combat. Even though small, they are not normally fast. Burly American NCO's in their thirties can sometimes outsprint every man in a Vietnamese company. But fighting without weapons is rare; muscles are not normally employed directly in battle today. The most outstanding physical disadvantage of the VC in this war is their inability to throw any form of grenade accurately or far enough. In other ways they are at least adequate physically.

There is every reason to believe that the VC benefit from their size. They certainly require less food and water and they may stand up better to long periods of exposure to conditions of jungle combat. They undoubtedly require smaller, simpler accommodations and can fight efficiently in smaller fortifications and tunnels. They move more easily and silently in the jungle and take cover more effectively. They do have foot troubles, however, and are not immune to their own tropical diseases. They may have less stamina than Americans.

Mental ability is more difficult to evaluate, but the educational level of both VC and ARVN soldiers is below U.S. standards. The VC hard-core units are said to contain few illiterates, but the average soldier probably has less than the equivalent of a fifth-grade U.S. education. The Communists are conducting training courses for their regular personnel. These are taken seriously; effort is good, but progress only fair. This may not be important. Education certainly cuts down the time required to learn about complicated modern weapons for conventional warfare. But guerrilla weapons are usually simple. If extra hours for instruction are necessary, they are easily found. There is some reason to believe that men who learn more slowly because these processes are relatively new to them attain a higher level of mechanical proficiency. Cunning and guile in combat situations appear not to depend on schooling at all.

The effectiveness of all soldiers depends on discipline and desire. Hard-core or regular-army VC are good soldiers because they have these qualities. To produce them there is a coordinated system that extends from boys of fourteen to junior and senior officers. Personnel at each level must qualify for advancement by hard work, demonstrated loyalty, and proficiency. Contrary to what has sometimes been written, the VC do not normally impress men into combat units. Young males who are drafted usually do only noncombat work.

The VC have built up their army carefully. They use an efficient system of propaganda to persuade youths to want to be VC, particularly the more daring and adventurous among them. Boys prove themselves by making booby traps, gathering simple military intelligence, showing a proper Communist spirit, and completing simple missions in the jungle at night. As they grow older, they become part-time, usually unarmed, guerrilla supporters. They are not paid, but do receive subsistence during full-time work. If they have a weapon at all, it is likely to be obsolete or homemade. Long knives are common at this level.

There are also slightly better organized VC units in some villages.

Members of these have learned to obey orders, live in the jungle, use camouflage, and patrol. Every man must know his area even by night and be able to act as a sure, quick guide. A unit of this type is sometimes used to provide labor in connection with an ambush or an assault of a Government position, but is not often relied upon heavily in combat. These men are not yet full-time, receive no regular pay, and live at home. But they are now full-fledged Communists living under discipline. They are ready to obey orders and fight as necessary, although their weapons are not good. They remain undetected by outsiders within the civilian population.

Gradually, depending upon local conditions, the better recruits will receive more difficult assignments. Training and indoctrinaton processes continue, often with these part-time VC guerrillas acting as their own instructors. With advisers from a higher level they take boys into the worst local terrain to maneuver at night. The boys' first efforts are probably crude, but they learn. At this stage they are still only militia; their logistic support is largely their own responsibility.

In many areas local guerrillas do have combat opportunities but these are carefully chosen so as to be within their capacity. They are particularly effective against declared local non-Communists, or wealthier people who are presumed to have a tendency in that direction. These militia are also useful against low-efficiency Government militia who have received a minimum of training. The VC almost surely improve because they engage in minor combat activities such as armed night patrolling and ambushing. Occasionally local guerrillas will undertake more ambitious offensive operations, but these have to be cleared through higher authority to guard against defeat.

The better men are taken from this guerrilla force, given better weapons, and promoted to a VC hard-core battalion. They become full-time soldiers; their training will go on, but under the direction of more qualified teachers. Small operations continue, not to accomplish anything startling on a national scale, but to give personnel combat experience and to establish a pattern of Government insecurity. Some able U.S. advisers say that these small actions are of extreme importance because they slowly waste away ARVN men, weapons, and morale. They are hard to counter effectively. U.S. units are also sometimes damaged by these small offensives, particularly the sudden sneak attacks and brief mortar shellings.

All men in hard-core VC units have demonstrated a loyalty to the Communist party and spent many hours learning simple guerrilla techniques. They are able to attack village fortifications suddenly, to ambush reinforcements, and then disappear. The VC have been taught by guerrilla war leaders from North Vietnam and Red China techniques of deception, anticipation of the enemy, and, when necessary, patience.

Hard-core VC usually become good instructors themselves in the hamlets where many spend a good deal of time. They learn to use ruthless cruelty not only against their enemies and the families of their enemies, but also against the civilian population to enforce obedience from them and to prevent any support for Government and U.S. forces. As taught by Mao, however, thc VC at all levels are scrupulously correct in their personal conduct. They are not allowed to take advantage of their positions to seduce local women or steal. In theory, at least, the VC help the peasants toward a better way of life. They don't have as much in material aid as Government representatives, but they are often more sincere and almost always have more time. They live with the people, and not, as Government representatives often live, in fortified compounds cut off from the local population at night.

Occasionally the VC in villages are forced, by conditions beyond their control, to order heavy taxation and forced labor, and even to draft young men for fighting, which ordinarily is not their policy. This sort of thing occurs particularly in an area where the people begin to return to Government control and no longer give freely all the Communists require. The VC will go to extremes before giving up an area.

The single most astonishing difference between the VC and ARVN is the former's ability to fight in the jungle and at night. The difference can only be the result of desire and training. A boy who lives in a tropical jungle hamlet and works in a rice paddy is not necessarily a jungle fighter; the Vietnamese peasant is more afraid of the dark than most Westerners because of his highly developed superstitions. In normal life the jungle is the enemy of farmers living in or near it. They travel through by the best road or path available and avoid dense vegetation as much as possible because of leeches, scorpions, and snakes. ARVN soldiers have all these tendencies more or less unchanged plus some new ones bred by life in cities.

VC recruits learn that night is the friend of the guerrilla and the enemy of the white man and his expensive weapons, particularly his aircraft and tanks. They learn that moving in jungle, even the roughest places in jungle, is much easier than they thought and that scorpions and snakes do not really present much of a problem. At some point early in their careers most VC suddenly achieve the moral ascendancy which comes to men who can move and be comfortable in the jungle at night over those who cannot. Once born, this idea flourishes with combat experience. The VC soon become good jungle fighters.

We must avoid, however, the idea that VC have all military virtues, or that their training is perfect. They are below Western standards in several respects. Their rifle marksmanship is atrocious. Few can hit a single enemy at a range of 150 yards even once in five tries. A U.S. Marine company commander in the Danang perimeter told me that his unit had been under sniper fire more than ninety times in the course of a month and had not sustained a single casualty. Part of the answer lies in poor small arms, but VC marksmen with the best Russian telescope rifles do not do a great deal better. So far, their marksmanship training programs—if they have them at all—are fatally handicapped by lack of facilities, ammunition, and competent instructors.

Another VC training disadvantage is the lack of uniformity. The step-by-step training program described is not always feasible. Educated recruits who in time may become well-rounded senior officers are also lacking. Academic training is not a requirement for military efficiency, but officers who do not have it are not normally as good as those who do. Mao's rise to power and efficiency in supreme command was undoubtedly aided by his education and wide reading. Ho and Giap are also educated men.

Guerrillas have always used a wider variety of arms than the conventional forces they opposed because the former have had to employ everything they could get. The VC are now receiving efficient modern weapons from their Communist friends, but they still have to keep obsolete materiel in service in their lower echelons because they don't have enough of the new arms for everyone.

The simplest weapons used are the booby traps. These "arms" can usually be set and left concealed; they require little except labor to produce. The cheapest are the sharpened bamboo stakes known as pungis, the tips of which are sometimes poisoned in various ways. In some instances long belts of these are set at an angle, presenting an impenetrable barrier thirty to fifty feet wide. Grass grows quickly to conceal their exact location. Other pungis have been hidden in holes in the ground which vary in size from something that will take a man's foot to something that will collapse and receive his entire body. Pungis don't work well under water, but homemade iron spikes do. These are usually common nails reforged into long, slender barbed points fixed in boards and concrete bases. Since the advent of the steel inner sole in U.S. combat boots, pungis or spikes in foot traps are arranged so as to do damage to the ankle and calf, or when a man pulls his foot out of the trap.

The pitfall idea, with or without pungis, has been worked in endless variety and size. They can be dug under a trail from the side so that the undisturbed "roof" has a carefully calculated strength sufficient to support a child, or even an unburdened Vietnamese, but not an ARVN with a weapon and pack, or a U.S. soldier. Against the French the Viet Minh even dug some of these for use against tanks.

Crossbows are set so as to discharge bamboo arrows when someone touches a trip wire. Old muzzle-loading firearms are sometimes substituted for these bows. Animal traps of local manufacture activated by steel springs from destroyed ARVN vehicles have also been used hidden on or near trails. These sometimes require more than fifty pounds of pressure to trip, but the big ones can take off a man's leg.

Up to about 1963 the VC also used massive, complicated booby traps of various kinds. Some of the crushing beams were so large that two elephants were needed to hoist them into place. A swinging device known as a Malay whip once took a whole ARVN patrol of thirteen men out of action at the same time. The swinging member, a slender beam, was over fifty feet long, armed with sharp bamboo spikes and powered by the resiliency of two jungle trees. This whip was supported at its outer end by means of a vine rope so that it swung throughout a 90-degree arc about three feet off the ground. The combined strength of many men operating through a system of pulleys was needed to pull back the arm and set it.

In spite of occasional effectiveness these devices were probably more valuable to the VC as morale builders than for producing enemy casualties. They were impressive; the many men who made them were proud of their work. Besides, this work tended to commit the workers irrevocably to the VC.

All these primitive devices cost a lot of time and hard work. Now that the VC can get explosives and have established themselves in most areas, they do not waste time on the big primitive machines. They still use some pungis, steel spikes, and animal traps, but explosive booby traps are not only more easily and quickly constructed, but can also produce more casualties. Recently, the VC have shown real imagination in connection with them. They will, for instance, mine an area likely to be occupied by an enemy patrol when fired on. A single VC who suddenly discharges a burst from an automatic weapon may cause an ARVN or U.S. unit to dive onto a natural depression nearby and be blown up or impaled on poisoned pungis.

Grenades are the most common booby-trap explosive, but other kinds are also used. The VC in Saigon employed fixed directional mines similar in principle to U.S. claymores in the floating restaurant tragedy which resulted in ninety-six civilian casualties—twenty-eight Americans were killed or wounded—and in later street massacres. Both types of mines use the force of a detonating, unconfined explosive to drive projectiles arranged on one side only. When properly set, VC mines discharge a large number of steel fragments in a conical pattern. In similar American mines the fragments are steel spheres which fly in a band pattern. The VC mines are not so precise; they discharge short pieces of reinforcing steel cut with a cold chisel and a sledge hammer in a conical pattern. Plastic explosive is also used in various ways, and sometimes in large quantities. In some instances these have been set off in Saigon mainly to provoke nervous U.S. or ARVN soldiers into firing their weapons in crowded streets. Civilians and friendly soldiers have been hit.

Captured 105-mm howitzer shells can be rigged for ambushes so as to be exploded electrically from a distance. In one ambush along Highway 13 a roadside line four hundred yards long went off simultaneously. The senior Marine killed in Vietnam in mid-1966 was a lieutenant colonel who stepped on a booby trap made of a U.S. 155-mm shell. The VC had dug a wide pit, set the shell in the middle of it, removed the protective cap, and put in a charge of black powder and an ordinary percussion cap on an improvised nipple. They then covered the pit with thin slabs of stone supported by a piece of bamboo in the middle over the shell and sprinkled earth and leaves on top. A man stepping on the stones anywhere within a circle about five feet in diameter would collapse the bamboo, explode the percussion cap, and detonate the shell.

The personal firearms of the VC have followed the same pattern as booby traps. Early in the conflict the VC were armed in part with village-manufactured shotguns, mostly muzzle-loaders. They also had weapons left over from every war fought in Asia in the last century. Hours of work were spent making one usable firearm out of parts of several badly damaged weapons. Sometimes a dozen different types of ammunition were needed in the same VC company, but there was rarely enough for anything save a short fight. The VC had to be at close range to be effective. The VC hard-core units always had the best arms, but even they had only mediocre nonstandard weapons through about 1962.

More recently Communist aid from the north has led to a rearming of all VC units. The best troops now have modern weapons of Russian or Chinese manufacture. Rifles are of several types. The most common appears to be the Chinese Type 53 which is a copy of the Russian bolt-action Model 1944 carbine with bayonet permanently attached, but not necessarily fixed. The original Russian-made weapon is also found. These arms are satisfactory in every way and stand up well under conditions in the jungle, but they fire full rifle power ammo, the 7.62 Russian-rimmed cartridge. The recoil is severe for soldiers weighing an average of about 100 pounds; full rifle power is not often needed in the jungle where ranges are short.

Another common set of shoulder weapons in the hands of the VC regular troops appears to be the Russian SKS semiautomatic carbine and the Chinese copy of it, their Type 56. These are not trouble-free, but are chambered for the 7.62 Russian Intermediate cartridge which has plenty of power for this theatre. Semiautomatic functioning is of value where fast single-shot firing from unorthodox positions is required.

The most modern rifle in the hands of the VC, and the one most frequently encountered in North Vietnamese regular units, is the Russian-designed AK assault rifle manufactured in China. This weapon is also chambered for the 7.62 Intermediate round and is capable of full-automatic fire from a thirty-round box magazine. The AK as manufactured in Russia now often has a folding stock. The Chinese weapons have wooden stocks which do not fold.

The U.S. M1 rifle and the French MAS 1936 are also plentiful in some VC units because so many have been taken from ARVN or were captured from the French Union troops in the earlier war. Both these captured weapons fire cartridges which have unneeded power, as much as the full-power Russian round. The M1 is too big for Vietnamese and is said by ARVN not to stand up well to jungle conditions, but the VC take better care of them and appear to have no serious problems in connection with reliability.

Submachine guns have been popular with all guerrillas since they became reasonably plentiful during World War II. The VC were particularly fond of a captured French weapon of this type, the MAT 1949. This gun fired the 9-mm Parabellum cartridge and was, when in good condition, an entirely acceptable personal arm for this type of war. But 9-mm ammunition became hard to get. Many were rebarreled for the 7.62 Russian pistol cartridge or even the 7.62 Intermediate and had their magazines altered slightly so as to hold the new rounds. The VC also use Russian-designed submachine guns chambering this 7.62-mm pistol cartridge and the U.S. M1 Thompson originally issued to ARVN which fires the Cal .45 ACP cartridge. U.S. M1 and M2 carbines are often used by good VC units and are probably best classified as submachine guns, although the M1 cannot fire bursts. Pistols have never been of great value to the VC, even though they have been of considerable importance in other post-World War II guerrilla wars. The most common appears to be the U.S. Model 1911A1—the so-called Cal .45 automatic—obtained from ARVN. But this weapon weighs more than three pounds, including the holster, and is too heavy for these men if they have any other small arm to carry. The VC also have Chinese copies of the Russian Tokarev pistol, but these are rare.

These personal arms make up over 90 per cent of those used by VC regular or hard-core units. Other weapons include German World War II materiel captured by the Russians or by the Viet Minh from the French Foreign Legion; U.S. weapons given to Nationalist China, taken by the Chinese Communists, and turned over to the Viet Minh; and modern small arms made in Western Europe. I examined an almost new Swedish submachine gun taken near War Zone D in September 1965. A fair number of these were brought into the country by a U.S. agency and are presently being used by both sides. All small arms made in this century that are still serviceable and in the hands of the VC are useful to them, but create serious ammunition problems in some instances. On the other hand, the muzzle-loaders and village manufacture breech-loaders of the early days have disappeared except when used in booby traps.

VC support arms have to be light enough to be carried on foot, although some have small wheels which allow human draft. By far the most important of the weapons served by crews are the various machine guns. Burst fire is needed more in armies where individual rifle marksmanship is poor than where it is good. The VC have a variety of light, medium, and heavy machine guns. The regular units now use Chinese copies of the Russian DPM and RP-46 LMG's mounted on bipods. All fire the 7.62 Russian full-power round. The Chinese Type 53 LMG uses the distinctive flat circular magazines;

the Chinese Type 58 normally uses metallic link belts, but can be adapted to the pan magazines too.

The favorite Viet Minh MMG's were the Chinese Nationalist copies of the old water-cooled Maxims, German Model 1908 chambered for the 7.92 Mauser. They were used with some success by hard-core VC units through 1964, but were not suitable for firing at aircraft. Besides, they just weighed too much and were too bulky for use in the jungle by small soldiers. The most common MMG now used is the Russian and Chinese Communist SG and SGM series, all firing the 7.62 Russian full-power round. There are several different modifications; the wheeled-carriage type is best for Vietnam. It is drawn and fired against ground targets on its wheels with a single composite trail, three members strapped together. It can be raised off wheels and go into action in seconds against helicopters or other aircraft from a high tripod made from the three trail members. This convertible carriage is most ingenious and has increased greatly the effectiveness of VC antiaircraft fire.

The Chinese Communist copy of the post-World War II Russian RPD belt-fed light machine gun, which fires the same 7.62 Intermediate round as the SKS and AK rifles, does not appear to have been used by the VC in quantity up to 1965. This model should be entirely satisfactory for a war of this type and is popular in Russia and China. It is standard issue, however, in North Vietnamese units; several were taken by the U.S. First Cavalry in the fall of 1965 in the central highlands. Several U.S. units encountered them in VC hands during 1966.

VC .50-cal. machine guns are something of a puzzle. They have often been reported by helicopter crews. Streams of .30-cal. bullets cannot reach up far with any degree of accuracy and effectiveness; 1500 feet may be about their limit. But helicopters have been brought down from greater altitudes. The VC certainly have not had any AA cannon in action so far (February 1967). The logical answer is a heavy of about .50-cal.; the Russian equivalent is the 12.7-mm. The VC are known to have the Chinese copy of the 12.7-mm Russian DSHK mounted on small wheeled carriages capable of both ground and antiaircraft roles. Some have been captured since

October 1965; there are probably a lot in Vietnam now, but the VC seldom lose crew-served weapons. The VC also have a number of captured U.S. .50-cal. machine guns, mostly from vehicles and aircraft. In at least one instance, a village blacksmith made a dual-purpose carriage for one of these. It was heavier than the Chinese model, but it worked.

The most common VC mortar is the 60-mm, a size not used by the Russians at all. These are either U.S. weapons captured from ARVN, the same type taken from the Chinese Nationalists, Chinese Communist copies, or locally produced weapons of the same size. The latter are the only significant survival of the old village-made arms presently used by VC hard-core units. They are light, rugged, and surprisingly effective with their 3.3-pound bombs.

The VC also have many Russian and Chinese Communist 82-mm mortars—often referred to as 80-mm in the newspapers. These can fire U.S. 81-mm shells in addition to their own. The Chinese 120-mm mortar was not used by the VC until January 1966, although the short 75-mm Japanese infantry howitzer was sometimes employed. The 120-mm mortar is a favorite of the Communists elsewhere and may be employed more often in future. It will add considerably to the range at which the VC can do damage, for instance, to aircraft on the ground. But foot mobility is a problem. The tube and bed-plate can each be carried satisfactorily by two selected Americans in such climate and terrain as that of the Aberdeen Proving Ground in Maryland, but jungle mobility in Vietnam would probably require four VC on each component. This would be clumsy. Besides the ammunition is extremely heavy.

The most common VC recoilless rifle is the 57-mm; it is usually a Chinese Communist copy of the World War II U.S. type. But some are U.S. weapons taken from either Nationalist Chinese or ARVN units. This weapon was unable to penetrate the relatively heavy faceplate of the M113 armored personnel carrier when using VC ammo. But new rounds rushed down from Communist China went into these lightly armored vehicles no matter where they were hit. The VC now have some heavier recoilless rifles similar to the obsolescent U.S. 75-mm, the Chinese Type 52. It was a round from one of these that penetrated the turret of a USMC M48A2 tank in the Star-lite operation.

VC launchers are of two types. They have the U.S. 3.5-inch rocket launcher or bazooka, which uses a slow-burning fuel contained in the base of the rocket for propulsion. The other type is the recoilless launcher. The projectile is shot forward as in a gun or recoilless rifle by the sudden inflammation of fast-burning propellant; the products of combustion go out the back suddenly and cause the projectile to move forward. This weapon is the Chinese copy of the Russian RPG-2. The 40-mm tube is not rifled; the 82-mm warhead is out in front of the barrel, like the German World War II Panzerfaust.

The VC have used flame throwers sparingly. Where an attack is to be made on a fortified hamlet which is usually constructed in part of wood, these weapons can be effective. But the weight of fuel, the damp condition of most village buildings including even thatched roofs, and the stubborn courage of some individual Government soldiers to stand against fire have limited their use.

The most effective single VC weapon—it has been called their secret weapon—is a thirty-inch piece of stout bamboo with a light flat steel blade about eight inches across. It's an ordinary shovel, but it is not fully appreciated by Americans. The VC, however, use it extremely effectively in both defense and offense. It is particularly good in fashioning narrow trenches and foxholes which are bigger at the bottom. Air-delivered grenades in even patterns do damage only when they go into these openings.

Not much is known of VC organization. Basically it is triangular and light. Extreme variation is, of course, possible in the field. A battalion has about 450 men divided into a headquarters and support company and three rifle companies. These usually have collectively four 81-mm and nine 60-mm mortars, thirteen medium machine guns, and nine or more recoilless rifles, rocket launchers, or Chinese Panzerfausts.

The VC appear to have two basic rules in choosing and planning their operations. First, they consider the political effect; this is more important to them than military considerations. Second, they try to fight only at a time, place, and under circumstances favorable to them. Even during 1965 against U.S. combat forces, they were able to adhere fairly closely to these rules, save for two instances. The U.S. Marines did catch the First VC Regiment in Starlite, inflicting severe damage. The VC did stand and fight in semifixed positions against the U.S. First Cavalry (Airmobile) west of Pleime; both sides lost heavily.

The VC have conducted two types of offensive operations more frequently than any others. They have attacked Government forces holding hamlets and villages. The VC have also ambushed ARVN and U.S. columns in many different areas. The Government forces, like the French, have chosen to defend many centers of population with perimeters of earth and concrete, barbed wire, and pungis. Garrisons vary from a platoon of semitrained local forces with small arms to a battalion or more of well-trained ARVN with efficient U.S. weapons and good communications equipment.

When a VC unit commander decides to attack a Government post, he follows a procedure established by Giap. First there is careful planning and rehearsing of the entire operation down to the last detail to make victory as certain as possible. Full-size replicas of enemy installations are often constructed in a VC-controlled area and used time after time. All the force that is considered necessary is obtained, or the attempt is not made. The VC emphasize always patience and preparation. All possible eventualities are considered and discussed over a period of weeks. If anything of importance changes, the operation is supposed to be given up, or replanned from the beginning.

The VC also endeavor to take advantage of their better system of intelligence and to use surprise to obtain a quick decision, if this appears feasible. They frequently lull a garrison into a false sense of security. But an assault can also be preceded by weeks of harassing fire and grenading at night to demoralize and tire out the garrison. A combination of these two is possible—harassing at first over a large area gradually circling around one site, but with the final assault on another.

A VC commander, once he starts, will try to follow Giap's four

Quicks; these are quick concentration, quick attack, a quick clearing and securing action, and a quick withdrawal. In recent months, these assaults have been supported by numerous heavy weapons—mortars, recoilless rifles, rocket launchers, medium machine guns —but these frequently begin their withdrawal when the riflemen and grenadiers reach their objectives. VC commanders realize that U.S. and ARVN units can move quickly also. They prefer not to risk their precious heavy weapons in combat with U.S. units perhaps supported by aircraft, artillery, and armor.

Not all VC attacks on fortified places are designed to take them. A strike may be intended to inflict casualties and damage, or to isolate but not actually capture immediately. The real purpose may be to ambush a relief column. Either way, barbed wire must be cut or blown up. Covering fire is necessary. If a real assault is to be made, it must be carried out with reckless abandon. Mortars, recoilless rifles, and flame throwers are used as available and required. Bangalore torpedoes—long pieces of pipe containing detonating explosives—can be pushed through a field of wire to clear a path through it. Bunkers are now usually attacked with recoilless rifles or rocket launchers which blow holes through the walls. If the defenders survive, grenades can be tossed through these holes or the machine-gun embrasures. Throughout Vietnam, firing openings in bunkers and other fortifications are protected with chicken wire to keep out grenades, but it usually won't stay in place when recoilless-rifle projectiles detonate close to it.

The VC endeavor to operate with as few casualties as possible. They are willing to take heavy losses where necessary, but have found that treachery within enemy garrisons can save VC lives. Defenders who change sides suddenly and either remove obstructions, or open fire on their RVNAF comrades, are obviously valuable to the VC. The Communists have shown considerable ability to recruit NCO's and officers of ARVN and insist that they prove their devotion to their new cause by helping to take the places where they are stationed.

Ambushes are the second important type of VC offensive maneuver. The VC can lay an ambush for Government and U.S. combat and supply columns practically anywhere, even in the open along the side of one of the main roads. They are masters of camouflage and patience. Ambushes can be of several different types technically known as area, V, L, or minuet. The object is always to inflict as much damage as possible with minimum loss. They can set up and spring any of these ambushes in unlikely places. The VC have frequently ambushed ARVN units when they were *returning* from an operation and close to their base.

If the VC commander does not have sufficient strength to deal with the forces to be ambushed, he does not spring it at all. The early jungle ambushes were often dependent on shotgun-type, muzzle-loading weapons, similar primitive breech-loaders, a minimum of automatic weapons, and personal arms. More recently weapons have included heavier weapons. Electrically detonated mines of large size have also been employed, particularly against vehicles. These same tactics can be employed in connection with artillery or mortar shells suspended over trails.

The ultimate ambush victory is complete destruction of the enemy, but this can be costly. VC commanders can usually disengage if their losses mount disproportionately. They bear in mind always the speed of a heliborne enemy reaction force. Quick retirement into the jungle with everything that has been captured has often been accomplished. As already mentioned, an attack on a Government fortification can be combined with one or more ambushes. The ambush will be laid along the most likely path for a relieving Government column.

There are some other VC offensive tactics which are of particular importance to U.S. forces. Suicide penetrations of perimeter defenses by a few VC with explosives have blown up aircraft. Larger units suddenly attacking necessarily thin outer defenses can get VC mortars within range of important targets such as U.S. aircraft on the ground. These have both been effective. When carefully planned and rehearsed and carried out quickly, they are hard to stop. But American loss in men and materiel may not be irreparable.

Occasionally the VC will fight an offensive action which is neither an ambush nor an assault on a fortified place. Until late 1964 these were generally chance meetings followed by a more or less standard attack; but the fighting could not last long because VC ammunition could not be wasted. They can now deliver a larger volume of fire and sustain it for some time. They often have more firepower and heavy weapons, battalion for battalion, than ARVN. If the size and composition of the enemy force are right, VC commanders may press an effort of this type to the limit. They like to achieve an encirclement and wipe out their enemies completely. So long as the VC are winning, they continue the fight. If U.S. combat forces arrive on the scene, however, the VC are often ready to retire and disperse into the jungle.

The capture of weapons, ammunition, and other items of equipment has always been a major consideration in all VC offensive operations. Formerly, costly assaults were undertaken primarily for this purpose. They still manage to carry off a very high percentage of their own weapons along with many of their killed and most of their wounded. They do this not only because of pride, but also to preserve their winning image in the minds of the civilian population and to conceal their losses from the enemy.

By far the most potent VC defensive tactic maneuver is just to disappear. Even battalions can fade away into the jungle quickly. The VC also have a lot of fixed fortifications. These do not resemble the strategic hamlets of the Government because anything that can be seen from the air, or even from the ground nearby, can be destroyed by bombing, artillery fire, or projectiles from infantry support weapons. All VC works are camouflaged or underground.

These fortifications vary enormously in extent. Every VC hamlet will have spider holes and tunnels. Base areas will have concealed systems of trenches, bunkers, recoilless rifle and mortar emplacements, and underground passages extending in some instances for miles. These are cleverly designed with many airshafts and exits. Sometimes entrances are underwater or below cookfires. VC tunnels are often too small for Americans to use. Fire can be delivered from bunkers or not, as desired. When the VC don't shoot, their installations often remain undiscovered.

The real value of these fortifications lies in the way they are used.

They are completely expendable in the eyes of VC commanders; they cost labor only and can be reproduced easily. They aid the Communists in creating enemy casualties, but are not held to the last extremity. The VC will open fire suddenly with every weapon they have on any ARVN or U.S. force that comes within range. If they are not immediately victorious, they will continue the fight only so long as they are not in danger of being surrounded. They are usually aware of what is taking place around them. If encirclement and destruction appear possible, they leave, probably through escape tunnels into the jungle.

Recent actions indicate that the VC have perfected a technique in which they draw U.S. and ARVN units toward these fortifications. A few VC soldiers will deliberately open fire on their enemies and retreat toward the concealed VC bunkers. When U.S. and ARVN forces are within easy range, the VC will open fire, sometimes with mortars and recoilless rifles as well as the inevitable automatic weapons. Young U.S. rifle platoon leaders and others have sacrificed themselves by assaulting these prepared positions which they assumed to be just a VC firing line in the open jungle.

The VC have shown a remarkable ability to defend themselves against new weapons and tactics. In a few cases they have developed something new themselves; more often they have adapted old techniques to counter new challenges. U.S. helicopters began to arrive in South Vietnam in quantity early in 1962 and gave ARVN the ability to attack quickly and with little warning. These attacks were successful at first; the aircraft seldom suffered serious damage. But VC units above platoon size stopped concentrating where they could be enveloped. Dual-purpose machine guns began to knock down helicopters regularly. In the early days of the armed escort helicopters, VC antiaircraft and ground fire was subdued. But they soon realized the comparative ineffectiveness of fire from the choppers and stuck to their machine guns.

The VC tactical reaction to local defeats has been interesting. Before U.S. combat troops were committed, an ARVN victory in almost any area was answered quickly by a successful VC assault against some Government post in the same area. As we have seen, the Marine Corps victory in Starlite led the VC to concentrate again ten days later to hit the Chu Lai airfield even harder. This resulted in another clobbering in Piranha. Since then, the VC have refused to concentrate close enough to the coast for the Marines to use their amphibious and heliborne skill and equipment for dramatic victories. The same general VC thinking appears to apply to U.S. Army areas; the VC will not come back for more the way they did against ARVN.

On the other hand, VC and North Vietnamese units now appear determined to fight for some territory where they do have adequate defenses and advantages in terrain and positions. Their bunkers, tunnels, and trenches are sufficiently extensive and hard to find to protect them from aircraft and artillery bombardment. If encirclement is not possible because of distance and jungle, they will stand. They are now willing to sustain severe casualties, if they can also create them in enemy assault units. They now have the weapons and ammunition, the skill in near conventional war tactics, and the individual dedication to kill until they get killed. But this type of defense has been encountered mainly far inland close to Cambodia and Laos.

The VC are not invincible. Not many neutral observers still believe that they can win in the field the way the Viet Minh beat the French. The VC still remain, however, extremely tough antagonists. Nothing increases the efficiency of a combat unit so much as actual fighting. Their leadership, discipline, and combat know-how will get even better. The VC don't expect to be rotated home after twelve months or to get five days in Hong Kong. They have known little except war for twenty-five years; they don't expect any other kind of life.

The great danger in fighting them is to judge their military potential from their appearance. The French lost to the Viet Minh in part because of this; the U.S. is not making this mistake, at least in training. A Fort Benning manual has this to say of the VC:

They have the strength which comes from long, patient, tough military training, an iron discipline of mind and body, and a true missionary zeal in their cause. They have been convinced by their leaders that they are right and that they will win. They, therefore, consider themselves "free men" fighting for a way of life which they are certain will soon prevail throughout the world for are they not communists, riding the "wave of the future"? The guerrilla has learned the hard way that he must out think, out perform, and, even more important, out believe his more heavily armed opponent.

VC recruits in adequate numbers may continue to be forthcoming. There appear to be about 48,000 hard-core troops supported by 130,000 guerrillas and 25,000 North Vietnamese. Logistic and political support from North Vietnam and the Chinese Communists is increasing. The VC hate the West, but they don't underrate anti-Communist combat ability. They have received too many pointed demonstrations of it. No one can tell how the war will end, but the enemy is worthy of the best efforts of the U.S. and its allies. They are first-class fighting men; many conditions in this war are favorable to them. So far, they have taken full advantage of almost every one.

7: South Vietnamese Government Forces

IIIIIIIIIIIIIIIIIIIIIIIIIIIIIIIIIIIIIIIIIIIIIIIIIIIIIIIIIIIIIIIIIIIIIIIIIIIIIIIIIIIIIIII

In 1955 South Vietnam began a long hard uphill climb economically and politically under the anti-Communist government of Ngo Dinh Diem. In spite of internal troubles, but with aid from many Free World countries, particularly the U.S., Diem's government gradually made headway. Gross national product was rising; Diem defeated two militant sects that fought against him. He was sincere and fanatically dedicated, but not popular in the villages. His government appeared, however, to be building an independent nation closely allied to the Free World.

This the Communists could not stand, and they began their own version of bargain-basement war in 1959. Diem and his colleagues were ill prepared for such a violent trial of strength, both politically and militarily. Not many in responsible positions in his government came from outside the relatively wealthy, literate classes of the cities. Diem personally reacted badly to opposition in this form. He gradually isolated himself from his people and became more autocratic. He did not have the rare faculty of choosing an organization which would make up for his own personal deficiencies. He was a deeply religious scholar, not a dynamic leader like Magsaysay or Templer, and he insisted on doing even trivial things himself.

Diem would not take U.S. advice. He did not realize that his policies were alienating most of his people because those he trusted gave him a false picture of what was happening. Enveloped personally in a cloak of righteousness, he condoned dishonesty, inefficiency, and cruelty in others. His chief advisers were his brother, Ngo Dinh

Nhu, and his sister-in-law, Madame Nhu. Both appear to have been power-hungry and to have had few redeeming virtues.

The U.S. made little headway in persuading Diem to make real changes in his government. In 1962 and early 1963 Diem was managing to lose the war in spite of an enormous amount of U.S. aid. He became so stubborn and set in his illogical ideas that high-ranking U.S. advisers were driven close to despair. A military coup of which the U.S. had prior knowledge, but certainly did not sponsor, took over on 2 November 1963.

The first government under General Duong Van Minh lasted until 30 January 1964 when General Nguyen Khanh came to power. Khanh was succeeded by other short-lived regimes until Nguyen Cao Ky with nine other military men took charge in June 1965. Ky weathered several political storms in his first year in power, and at this writing (February 1967) appears to have weathered another even more serious one. He is a young man with considerable military ability; he has been head of the Air Force for some time. He may develop into an able politician and has a lot of personal appeal. He is intensely anti-Communist and strongly allied to the U.S.

None of these South Vietnamese governments has been democratic, nor have they been able to generate much loyalty in rural areas. The recent struggle for power between Ky and Buddhists could still lead to real civil war. But democratic elections are at least promised. The U.S., Ky's Vietnam, and other less numerous allies are presently fighting a joint war against a common enemy, the VC.

Grand strategy in this bargain-basement war has varied considerably. Under Diem the Government attempted an extremely broad program of strategic hamlets similar to those used by the British successfully in Malaya. The same British advisers were sometimes actually in over-all control. Other counterguerrilla experts from the Philippines and elsewhere came in to tell U.S. advisers and the RVNAF how to win the war. Many procedures that had worked in other places were tried in South Vietnam without much progress. The hamlet program failed because too much was attempted with too little attention paid to winning over the people and teaching them how to protect themselves. Some economic, medical, and social improvements were made, but the success of these may have been exaggerated. Politically the war has not always gone well. Both Diem's government and its successors have lacked real ability to communicate with the people in the villages and weld them all into a nation. General Thi of the I Corps Area might have had a better chance of doing this than Ky, but he was removed from the supreme council. Unlike Thi, most government representatives in the villages cannot even speak the local language. Thi, a Buddhist, was a real leader of the people of the rural areas and one of the few high officers who came from the countryside.

The RVNAF now include almost 700,000 fighting men of all descriptions, one of the largest armed forces in the anti-Communist world. Victory in the war depends on them. U.S. combat troops and the Australian, New Zealand, Korean, and Philippines units deployed in the country under U.S. leadership can help, but a meaningful victory over Communism can be won only by the South Vietnamese themselves. Only these people can establish a strong anti-Communist government.

The RVNAF consists of ARVN (the army), an air force, a navy, and several smaller independent organizations. There are about 300,000 regular troops in ARVN, but this total does not include the Regional Force of about 123,000 under arms on a full-time basis, or the Popular Force, which numbers over 135,000 local militia. The Vietnamese Special Forces (LLDB) is also virtually independent of ARVN and contains an additional 23,000 Vietnamese, plus mercenaries mostly from other ethnic groups like the Cambodians and the various hill tribes often called collectively Montagnards. In addition, there are 50,000 National Police and 40,000 Armed Combat Youth.

The men who make up these forces are not without their weaknesses. To pass over them without comment would leave a false impression. The Vietnamese are as small physically as the VC and not usually in as good condition. They are no better coordinated and have the same physical advantages and disadvantages already discussed. Their morale is not so high, on the average; they do not normally have so strong a desire to win. There have been reports of

ARVN units that would not attack, but instead threw away their arms in retreat and lost strong positions to inferior enemy forces. These things have happened, but some other units, and even the same units at other times, have done well. Americans who know ARVN best say that they do not lack personal courage. Individuals have been extremely brave; small units have been burned to death by VC flame throwers without surrendering. Some native Vietnamese soldiers performed magnificently under the French.

ARVN soldiers don't always use U.S. equipment properly, and sometimes behave barbarously to their own people. They have an abundance of patience, but little sense of urgency. They let opportunities slip through their fingers because they are not prompt either in military maneuvers or in their personal lives. Promotion is not always based on merit, or on any regular system of seniority. Field officers are usually from the wealthier town families, know little of the people living in villages, and don't even speak their language. Yet capable men often do get important jobs. A good commander means a good unit; some are entirely satisfactory even by Western standards.

There is an even more serious handicap to effective military effort. South Vietnamese do not cooperate well with each other. Commanders of units tend to become rivals; personal jealousy often prevents full assistance and information sharing. The RVNAF are still separate and do not subordinate themselves to the common good. Even after the introduction of U.S. and other allied combat forces, the Vietnamese refused to consider a joint command. U.S. advisers are in reality just that; they are rarely allowed to control. When U.S. Army and ARVN units participate in joint action, there is no one local commander in chief.

This is a strange situation, almost unbelievable actually, because of the obvious difference in military ability and efficiency. Historically, a nation with a long-established, efficient professional army when fighting alongside a younger, less competent ally has usually taken over operational control of the ally's army. It would be more efficient for the U.S. to control ARVN and the other RVNAF. But Vietnamese hate anything that resembles colonialism; military subordination to a Western power would create an extremely bad public image. The U.S. is now committed to the war; American commanders are doing their level best to win it with the present system.

There have been two small exceptions to this lack of joint command. U.S. Marines under General Walt in the I Corps Area have tactfully insisted on commanding ARVN and South Vietnamese Marine units which they took into combat with them aboard U.S. landing craft and helicopters. This system has worked well and might perhaps be the opening wedge to something more permanent. The Marines and the I Corps RVNAF, formerly under General Thi, get on well together.

The other exception to the general rule of separate commands is in connection with U.S. Special Force strike commands in the same area. In most Special Force situations, U.S. soldiers are really only advisers with a bit more control of those they are advising than usual. The Vietnamese Special Force officers usually command, but there is at least one non-Vietnamese mercenary force in I Corps Area which is permanently under the command of a U.S. Special Force A Team assigned to it. The Montagnards—another ethnic group who live in the hills and mountains—have shown a greater friendship for and loyalty to the U.S. Special Forces than to similar LLDB units. This arrangement of U.S. command of Montagnard units may well become more common. The mountain people just don't get on well with most city-bred Vietnamese, but do with both Australian and American Special Force soldiers.

When the U.S. began to supervise the South Vietnamese military training program in 1955, triangular infantry divisions were formed with some tanks and artillery in each. There were three rifle regiments in each division with three rifle battalions plus some heavy support weapons in each larger unit. This conventional arrangement was designed to stop a military penetration by the Army of North Vietnam across the Seventeenth Parallel. Both Diem and top U.S. officers expected such an effort. But the Communists had enough of straight-ahead conventional fighting in Korea; the vast productivity of U.S. industry gave that nation too much of an advantage in this type of war.

ARVN divisions were nearly useless for fighting guerrillas in the war which began about 1959. Battalions were the largest units which could usually operate efficiently against the VC. Each rifle battalion consisted theoretically òf a headquarters and support company with an 81-mm mortar section and a 57-mm recoilless rifle section, each with two weapons, plus three rifle companies. Each of the latter had a headquarters, three rifle platoons, and a weapons platoon with two 60-mm mortars, two 3.5-inch rocket launchers, and two medium machine guns. Each rifle platoon consisted of a headquarters, three rifle squads, and a weapons squad which had two BAR's. A rifle squad normally contained only riflemen; this arrangement of platoon weapons is similar to that of the U.S. Army early in World War II. The ARVN organization seemed to call for eleven-man squads with four men in platoon headquarters; this leads to a rifle platoon strength of from 48 and a total company strength of about 200. A battalion would be above 700 men at full strength.

But the average ARVN rifle battalion shrank in 1963, because of casualties and desertions, to the smallest in the world, sometimes less than 300 men. Some changes obviously had to be made; the usual expedient was to drop from three to two units at each level and/or combine the support unit with the rifle units. After several years an under-strength table of organization and equipment has been established which calls for a standardization in all units. Each rifle platoon consists of a headquarters of one officer and one enlisted man and three eight-man squads. Two of these are called fire squads because they contain a BAR; the other is the maneuver squad because it contains only rifles or their equivalents, carbines and submachine guns.

On this basis, an ARVN rifle company or other similar unit contains about 100 men, and a rifle battalion about 400 to 450. RVNAF are trying not only to fill up their ranks, but also to increase the number of combat rifle battalions. There are about 130 of these now, with an additional 17 in training and 14 more planned. ARVN commanders would also like to add an extra BAR, medium machine gun, rocket launcher, and 60-mm mortar at appropriate places in each company in order to have three rather than the present two per unit. They would like to add a 57-mm recoilless rifle and an 81 mortar to their battalion support arms also for a total of three each. U.S. advisers often feel, however, that the increase of 50 per cent in support weapons and ammunition would not be desirable. In spite of some Vietnamese being able to carry heavy loads, 26, 100, and 450 ARVN's just can't carry as much as the same number of Americans, even in tropical jungle. Extra support arms would decrease already limited mobility and probably lead to even greater losses of weapons during retreats.

The Regional Forces are organized no higher than battalions; even at this level they are most irregular. A provincial (sector) chief, usually an ARVN lieutenant colonel, has all his Regional Force companies in a loose battalion formation. They may number from three to more than ten, but they rarely operate together. One or more companies are permanently assigned to each district (subsector) chief who is normally an ARVN major. Each company usually consists of a headquarters, a weapons platoon, and three rifle platoons more or less like those of ARVN. Some companies have numbered even more than 150 men for short periods. But many shrink to under 100 and lose subordinate units in the process; a squad of three or four men, or a platoon of two weak squads, does not make sense. Two under-strength units are frequently amalgamated to form one of acceptable strength. Platoons consisting of two squads, and companies which have but two platoons are not unusual.

Popular Forces are organized in a similar manner, but one level lower. There may be as many platoons as there are hamlets in a given village, plus one or two for the main population center, if there is one. This means usually from three to nine platoons which form one loose company. Platoons are irregular in strength, but generally have three or four squads plus a slightly larger than standard headquarters. There are no larger units. The LLDB's have an organization quite different from this, but similar to U.S. Special Forces. These units will be covered in some detail in the next chapter.

ARVN, Regional Force, Popular Force, and LLDB units are now armed with U.S. World War II types of weapons. Other small arms, including some from France and Germany, are in the hands of Government forces, but these have been passed along to police units and the Armed Combat Youth. The term "rifle" in Vietnamese units is vague. An ARVN maneuver squad is supposed to have two M1 carbines, an M1 Thompson submachine gun, and five M1 rifles. The average soldier prefers a Thompson or a carbine to the M1 rifle which is just too big for him. An M1 rifle will be carried cheerfully only if the weapon is equipped with a grenade launcher; a young soldier who receives this combination feels that he has been given something special, a kind of a status symbol, and will work hard in order to keep it with him. But if he should try to fire a grenade from the shoulder, he may injure himself severely. There is, theoretically, one grenade launcher in each squad, but an M30 grenade launched from it has about three times the recoil of the same rifle with ball ammunition.

This preference for Thompsons and carbines is even more decided in Regional Force and Popular Force units. Not many of these soldiers who have a chance to get these continue to carry M1 rifles. The Thompson is particularly popular because of its burst-fire capability. I saw many RVNAF soldiers with Thompsons. They also may prefer them because of the American movies they have seen.

Shotguns have been issued, but I received conflicting comments on their efficiency. Lack of range is probably not important; these weapons have been less effective in combat than they might have been because issue ammunition is wrong. The 12-gauge shotgun shells in use discharge only eight pellets of 00 Buck; the same weapon can fire satisfactorily forty-one pellets of #4 Buck, a much more guerrilla-effective load. Forty-one pellets obviously have a greater chance of hitting than eight; one is enough to wound seriously. Shotgun ammunition loaded with a cluster of small steel arrows is being used in Vietnam, but not so far by RVNAF. Another disadvantage that U.S. shotguns have for Vietnamese is that their arms are too short to operate the pump action satisfactorily. In their hands, a fine Remington Model 870 repeater becomes little better than a single shot.

The ideal rifle now available for the South Vietnamese is the U.S. M16 because it is light enough for them to carry, fits them better, and is sufficiently powerful at all useful combat ranges. These arms have been somewhat more difficult to maintain and use a lot of ammunition because of their burst-fire capability, but they are extremely popular. Individual ARVN soldiers, mainly airborne, who have been issued AR-15's are said not to have lost a single weapon to the enemy—a rather astonishing record. Some ARVN units in retreat have thrown away M1 rifles and BAR's, confident that they will receive new weapons quickly when they return to their bases.

The BAR in ARVN is definitely a crew-served weapon; it's a brute for the little fellows to carry complete with ammunition, but two of them with one gun somehow manage to struggle through even on long marches. This arm is also something of a status symbol because of its combat importance. Medium machine guns in ARVN are now limited to the U.S. air-cooled Brownings (Model 1919A4's and A6's). As originally made, the A4 was for use with a tripod and without the buttstock; the A6 was the bipod mount, buttstock model. These are sometimes used as originally intended, but more often combined. Weapons of both types—they are not quite the same internally—are used with mounting features of the other. ARVN gunners like the tripod and the buttstock incorporated into the same weapon; they think they can control it better.

Other infantry support weapons are current U.S. models such as 81-mm mortars and 3.5-inch rocket launchers plus the recently abandoned 57- and 75-mm recoilless rifles. The 75-mm is not popular; it weighs more than the 57 and is not appreciably more effective against most VC targets. I ran across more than one ARVN soldier with a U.S. M79 grenade launcher, but this issue was probably *sub rosa.*

The U.S. 60-mm mortar is used by the Vietnamese. It is valuable for combat in terrain like that of South Vietnam. There are also 81-mm mortars in ARVN and Regional Force units. Armored personnel carriers, although strictly speaking not infantry weapons, have been assigned to some provincial chiefs. Many district chiefs have received 105- and even 155-mm howitzers complete with ARVN crews.

Village and hamlet fortifications are extremely important to the Vietnamese war effort and depend heavily on U.S. infantry support weapons. Trenches, barbed wire, pungis, and weapons emplacements can be built around almost any inhabited area; these are normally irregular because the villages vary in size and shape. Two standardized small-defense systems—both actually of French origin—are popular; these are called stars and triangles. In the star the trenches connect each of the terminal bunkers directly with a central hub. In the triangle the trenches connect the terminal bunkers directly with each other. A small group of buildings may be placed inside the star.

Somehow, U.S. advisers have usually found three automatic weapons—two BAR's and one medium machine gun—and a 60-mm mortar for each of these small fortifications, although garrisons are normally only a Popular Force platoon. The wide trenches—the garrisons usually live in these with their families—allow all three automatic weapons to be concentrated and fired from any terminal bunker; each has three openings, or an open parapet. Riflemen alone can hold the other bunkers against sneak secondary attacks until the return of a temporarily loaned medium machine gun or BAR. The 60-mm mortar is set up in a sandbagged or even a concrete emplacement in the triangle, but is located in a similar position outside, but close to the hub in the star.

These stars, triangles, and larger fortifications are the basis of South Vietnamese ground force defensive tactics. The country, save for areas completely Communist-dominated, is presently divided into provinces and districts. A district is roughly about 150 square miles in area; each is under a chief, as already mentioned. These ARVN majors have both political and military duties. Each usually has one or two Regional Force companies plus the ARVN artillery. Two 105-mm howitzers are customarily assigned, but where the VC are strong, or the district large, there will be 155-mm howitzers, either in place of the 105's or in addition to them. This artillery plus the Regional Force 81-mm mortars will normally be inside the defenses of the district "capital," often only another hamlet. Most or all the area within a district will be within the range of these centrally placed support weapons.

Each district chief will organize his villages and hamlets as he sees fit, but will have the assistance of a U.S. adviser team of about ten officers and men. He will usually garrison his outside fortifications with Popular Force platoons, but keep his Regional Force units near his central headquarters. The entire command is interconnected by two-way radios.

Ideally, each district chief should hold all his fortifications with a portion of his force only and go out on night patrols and ambushes with the remainder so as to keep down VC activity. In actual practice, this is difficult to do. The VC can bring in one of their hardcore battalions temporarily and overwhelm a local ARVN officer who tries fighting at night in the open with his Regional Force and Popular Force units. Most district chiefs concentrate all their forces during darkness inside their defended perimeters and support each other in the event of a VC attack with high-angle fire. This is limited by range only, since projectiles travel through arcs high above the jungle.

A reaction or strike force could be sent out to relieve a hamlet under attack at district level, but the chief has no helicopters or armored personnel carriers. If he moves on foot, or in thin-skinned vehicles, he may be ambushed. Some provincial chiefs have ARVN rifle battalions and personnel carriers, and they can get helicopter transportation. But by the time these forces can be ready and sent to where they are wanted, the VC have usually done their jobs and faded away into the jungle. Provincial forces can also be ambushed if they move out without proper security precautions.

The Government has lost control of most land communications in Vietnam and more than half the people in the villages. The roads that are still used by U.S. and ARVN convoys are often mined; almost every one is subject to ambush. Railroads seldom run at all. In the Mekong delta in the south, ARVN thought that the answer was to send convoys with armored personnel carriers as escort vehicles. This worked for a time, but additional Chinese 40-82-mm launchers, 57- and 75-mm recoilless rifles, and more effective ammunition for these weapons has reduced the effectiveness of the carriers. One ARVN unit lost ten M113's, essentially because the men inside tried to use these fine light vehicles as pillboxes, rather than move and fight from them in the manner that U.S. advisers suggested.

If a fortified hamlet or larger place is hit by the VC, the garrison will open with all it has in the general direction of the enemy. If radio communications don't break down, a call for help goes through to the district or provincial chief. A Popular Force or Regional Force garrison plentifully supplied with ammunition and supported by high-angle fire already zeroed in can be a tough nut to crack.

I was fortunate in being able to visit a star fortification that had been hit the night before by an entire hard-core VC company with some local Communist guerrilla reinforcements. A single Popular Force platoon of an initial strength of thirty-eight held off this attack in spite of the defection of its leader and one NCO to the enemy. Before these two left they placed two mines, one under the radio in the center of the star and the other in the adjacent nonstandard headquarters building. They fired the mines electrically from the outside and wrecked the communications and command system of the small garrison. The two defectors also removed the obstructions in the passage through the barbed wire and pungis. The hard-core VC company poured into the fortification as soon as the mines were set off.

In this crisis the lives of the remaining Popular Force soldiers and their families hung by a thread. A soldier of seventeen—he looked about fourteen—tossed a grenade ten feet across a concrete barrier into the Command-post entranceway. He was dizzy from the concussion of the mines, but his bomb killed the first four VC who were coming in and blocked the passage with their bodies. A burst from a Popular Force BAR hit the VC company commander in the chest; he fell inside the star. The Popular Force platoon's other BAR and its medium machine gun cut loose too; the VC fell back. Somehow, the platoon pulled itself together, mostly by instinct; they regrouped to cover the weaknesses in their defenses.

The twenty-three Popular Force soldiers who survived the initial mine blasts and first assault fought with a tenacity based not only on patriotism and individual bravery, but also on the certain knowledge that they and their families would be tortured to death if the VC overran them. The garrison was not in communication with district headquarters because the radio was gone, but the chief opened with his 81-mm mortars and 105-mm howitzers anyway. He could hear the fighting and placed a belt of fire around his sorely tried platoon.

Four hours of darkness remained; the hamlet that had been hit was only two miles by road from the district capital, but the chief and his U.S. adviser refused to go to the rescue on foot or in jeeps and trucks. They could hear the firing, particularly from the Popular Force machine gun; they kept up their mortar and howitzer support. But they did not move out of their own defenses. When reinforcements were flown in the next morning, they did advance down the road toward the star fortification. They found out then how right their decision had been not to go to the rescue. One VC company had hit the small fort. Two more had entrenched themselves in an L-shaped ambush position along the rescue route to the district headquarters, but had retreated at daylight.

The Popular Force platoon had lost eight of the men who survived the initial attack. The enemy managed to collect all their own bodies, save for the five men who had been killed deep inside the defenses, but blood and some dismembered parts of other VC bodies indicated severe additional casualties. Even more conclusive proof of the extent of the small victory were seventeen captured VC weapons, an extremely large number for an action of this type. These had probably been blown into the jungle and could not be found in darkness. The 105's and 81's had done remarkably well in shelling close to the barbed wire and pungi-studded perimeter without going into it as sometimes happens. They had plenty of ammunition and had fired many thousands of rounds; VC reinforcements from the two ambushing companies which also attacked the star after the first attack failed brought with them at least one 57-mm recoilless rifle and two 60-mm mortars. But these were not able to fire effectively on the three bunkers, although the recoilless rifle did smash holes in the abandoned headquarters building.

This small but resounding victory was due to the courage and the fighting ability of a Popular Force platoon, the military judgment of a good district chief, high-angle support fire from a distance, and some luck. If that first grenade had gone astray, the fort might have fallen in sixty seconds. But luck has always been important in war. The areas where the Government is still strong enough to have integrated systems of district defenses like these may easily return to complete Government control, if a few victories are won in the field.

RVNAF offensive tactics are more difficult to understand, perhaps because they have varied greatly. ARVN commanders first tried to conduct counterguerrilla operations with conventional divisions and smaller organic units from them. These were not able to go out into the jungle and find the VC, much less fight them. But frequently on the way home they were ambushed. A great deal of time was spent by U.S. advisers and ARVN commanders in makeshift counterinsurgency training with far from perfect results.

ARVN can launch an infantry attack with support from all weapons that can reach the combat area. Battalions, companies, and platoons move under cover of their own fire. Regular units have air and artillery support and often armor. Armored personnel carriers can be used over a wide range of terrain and perform fairly well as substitute tanks where the heavier vehicles cannot be used because of paddy, swamp, or mountains.

Divisions and regiments don't often go out into the jungle. Offensive maneuvers by ARVN battalions are usually still slow, not always well planned, and seldom driven home viciously. Worst of all, the VC sometimes know ahead of time where ARVN units are going to attack. The VC will either disappear or concentrate and fight ARVN toe to toe. Bernard B. Fall compiled a long list of ARVN defeats by VC units of the same or smaller size in his book *Street Without Joy*. Helicopter envelopments by ARVN units alone were effective in 1962 and 1963, but seldom worked in 1965 and 1966.

On the other hand, the larger ARVN offensive operations began to benefit in 1965 from the presence of U.S. combat forces. The VC began to realize that if they opposed ARVN too strongly, Americans would be committed imaginatively. Slugging matches had to be avoided by the VC even when no U.S. units were engaged because they might come in at any time accompanied by support weapons, artillery, and air power in all its devastating forms.

In small offensive operations, however, RVNAF have continued at a disadvantage. The VC are superb jungle and night fighters; their system of intelligence is much better than ARVN's. In spite of a few dramatic exceptions, local Government forces don't normally have the training, experience, and desire to find, fix, and kill the enemy. The VC have confidence in their ability to use the hours of darkness.

Government forces will also improve, especially in leadership. The ARVN Infantry School turned out better than 6000 platoon commanders in 1966. All demonstrated an ability not only to master academic subjects, but also to lead men in the field. Unlike many ARVN officers commissioned in the past, the new ones must be tough physically. They have an obstacle or confidence course of the U.S. type which must be conquered before graduation. It requires real muscular strength, coordination, and more than normal courage. A serious effort has also been made to imbue the trainees with patriotic dedication of the kind Magsaysay instilled in his young officers.

A discussion of Government tactics must include those of the LLDB, the Special Forces. Units are located not only in primitive areas such as the Central Highlands, but also near Communist strongholds of long standing. These forces are, of course, patterned after U.S. Special Forces; each LLDB battalion has a U.S. Special Force A team assigned to it. The U.S. team does not usually command, but does come closer to it than in other cases because the American Government supports the battalion logistically. Pay comes directly from the U.S. A team.

I visited one of these Special Forces areas not far from War Zone D north of Saigon, a Communist stronghold for more than twenty

Dept. of Defense (USMC)

U. S. Marine riflemen and M48A2 tanks collaborating in a search and clear operation. The tanks supply heavy firepower which is particularly effective against VC fortification. Marine riflemen protect the tanks against short range VC attacks with AT weapons.

Marines in a VC trench during Operation Starlite. The Marine in center foreground has an M79 grenade launcher, one of the most successful of the new U.S. weapons being used in Vietnam.

Marine infantryman, an M48A2 tank, and an HU-34 helicopter during Operation Starlite. Where these components can operate effectively, they are unbeatable.

A Gurkha soldier in a bivouac with a Cal .303 British Bren light machine gun.

The large, slow-flying British Beverly transport plane has been highly useful in Borneo. It can carry ninety-six paratroopers, or machinery for clearing tropical jungles. Where landings are impossible, it can drop a medium-sized bulldozer by means of three sixty-eight-foot parachutes.

Three Gurkha soldiers armed (left to right) with the British SLR, the 7.62 NATO Bren light machine gun, and the 9-mm Patchett submachine gun (L2A3). This photograph was taken outside one of their base camps in Borneo.

Gurkha soldiers with the .303-cal. British water-cooled Vickers. This weapon has proved to be the most effective medium machine gun for use in Malaysian base camp bunkers. Rugged and reliable, it delivers almost continuous fire without changing the barrel.

Republic of Philippines Army crew with a 4.2-inch mortar.

This VC mantrap was hand-forged in a village using springs from a U.S. jeep. A pressure of forty-five pounds is required to spring it. The sixteen-inch jaws are probably capable of taking off a leg.

Part of a shipment of Communist weapons which did not reach the VC. In the foreground are potato-masher-type grenades. The light machine gun behind them is said to have been manufactured in Czechoslovakia. The rifles are German World War II Mausers.

Dept. of Defense (USN)

A demonstration VC pitfall trap from the U.S. Marine Corps Jungle Training Center on Okinawa. The Marine who appears to be impaled on one of the sharpened stakes is astonishingly realistic until he has to take a breath.

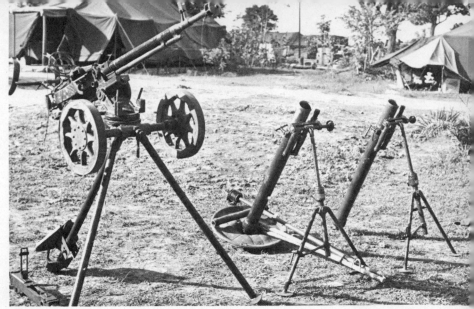

Two captured VC mortars and a heavy Communist medium machine gun which can be used either against ground or air targets. The gun is set up for firing at aircraft. Note particularly the rear sight.

U.S. Marines looking into a VC spider hole. The Marine has had to enlarge the opening before investigating inside.

A Marine lieutenant colonel displays two VC souvenirs. The board with the reforged barbed nails must be tied in place under water. The grenade is of village manufacture.

One of the hundreds of old French concrete blockhouses still being used by U.S. and allied forces in Vietnam. These are particularly valuable if situated near airfields and similar installations.

Two Popular Force soldiers in a star fortification bunker outside a Government subsector capital. The weapon is a U.S. Model 1919 medium machine gun. The men are ready to fire on any VC they see.

Typical Delta country as seen from a helicopter. The tracks in the background are where armored personnel carriers ended a reconnaissance and turned around. Transportation in this country is mostly by boat, although amphibious, lightly armored vehicles can negotiate some of it.

A U.S. infantryman with his 3.5-inch rocket launcher in the outer perimeter defense around the Bien Hoa airfield near Saigon. Living in this area during the rainy season is not easy. Troops must be ready for action at any time, day or night.

Another view of Bien Hoa perimeter showing an 81-mm mortar. The troops holding these positions are from the U.S. First Infantry Division.

Three U.S. soldiers in a jeep with a U.S. M60 medium machine gun on a swivel mount.

A UH1B U.S. Army helicopter. The rocket at right has just been discharged. Two medium machine guns in fixed mounts are shown beside the door. A soldier with a flexible-mounted M60 is watching for a ground target opportunity.

A U.S. 4.2-inch mortar and crew firing a mission in Vietnam.

Two Air Force F-100's. These jet fighter-bombers can roar in on call from light reconnaissance planes and deliver several types of ordnance.

General Lew Walt, USMC, and ARVN General Thi, the I Corps commanders for their respective nations. General Thi has since been replaced. He was one of the few top RVNAF commanders who spoke the language of the village people.

years. I went first to the enclave which contained the U.S. and LLDB B teams. This would correspond about to a province chief's headquarters in other areas. There were two 155- and four 105-mm howitzers, all with regular ARVN crews, mortars, 3.5-inch rocket launchers, and many medium machine guns. Because of its logistic support function, the U.S. B team had a separate but adjacent fortified compound.

I also visited a typical LLDB battalion and its attached U.S. A team. This unit lived in a strongly fortified compound of its own. The outer perimeter of barbed wire, pungis, and booby traps was supported by sandbag bunkers and trenches. There were several tripod-mounted A6 medium machine guns and protected firing points for BAR's, rifles, and submachine guns. Some rocket launchers normally used on armed helicopters had been mounted on the walls. The buildings inside the perimeter were laid out to aid a defense of the place. The command post was strong enough to resist mortar fire and was protected from enemy recoilless rifles. The U.S. A team commander had a group of men and women making solid concrete blocks for use in even more secure defenses.

The civil effort of U.S. and RVNAF was also working well. It included American movies shown twice weekly and a small but surprisingly efficient hospital open to civilians. Two Special Forces medics were saving more lives in a week than many U.S. doctors do in a year. Almost all civilians within a considerable area were friendly. The best of the local young men had been organized into three fine companies, the mercenaries referred to earlier.

This post was close to perhaps the strongest Communist area in the entire country, but its condition was extremely encouraging. The U.S. A team and their LLDB counterparts were enthusiastic, efficient, and proud of what they had accomplished. Their mercenaries were in part Cambodian; all weapons were clean and individual soldiers bore themselves well. I watched one company begin a three-day patrol into enemy territory. Saigon inefficiency is forgotten in the presence of these back-country fighters.

The VC, like other guerrillas, can be beaten. The basis for victory is, of course, an integrated military and civil program. One without the other is always useless. The all-important area of conflict is in the minds of the village people, but the best way to be understood there is to beat the VC. Both terror and good works will fail, if the people believe the side responsible for them cannot also win the fighting.

Perhaps the most interesting ARVN action, from the point of view of the West, was the reaction to the VC winter and spring offensive of 1964–65. ARVN did not do badly, but the final result was the U.S. decision to commit combat troops. If these had not come in, the VC would have won the war.

The first phase of this action occurred in December at An Lao near the coast north of Qui Nhon. A regimental strength VC unit took the place and dug in; when ARVN counterattacked, the enemy held their ground stubbornly in spite of U.S. tactical air support. The VC finally withdrew, but only after several days of toe-to-toe slugging. This was the first time a VC unit of regimental size had done this.

Early in February the VC again attacked not only on the coast, but far inland around Pleiku. VC and North Vietnamese units were shifted from place to place with surprising speed. ARVN troops on the coast were isolated in Bong Son and Phu My; they could be re-supplied only by air. The rest of the coastal area north of Qui Nhon slipped into VC control even during daylight. The VC also attempted to cut the vital Route 19, the only ground supply line for the central highlands from the large port of Qui Nhon. This road has seen a lot of fighting over the past twenty years. If this VC plan had succeeded, Pleiku and Kontum would have been isolated.

A 14 February 1965 ambush here was partially successful. It occurred west of Mang Yang Pass where French Mobile Group 100 was finally destroyed. RVNAF units were soon engaged in bloody fighting at several places on Route 19. LLDB-U.S. trained mercenary companies were occupying fortified bases along Route 19; ARVN columns set out to relieve them from both Pleiku and An Khe. Both were ambushed. In heavy fighting Forward Operational

Base 2 was surrounded and subjected to considerable VC pressure. The ARVN force from An Khe was finally able to defeat their ambushers in bloody fighting and forced their way through to the base. But on the return journey the next day they were badly hurt. A second reinforcing column from An Khe was stopped by 82-mm mortars carefully and accurately handled. Route 19 was again closed, as it had been before.

Confused fighting continued along Route 19 for several days. ARVN and LLDB units received powerful assistance from U.S. tactical air units including armed helicopters. An Eagle flight—U.S. helicopters in the air with ARVN infantry waiting for a definite objective—was called in advantageously; an entire ARVN Ranger battalion was used effectively. But VC and North Vietnamese units dug in along the vital road and fought hard. Survivors from several RVNAF units were finally isolated at Base 2. A small Dien Bien Phu was in the making in spite of ARVN reinforcements from Saigon arriving at both Pleiku and An Khe. These just could not force their way along Route 19 from either end. Soldiers in Base 2 were outnumbered, disorganized, and demoralized. A VC victory seemed imminent.

But it did not happen. This time U.S. air power was decisive. General Westmoreland used U.S. jets for the first time in tactical support of ground troops. The VC and North Vietnamese were plastered. Transport helicopters defended by armed choppers took out every RVNAF soldier from Base 2. The operation was a dramatic success; the VC was so badly hurt by the jets that only the last two or three choppers were even fired at. ARVN morale rose sharply.

Slowly the ground battle fought at several places along Route 19 turned in favor of the Government. The road was open to civilian trucks by mid-March. Bong Son and Phu My were relieved. But the operation had been touch and go for more than a month. The VC had come out in the open and fought hard in large units for the first time. U.S. air power had helped RVNAF weather this storm. But there was no question that the VC and their North Vietnamese allies were entering Mao's third stage. The balance of military power was swinging to the Communists. U.S. ground support was fully committed before these actions were over.

RVNAF have improved somewhat since March 1965, but they still have a long way to go before they can be considered completely efficient. An army is never created overnight. In spite of their shortcomings, they are accumulating morale, experience, and combat know-how. They came late into conflict with an enemy more mature, more adventurous, and better conditioned for jungle combat, particularly at night. Americans must be patient and realize the problems faced by RVNAF. With U.S. help, they can do their part against the common enemy. Their army is as good today, in the opinion of many who have known both, as most of the South Korean Army was in 1953.

8: The U.S. Army in Vietnam

IIIIIIIIIIIIIIIIIIIIIIIIIIIIIIIIIIIIIIIIIIIIIIIIIIIIIIIIIIIIIIIIIIIIIIIIIIIIIIIIIIIIIIIIIIIIIII

The U.S. Army has been in South Vietnam in an advisory capacity continuously for many years. Some American soldiers were assigned to duty with the French in connection with U.S. materiel as early as 1952, and an American training mission took over when the French left South Vietnam in 1955.

U.S. advisers have been with some RVNAF units from the beginning of the VC war, but there were no more than 7000 U.S. military personnel in the country when the U.S. Military Assistance Command, Vietnam, was created in January 1962. This number was increased to about 25,000 just before U.S. combat troops were committed in March 1965.

The most important thing that a foreign ally can do for a country cursed with a bargain-basement war is help the government win the minds of their own people. This task in South Vietnam is extremely complicated, but the U.S. is doing its best. There are presently Americans in South Vietnam who are specialists in almost all nonmilitary fields. Cultural anthropologists and similar men with special training, some of them in uniform, are giving everybody advice. Sometimes these deep thinkers appear to be too theoretical and not always in agreement among themselves. For example, according to one view, defense in the strategic hamlets should be provided mainly by the people in them; according to another, it should be the responsibility of a relatively strong ARVN unit. The U.S. is also giving away millions in many different forms of civil and economic aid.

Another large area of American nonmilitary responsibility is the way that U.S. personnel influence national and local government. U.S. military men try not to meddle in politics, but in practice this has not always been possible. Without a stable government, South Vietnam can be but a poor ally. The Ranking Americans, both in and out of uniform, don't really care who runs the Government, so long as it is anti-Communist and reasonably efficient. It would appear likely that these men have sometimes been forced to take some political action. The Embassy at least informally approved of the removal of Diem, but Ky has apparently been on his own most of the time. As this is being written, the situation is improving. RVNAF are now able to handle their war effort more competently because the 1966 series of crises appears to be over.

In the larger aspects of combat, U.S. air power is said to be most important. Strategic bombing is conducted from airfields as far away as Guam. The power of the B-52's is obvious. Each can deliver 28 tons or more of high explosives—as many as 84 500-pound and 24 750-pound bombs in one arrangement—in the general vicinity of VC targets, but damage done to the enemy has been hard to verify. In some instances the bombers have softened up VC base areas in preparation for later ground attacks by U.S. and RVNAF troops. Some surrendering VC have mentioned the nervous tension created by the threat of such air raids.

On the other hand, Americans in Vietnam who know the situation well say that many of these bombings are either wasted or have fallen on civilians who had no close affiliation with the VC. The latter is deplorable for humanitarian reasons; it also turns the civilian survivors against the U.S. and the South Vietnamese Government. In World War II strategic bombing was a means of doing great damage to the industry of the enemy; there was at least an excuse for killing civilians, too. But the VC has almost no industry which can be seriously damaged from the air; they and their sympathizers are often dispersed among people with no great loyalty to either side.

The mere presence of these great planes within range of South Vietnam does prevent the VC from concentrating in strength for an extended period as the Viet Minh did against the French. Weather is said not to affect the accuracy of B-52 bombing. Air power specialists say that only a small fraction of the Strategic Air Command potential has been employed so far. There are bases for these planes closer to Vietnam than Guam.

A heavy weight of bombs has also been delivered on VC targets by smaller U.S. and South Vietnamese aircraft; fighter-bombers also use cannon, rockets, and napalm. These planes are based on airfields inside South Vietnam, in Thailand, and on U.S. carriers operating in the China Sea. This relatively short-range air power has been employed both against military targets in North Vietnam and to attack VC strongholds in the South. The careful control of the attacks on North Vietnam has limited their effectiveness in accordance with plans announced in Washington. This attacking of more or less nonvital targets in a country not formally classified as a belligerent to force negotiations is a new idea. But at worst, it will decrease Communist aid to the VC from the north.

Many air attacks are conducted entirely by planes based within the country. The problem is to determine precisely where the VC are. They are good at camouflage and in protecting themselves in tunnels and bunkers. Even in their famous base areas such as war zones C and D, hard-core personnel appear to be widely dispersed during the day most of the time. They sometimes march long distances in the early evening for offensive concentrations. Bombs dropped at random in the jungle in the hope of injuring VC are usually ineffective. Villages can be destroyed. But is an entire village ever completely hostile? Most villagers not only have no freedom of choice, but don't even have any real means of learning the truth about the war or their own political problems. Even though the South Vietnamese Air Force is not under U.S. control, many civilians blame all air mistakes on the Americans.

The most valuable use of U.S. air power has been in support of ground units. Tactical air power has often been the difference between winning and losing both offensive and defensive actions. U.S. reinforcements can sometimes move fifty times as fast as those for the enemy. A pair of armed helicopters can give a rifle company commander in combat the quickest and most flexible fire support that has ever been available. Americans have an enormous advantage in air power and have used it efficiently. Darkness and bad weather, however, decrease its effectiveness.

U.S. air power has also been used for mobility and logistic support. The completely airmobile U.S. First Cavalry Division can move all its combat units, together with 105-mm howitzers, by air. This concept is new and quite different from the airborne tactics of World War II in which paratroops and gliderborne forces were delivered on a chosen objective. An airborne division could go into an area quickly and with a fair amount of support weapons. But once it was committed, it became relatively immobile. The table of organization and equipment of the First Cavalry calls for 428 helicopters, some of the largest size. These allow continuous mobility by air, even tactical mobility. In one operation in the Central Highlands one or more pieces from one battery of 105's were moved thirty-six times in a single day.

The ability to move even short distances by air can reduce the VC advantage in intelligence. It can also counter their better foot-mobility in the jungle. Combat units of the First Cavalry can move unpredictably into new areas, make the VC fight when they are not prepared to do so, and keep the enemy off balance. The VC will not be allowed to concentrate at the right place at the right time. Airmobile strikes of battalion or regimental size with tactical air support can be extremely effective. The VC now have installations which they can ill afford to abandon. The only alternative is to fight for them at a time and place of the enemy's choice.

Airmobility has certain disadvantages. The First Cavalry by the very nature of its organization and training operates most efficiently in middle strength. It has no armor at all. It does not have the heavy support weapons required for sustained fighting; this must be supplied by the Air Force. Airmobility also appears to be impractical in combat situations where platoons and even companies operate independently because the noise of helicopters advertises their movements. Furthermore, the original airmobile theory has had to be modified slightly in regard to logistics. The enormous consumption of supplies including gasoline—as much as 500 tons per day if the entire division is in combat—cannot be handled entirely by air. The principal First Cavalry base at An Khe is mostly supplied from the port of Qui Nhon by convoys of trucks.

The U.S. Army in South Vietnam is presently deployed so as to operate throughout the country. U.S. combat troops could be sent into any area in a few hours; even the First Infantry Division is astonishingly airmobile. But for security, logistic, and strategic reasons major U.S. strength has tended to be concentrated in semipermanent bases. These have changed from time to time and will be further modified as new units arrive. But in general, U.S. Army strength is presently concentrated in the II and III Corps Areas. Marine units are in the I Corps Area; the IV Corps Area is still largely the responsibility of RVNAF.

The First Cavalry Division is able to operate quickly and efficiently from its base at An Khe to anywhere in the Central Highlands. The First Brigade of the 101st Airborne Division is at Tuy Hoa with a secondary base at Pleiku. The Republic of Korea's Capital and Ninth Infantry divisions and some other units, plus a reinforced brigade of Korean marines, are under U.S. control along the coast between Qui Nhon and Cam Ranh Bay. The U.S. First Infantry Division—the Big Red One—along with the 173rd Airborne Brigade and the Australian and New Zealand troops, operates mainly from several bases near Bien Hoa, twenty miles northeast of Saigon. The U.S. Twenty-fifth Infantry Division is at Pleiku; the Fourth Infantry Division soon will have one brigade near there with the other at Cu Chi west of Saigon. The special independent light infantry brigades, the U.S. 196th and the U.S. 199th, have been added, as has the U.S. Ninth Infantry Division. All these were organized and trained for the Vietnam war before leaving the U.S.

These U.S. units vary considerably from each other. The First Infantry did not bring its tanks with it, but now has some. The Twenty-fifth and Fourth brought or are bringing all their organic armor. Some divisional artillery, including even 175-mm guns, is on hand, but brigades often have two rather than three rifle battalions. Airborne soldiers—paratroopers—are scattered throughout the U.S. Army, but only one battalion as a whole is so qualified in the First Cavalry Division.

The U.S. Army is now using three types of battalion organization in Vietnam, two in regular units and one for the Special Forces. Tables of organization and equipment are not followed precisely, but changes from them have been fewer than one might expect.

U.S. Army standard rifle battalions (39 officers and 791 men) now consist of a headquarters company (21 and 269) and three rifle companies (6 and 174). The First Cavalry rifle battalions (38 and 729) are divided into a headquarters and headquarters company (15 and 119), three rifle companies (6 and 164), and a combat support company (5 and 118). Heavy weapons are almost the same for both battalions: officially, eight 106 recoilless rifles and thirteen mortars. The standard rifle battalion has nine 81-mm and four 4.2-inch mortars, as compared with thirteen 81-mm mortars in First Cavalry battalions.

A First Cavalry rifle company has 6 and 164; the standard rifle company has ten more enlisted men. Rifle platoons (1 and 43 each) are the same in both organizations and have a headquarters (1 and 2), a weapons squad (0 and 11), and three rifle squads (0 and 10 each). In theory, both weapons squads have two M60 general purpose machine guns, which may be used either with their integral bipod mounts or on tripods, and two 90-mm recoilless rifles. Each rifle squad consists of two fire teams with a grenadier in each.

The weapons platoons of First Cavalry and regular infantry are different; both have three 81-mm mortars and crews, but the latter have two 106-mm recoilless rifles, and the airmobile units have none at company level. This accounts for 9 of the 10-man differential in total company strength. The tenth man is in company headquarters; the First Cavalry has 2 and 9 compared with 2 and 10 for regular units.

The Army Special Forces organization is also important. The most unusual feature of these U.S. soldiers is their magnificent training. Each A team (2 and 10) contains specialists in communications, intelligence, heavy and light weapons, infantry tactics, demolitions, and practical medicine. Each team member is cross-trained in at least one other field. These men have graduated from tough courses in teaching others and in personal leadership. Several A teams are loosely organized under a B team (6 and 16), but B teams actually operating in Vietnam are augmented to fit conditions and responsibilities. Both communications and aviation units are sometimes organic parts of larger Special Forces operations.

Each A team can, if allowed to do so by the political situation, recruit, train, organize, and direct in combat a light battalion of local personnel of 400 to 600 soldiers. Such a unit would have a battalion headquarters of 27 with an attached mortar platoon (four 81-mm's) and a recoilless rifle platoon (four 57-mm's) for a total non-U.S. personnel of about 100. There would also be three rifle companies numbering about 170 each. Each company consists in theory of a headquarters (16), a weapons platoon (40), and three rifle platoons (38 each). The weapons platoon might have two 60-mm mortars, two 3.5-inch rocket launchers, and two medium machine guns. Each platoon would have a headquarters (4), three rifle squads (8 each), and a weapons squad (10) which would probably have two BAR's.

The basis of all combat is weaponry. In Vietnam the more important weapons are those used at battalion level and below. The infantry rifle leads all others, both numerically and in its effect on the enemy. But in this theatre there is some question about what an infantry rifle actually is. ARVN and other units have not only rifles, but also carbines, submachine guns, and shotguns as primary personal arms for combat soldiers.

Even U.S. riflemen now have two different weapons. The U.S. M14 is still being used, but the M16 is now standard in airborne and airmobile rifle battalions and is often encountered in Special Forces units. The M14 has been criticized publicly and privately by many people, some of whom have little basis for judgment. It is essentially an altered form of the U.S. M1, which has been almost universally acclaimed as the best infantry rifle of World War II. The M14 fires the 7.62 NATO round which is slightly smaller and lighter than the .30–'06 used in the M1, but both rounds have the same power. The M14 is about .8 pounds lighter, but is an inch longer; it employs twenty-round magazines which can be changed while the weapon is ready to fire with a round in the chamber. The controversial feature of the M14 is its ability to fire full-automatic. The burst-firing M14 Modified is essentially the same rifle, although some of these Modified types are now further modified to permit slightly more accurate burst fire. Any M14 can be altered by an armorer sergeant in a few minutes to enable it to deliver bursts.

In spite of what has been said against it, the M14 is, in my opinion, a fine weapon for firing single shots. It is accurate, reliable, and fits the American physique and tradition of rifle marksmanship. It looks like a rifle and is a worthy successor to the M1. Some of its good features as a rifle, however, make it a poor light machine gun. Its lightness, rifle conformation, high rate of fire, and powerful cartridge inevitably cause it to be highly inaccurate in bursts.

The U.S. M16 rifle was the first of several new weapons to fire successfully the 5.56-mm cartridge (.223-cal.). Like most pioneer weapons, it has some imperfections. These are minor compared to its advantages. General Westmoreland, the U.S. Commander in Chief in Vietnam, has asked for more M16's because they are better than the M14 for the conditions of war in Vietnam. Even the Marine Corps has finally requested them. Not many with a right to an opinion disagree. The principal advantages of the M16 over the M14 are in connection with weapon weight and length and ammunition weight. The M16 fully loaded weighs 7.3 pounds and is 38.7 inches long as opposed to 9.6 pounds and 44 inches for the M14. A magazine of twenty rounds of 5.56-mm ammo can weigh .65 of a pound (aluminum magazine) as opposed to 1.65 pounds for the M14. A thirty-round magazine can be supplied for the M16 which is only slightly longer and still considerably lighter when loaded than the twenty-round M14 type.

A soldier can have more than twice as much ammunition for the same weight of load when he goes on patrol with an M16 without sacrificing range, accuracy, or killing power. The additional ammo is extremely important. U.S. Army combat units have been wiped out in Vietnam because they used up all their cartridges. This occurs particularly in ambushes. In spite of American logistic capability, immediate resupply of ammo is sometimes impossible. The number of rounds a soldier has with him may easily determine whether he lives or dies.

The M16 can fire bursts. These are not as accurate as they might be because the weapon is too light, fires too fast—at a rate of about 1000 rpm with present ammo—and has a stock which is not really in line when fired by the average soldier. But the M16 is much more accurate full-automatic than the M14 fired the same way.

Burst fire also wastes ammo and causes relatively few enemy casualties in proportion to the number of rounds expended. Infantry rifles probably should not be fired full-automatic, even from a prone position with a bipod. But soldiers throughout the world think that burst fire is effective. The sound of it is important psychologically, particularly in gaining fire superiority which is usually a prerequisite for movement. If U.S. troops must have full-automatic fire, the M16 can deliver it more accurately and for less ammunition weight.

How does the M16 fit into the U.S. Army two-fire-team rifle-squad organization? There are now two M79 grenade launchers and eight identical M16's in each rifle squad. The automatic rifle in its tactical sense has disappeared; the fire teams can no longer function around a light machine gun able to deliver relatively large amounts of accurate fire, but this situation has not really existed since the BAR was replaced by the M14 Modified. Many U.S. soldiers in Vietnam think that spraying the jungle with bullets is effective. Almost surely, this is closer to the truth than some men who grew up honoring accurate long-range rifle fire will admit. In an emergency an M16 armed unit can figuratively explode with streams of bullets. Some of them are said to be effective.

Even though the Army wants the M16, each rifle platoon so equipped will need four types of ammunition: 5.56-mm for the M16's, 7.62 NATO for the M60 general purpose machine guns, Cal .45 ACP for the pistols, and 40-mm cartridges for the M79's. This situation is not ideal; considerable ammo flexibility is possible if rifles and machine guns fire the same cartridge. An efficient machine gun firing the 5.56-mm round is available. It is discussed in the next chapter.

The M14 and M16 are by far the most numerous shoulder arms

in the hands of U.S. troops in Vietnam, but a fairly large number of other similar arms are also used. Where unit discipline is strict, soldiers can't abandon their M14 and substitute some other arm. But men who carry only a Cal .45 pistol are always allowed to add a shoulder weapon. I saw both M1 and M2 carbines, M1 and M3 submachine guns, and various types of shotguns. Occasionally, particularly in U.S. Special Forces, there are foreign weapons.

Even if the M16 becomes standard for all, these substitutions will probably continue to some small degree because of the perversity of human nature and lack of weapons experience among young soldiers. But there is at least one weapon presently used by a number of U.S. soldiers that may have a valid excuse for continuing. The unauthorized conversion of the U.S. M2 (full-automatic) folding-stock carbine has several advantages. With the stock folded it is only 18 inches long and weighs less than 6.5 pounds loaded with thirty rounds. It lacks power and range compared to the M16, but is a lot easier to carry.

We should also mention the submachine-gun version of the M16 as evolved by the Army and the Colt Company. It's a little lighter, shorter, and because of the shorter barrel, fires somewhat more slowly. A limited trial in Vietnam is said to have been entirely successful. I like the weapon: I can fire bursts from it more accurately in a standing position than with the M16.

The .45-cal. semiautomatic U.S. Model 1911A1 is by far the most frequently encountered pistol, but I saw at least a dozen other types. Men of all ranks have managed to buy or borrow revolvers of several calibers, including even Smith and Wesson and Ruger .44-cal. Magnums. Pistols are often carried in non-G.I. holsters. Many of the holsters are purchased locally. A few men have short-barreled police-type .38 Special revolvers in compact rigs normally associated with detectives. A weapon and holster of this type are not as showy, but appear more practical. They are light, hardly impede normal movement, and keep the weapon available for immediate use. If a pistol is necessary—the number of American soldiers carrying them would certainly indicate that they are—it should be light and easy to carry. A .44-cal. Magnum "cannon" does not appear necessary. A .38-cal. Special bullet is powerful enough to stop most men.

Americans in Vietnam have shown a desire for knives also, perhaps for personal defense. Often these are just bayonets of the new short type for either the M14 or M16. But there are also G.I. sheath knives and commercial hunting knives. I even saw two expensive hand-forged knives.

Knives and pistols do not kill many VC, but they may add considerably to the self-confidence of U.S. soldiers. Occasionally they are useful. One combat unit made the headlines by employing some hatchets in defeating a VC ambush.

The U.S. M79 grenade launcher was new to combat when U.S. units first used it in Vietnam in 1965. No similar arm is organic in any other army. Many people doubted its effectiveness because of the small amount of explosive contained in its little bombs. These weigh only 6 ounces, but the bursting charge of 1.25 ounces of tetryl inside a sphere of notched wire sends out 300 fragments traveling at about 5000 feet per second. This compares to about 1000 slightly larger fragments moving initially at 4000 fps for the new standard (M26) hand grenade. All things considered, the M79 has been a success. It is effective in combat; its usefulness outweighs its disadvantages. The Army distribution of two in each rifle squad also appears sound. They can lay down accurately a number of the surprisingly powerful small shells even at ranges of 200, 300, and 400 yards. At short range, they can be shot almost as precisely as a rifle. Grenades from them have been shot into the openings of VC bunkers.

The principal disadvantage of the M79 was that the weapon was no good for personal defense. The bomb did not arm itself until it had traveled twelve or more yards. It had no great penetration, not enough to go into the chest cavity of a strong man, or through heavy growth. The long-awaited packet-of-arrows round for this weapon has not yet appeared in Vietnam, but a buckshot load is now available.

At rifle-battalion level and below, the most important crew-served weapon is the U.S. M60 machine gun. It has now been thoroughly tested in actual combat and has been found satisfactory. As originally issued several years ago, its reliability was questionable, but a few modifications in material and heat treatment have remedied these defects. It is one of the most accurate of modern general purpose machine guns on a tripod mount. It is lighter than most other bipod-mounted weapons that can place bullets precisely. Although it fires faster than the old BAR and the British Bren, it does not consume ammunition at the astonishing rate of the new British and West German general purpose machine guns.

The new 90-mm recoilless rifle is presently the least appreciated U.S. infantry support weapon in Vietnam. I saw none of these there and understand that only a few are in use. One battalion commander is said to have had all his 90's rendered unserviceable and then dropped into deep salt water. Those arms are primarily anti-tank weapons; the enemy has no armor. They do have secondary effectiveness against fortifications and enemy personnel, but they are not popular for these uses. The weapon and its ammo are heavy, 35 pounds and 9 pounds per round respectively, and cut down the capacity of the weapons squad to carry ammo for its two general purpose machine guns. There are no targets in Vietnam which require the power and accuracy at long range of the 90-mm. At platoon level, the old 3.5-inch rocket launcher is equally effective and much lighter. One able battalion commander in the Big Red One suggested a token compliance with the table of organization and equipment by substituting a LAW (light antitank weapon) for each 90-mm. The LAW is a one-shot nonreloadable rocket launcher which weighs only 4.5 pounds complete. But a more recent Fort Benning directive mentions the advisability of replacing both 90-mm's with an additional pair of M60 general purpose machine guns.

Mortars are important in counterinsurgency operations because they represent the only type of high-angle firepower that is foot-mobile. Standard U.S. rifle battalions contain four 4.2-inch mortars, but these controversial pieces are of limited value because they are far too heavy. This leaves only the 81's, for the Army has been slow to re-equip its units with the temporarily abandoned 60's. The three

81's in each rifle company are fine, powerful, long-range weapons. When all these mortars in the battalion are integrated into a single fire-control system, they can deliver a lot of support fire, particularly in defensive situations. But the need for this type of tactical employment in U.S. Army units is limited; large-scale defensive operations are rare.

Offensively the 81's have disadvantages. Three of them with ammunition at company level would crucify foot-mobility in the hot, humid Vietnamese climate and jungle. The tubes and base plates can be carried by selected Americans regardless of conditions. But a full supply of ammunition is beyond human capacity out there, if foot-mobility is to be retained. Because of the value of well-handled 81's in combat, they have been carried, but usually only one per company with no more than twenty to sixty rounds for it. The smaller mortars are coming back essentially because a 60-mm round weighs 3.9 to 11.2 pounds for one of the larger size.

There is little to say about the 3.5-inch rocket launcher. This arm is light and folds in the middle. Its ammo is heavy and bulky, but even two rounds can be extremely useful. They are often carried in Vietnam because they can knock holes in enemy bunkers. Both white phosphorus and antitank war heads are also effective against personnel.

Another weapon of marginal value in U.S. Army rifle battalions is the 106-mm recoilless rifle. The recoilless-rifle platoon at battalion headquarters has often turned in its eight 106's and been issued M60's so that it can function as a heavy weapons section for the headquarters security unit, another extemporized force. The limited use of the big recoilless rifle 106 is in contrast to the considerably greater employment of it by the Marines in the I Corps Area.

Actual combat in Vietnam has been mostly at company level or below, but veterans often say that they have not used what they learned in training about fire-team, squad, and platoon tactics. This appears to be an exaggeration; sometimes fire and movement at low level has been applied by the book. These instances are rare, but have happened. Company and battalion commanders recognize them more easily than members of the platoons involved. Jungle, village, and rice paddy are not like tactical training areas at Fort Benning, but war has always been different from even the best conceived practice for it. World War II rifle-platoon leaders in Africa, Europe, and the Pacific have told me they never used anything they learned in training.

In Vietnam, as elsewhere, sound principles of small-unit tactics must become instinctive for top efficiency and top chances for survival. Soldiers must take care of themselves physically, guard against surprise, and move, fight, and communicate. In infantry combat of any type the first tactical objective is fire superiority. U.S. rifle units with their personal arms and organic support weapons are usually able to gain this quickly and then move to close with, kill, or capture the enemy, if—and this is a big if—they can find the VC in about equal strength or less, in the open. They must also know or learn where the VC are and prevent their disappearance until an attack can be delivered. So often the VC cannot be precisely located because of jungle or camouflage; they tend to disappear as U.S. fire support begins to be effective.

Precise target identification is important, particularly at squad level. Properly directed, U.S. M14's, M16's, and M79 grenade launchers can be extremely effective. But blazing away at valueless jungle can be overdone. Once contact with the VC has been made, this relatively rare opportunity must be used to maximum advantage, even though the enemy often has the initial advantage. In the absence of orders from higher level, a squad leader will gain fire superiority and then move under cover of his own fire, either to improve his position or to close with the enemy. He is able to do this in various ways, basically firing with one element and moving with another, or with all assaulting together.

A U.S. rifle unit frequently comes under fire unexpectedly. This can occur in connection with several roughly similar missions, search and clear, clear and hold, search and destroy, and others. They all involve moving rifle units on their own feet through terrain favoring the enemy. A unit commanding officer, when surprised, seldom has a clear idea of the extent and configuration of the enemy position. He often does not know what to do, but he has been taught that the worst possible reaction is to take cover and do nothing. He orders his unit to return fire immediately and in as heavy volume as possible. He also decides on some positive action, most likely an attack. Junior officers and NCO's often lead heroic assaults in the direction from which the enemy fire comes, with tragic results. An older, more experienced man might not expose himself so rashly, but many young Americans demonstrate personal bravery, as they did on Iwo Jima, at Sharpsburg, and on Long Island in 1776.

After the first few minutes U.S. leaders who survive will probably find out where the enemy is and in what strength. Once this is known the VC may be in for a clobbering by riflemen supported by mortars, artillery, armed helicopters, and tactical air. But if the enemy is not protected against these to some extent, he will probably slip away.

The most important U.S. problem in an action of this type is to avoid heavy initial casualties; any movement that reduces these is desirable. As always in war, there is a great deal of value to the indirect approach, an assault on the flank or rear. This is possible even at squad level, but becomes progressively more practical with larger units. Support fire becomes more complicated, however, as more crew-served weapons are added, and takes more time to arrange. The local problem of jungle, poorly defined enemy positions, and ambush situations even in close combat areas all complicate by-the-book reactions.

During 1966 VC opposition to U.S. ground operations sometimes took on a more stubborn character, particularly where concealed fortifications and the remote location of the combat area prevented envelopment. U.S. units frequently cannot rely on heavy weapons and air power to make up for obvious VC advantages. Commanding officers may not make the best choice of a reaction. Combat intuition which some men seem to have will help, but better intelligence will be more effective on a regular basis. Americans win these head-on collisions more often than they lose, but victories are sometimes more costly than they should be.

Most U.S. defensive tactics in Vietnam are designed to meet various types of ambushes. The VC still catch American rifle units on foot more often than the Americans catch VC. In a VC ambush every U.S. soldier is likely to let fly with a hail of bullets. Movement is supposed to be toward the enemy for two good reasons: first, the area the enemy occupies won't be booby trapped or full of pungis; and, second, a vicious hand-to-hand clash can interfere with the enemy commander's plans. He always has something unpleasant in mind, which has probably been rehearsed. But if he loses control of his men, he may immediately order a retreat. Where U.S. foot-mobile units are ambushed, leadership, discipline, aggressive offensive spirit, and effective weapons handling can usually defeat the enemy.

The VC can also ambush larger U.S. forces including armor. Opportunities for these operations are increasing as U.S. Army units get more tanks and armored personnel carriers and move more on the ground in areas where the enemy may be. But the VC is having extreme trouble with these large ambushes. Initially they can do some damage, but U.S. firepower and quick, sure combat reactions limit this. Within minutes artillery fire, air power, and heliborne reinforcements can completely change the entire character of such an operation. Several large ambushes of this type in the summer of 1966 were turned against the Communists, who left large numbers of dead, wounded, and weapons in their initial ambush positions and along their line of retreat. The U.S. First Infantry Division actually offered an armored column as bait and then hit the ambushers from several directions.

Another type of ambush has been more difficult to handle efficiently. The VC sometimes use electrically controlled mines of large size and perhaps one or two automatic weapons against a supply convoy. Damage is done suddenly from hiding. No further serious action is contemplated. The enemy will try to pull out as soon as he blows his mines. Even if caught, their loss is probably smaller than that which they caused. Where ground communications must be kept open through the jungle, as the Allied units have to do between Qui Nhon and An Khe, this sort of thing is a continual drain. But the VC who control the mines are now sometimes being discovered by friendly forces before they can attack a convoy.

Another similar and almost unbeatable VC ambush is based upon one or more directional mines similar to the U.S. claymores. Properly concealed on a route which will be used by a foot-mobile U.S. unit and handled by a dedicated, alert VC control party, such an ambush makes reaction time, discipline, and leadership almost useless. The damage is done instantly.

Ambushes can be avoided in theory. Any platoon leader can diagram a formation for foot-mobile or vehicle-mounted rifle units with advance, flank, and rear guards that is almost ambush-proof. But these can't be used in the jungle, if a unit is to move more than a mile or two a day. Actual timings indicate a speed of about 400 meters per hour, if security is not sacrificed. Usually a company or platoon marching in the jungle will have to follow a single trail and leave its flanks unprotected. At best, a VC ambush can be turned into a small American victory. Fire and a vicious reaction will win most of the time; support can arrive quickly and devastatingly. At worst, however, U.S. combat units will expend all their ammunition and be wiped out before help can reach them.

The most important thing in defeating an ambush of any size is early intelligence on it. An ambush which can be exposed before friendly troops are in the killing zone has obviously failed. This can be accomplished in widely differing ways. VC defectors sometimes know what is planned by their headquarters for the next few hours. An alert U.S. rifleman at point in his squad column can also discover danger before even he is committed. Helicopter pilots can do the same for a vehicular convoy, but VC concentrations are not now easily spotted from the air. Ambushes discovered early are frequently vulnerable to swift counteraction.

U.S. units of all sizes appear to be doing better against ambushes than the French did and much better than ARVN units in similar predicaments. This is due in part to the quick reaction time for supporting elements. The rescue force may be another rifle squad in the same section of jungle alerted either by radio or the sound of the action, or an airborne battalion complete with attached 105-mm howitzers and tactical air power.

U.S. soldiers are striving hard to learn to fight in the jungle at night. Men used to high standards of living, including electric lights, balanced diets, cleanliness, and vehicles, are at a disadvantage fighting in a foreign country against an indigenous enemy who knows every tree, rock, and stream and who closely resemble the civilian population. A native can move swiftly and silently even at night. The VC take full advantage of these things.

Perhaps the greatest error that a Western nation can make in a bargain-basement war is to hope that its money alone will counteract this enemy capability. The right answer is for Americans to go into the jungle on a man-to-man basis at night and beat the VC. It can be done, but leadership, training, real desire, and high professional quality in officers and men are required. Many have worked on the problem, but two relatively young, extremely capable lieutenant colonels seem to me to be outstanding in this area. One went to Vietnam early in 1965 and volunteered to stay on past his normal relief date. I can do no better than paraphrase his words on low-level intelligence, fighting at night, and individual weapons for it:

We can use some sophisticated detection devices, but we must rely mainly on the eyes and ears of the foot soldier. He is the best source of useful intelligence. I feel that we do not always employ the foot soldier to his maximum capability. Properly trained and led, small reconnaissance patrols could roam the country in depth and could provide a wealth of information. Our old Ranger companies of Korean days and Special Forces mercenary patrols *under U.S. command* could do a superior job along this line. We could, and should, enhance their ability by introduction of the Katusa [Koreans in U.S. units serving in South Korea] system.

Night operations don't require comment; they require doing. The average American seems to have an innate fear of darkness and will avoid night operations whenever possible. This applies alike to new recruits and officers in high commands. Moving and fighting at night takes training and professional expertise, but some U.S. units have developed this capability. They have conquered their fear of darkness and learned how to make the night work for them. Morale in such a unit soars. But until we can teach every U.S. soldier to consider darkness an advantage, the night will belong to the VC.

If I were Chief of Staff, I would see that the work of one month in three was done entirely at night. All training including classroom exercises, close-order drill, and so on would be done during darkness and with a minimum of artificial light. When we conquer this fear of the night, we will minimize our defensive thinking and move out of our camps at sundown, not into them.

We must consider weapons in this same connection. Rifles are as good as the men who pull the triggers. Each soldier must consider his weapon in the same light as he considers his right arm; together they are a team. Psychological indoctrination must be integrated into weapons training as it used to be in bayonet training. Learn it well, it may save your life. Few Americans have a natural feeling for weapons; fewer still have it when they are firing at other humans. This feeling can be overcome by constant and persistent training. One must believe in the weapon he is using. A bolt Mauser known and loved is better than an M16 one doesn't trust!

An analysis of combat actions in Vietnam indicates that ranges vary from a few yards in dense jungle to a hundred yards in the open. All available weapons are effective within this range span. No one weapon or group of weapons will solve the problem. An offensive spirit remains the best defense. Whereas bigger and better weapons—gadgets if you will—will give you more reach and a greater feeling of security, there is nothing that will beat the eyes, ears, and brain of the foot soldier in increasing defensive efficiency.

This emphasis on a foot soldier gathering information, fighting at night, and using his rifle in an environment that he has made his own is the way to control both territory and the enemy. The British did it in Malaya and Malaysia; the Filipinos did it under Magsaysay. The French failed in Indochina because they relied too heavily on concrete and roadbound, supposedly mobile columns.

The other brilliant lieutenant colonel can be named because some of his story has appeared in the 23 May 1966 issue of *Newsweek*. He is Henry "Gunfighter" Emerson, Commanding Officer of the Second Battalion, 502nd Regiment, 101st Airborne Division. He learned of a PAVN—Peoples Army of North Vietnam—ambush before it caught his force.

The tough, hawk-nosed battalion commander radioed to his scattered units, moving them into place and finally surrounding the would-be ambushers. After a shattering battle, in which artillery and air strikes were called in to support Colonel Emerson's troops, the PAVN's withdrew, leaving at least 100 of their dead on the field.

It had been a brutal fight, and it illustrated how tough these American troops can be. The 101st is a crack outfit. Colonel Emerson's units, however, are unique; they have been sharpened into what amounts to a counter-guerrilla spearhead. They slink through the jungle at night as well as day, operate independently in squad-size units or smaller, live on rice in the field and lay ambushes as stealthily as the enemy.

It is a fast-moving, exhausting, subtle style of war, requiring heavy firepower even in a small unit patrol. The men in the Second Battalion are walking arsenals, carrying everything from lightweight M-16 automatic rifles and M-60 machine guns to grenade launchers, hand grenades and sharp-bladed Bowie knives. As often as possible, they operate by darkness. Each soldier carries one or two cans of meat rations and 2½ pounds of rice—enough for five days. "I try to get my men to sustain themselves for five days without resupply," says Emerson. "My effort is to try to beat the damned guerrilla at his own game."

Emerson and his men took a prominent part in Operation Hawthorne, a U.S. Army operation in late spring. General Westmoreland conceived Hawthorne and had it worked out by his staff. The First Brigade, 101st Airborne Division supported by the First Cavalry and other troops was to be lifted into blocking positions around an area that probably contained a PAVN regiment near Tou Morong north of Kontum and Pleiku. The objects of the attack were to take pressure off Tou Morong, defeat a veteran North Vietnamese unit, and cause the enemy to waste prematurely strength which they might otherwise employ in a monsoon offensive.

This sixteen-day battle began the first week in June 1966 when Emerson's battalion was set down almost on top of the Twenty-fourth Regiment of the 304th PAVN Division; this unit played a prominent part in the Viet Minh victory over the French at Dien Bien Phu—twelve years before. The elite U.S. soldiers were really tested in steep jungle. The PAVN's were extremely pugnacious and fought well in an environment where normal air support was difficult. At one time Emerson's three companies were each fighting a different enemy battalion. Before the actual configuration of the enemy position was determined, Company C was moving up a draw and was suddenly hit from three sides. Hastily established perimeters were broken through; the entire unit was being overrun.

The company commander, Captain Bill Carpenter, who had been West Point's All-American lonely end on Earl Blaik's last fine team, called in air strikes on top of his own position. The usual low-level tactical air support, which lands close to, but not on, friendly troops, could not be delivered in this terrain. The napalm bombs and rockets which arrived caused some U.S. casualties, but they plastered the enemy. This air strike turned the tide in favor of Carpenter and his gallant force, who had never stopped their fighting. When reinforcements arrived, they were reorganized around a bit of jungle which they were holding in strength. There were more PAVN bodies—almost all with their weapons—than U.S. killed and wounded by 3 to 1.

After ten days of confused fighting U.S. leaders had determined more or less what the PAVN situation was in spite of terrain and enemy mobility. A semi-envelopment was achieved, but frontal attacks would be extremely costly and probably produce a disappointingly small number of enemy killed, wounded, and prisoners. VC and PAVN's can slip away into the jungle with extreme facility.

Instead of attacking, Westmoreland and his subordinates lifted out U.S. forces from the immediate area, plastered it with bombs from B-52's who were, of course, on the way, and brought back the infantrymen. The PAVN position was carried easily; enemy survivors were still dazed by bomb concussions. A total of 533 PAVN bodies were counted during Operation Hawthorne, most of them easily identifiable because of their distinctive uniforms. There were surely many more enemy killed and wounded.

Operation Hawthorne is anti-insurgent war at its best. Full advantage was taken of U.S. materiel, coordination, battle know-how, and logistics. But the victory really belonged to Emerson, Carpenter, and men like them who beat the victors of Dien Bien Phu face-to-face in the jungle. After reviewing the operation with the Screaming Eagles, General Westmoreland scrambled onto a mass of supplies, talked to the men briefly, and then said, "Soldiers, I salute you!" He came to attention and brought his arm up with the same precision and snap as when he was West Point's first captain.

There have also been other great first captains of the Point including MacArthur, Pershing, and Robert E. Lee.

9: The U.S. Marines in Vietnam

The U.S. Marines are fully integrated into the American effort in Vietnam. Their aims and over-all procedures are the same; all operations are ultimately controlled by General Westmoreland and his headquarters in Saigon. On the other hand, Lt. Gen. Lewis W. Walt, Jr., USMC, not only commands all Marines, but all other U.S. forces in the I Corps Area.

The Marine Corps functions almost as an autonomous force in this war. Their weapons, organization, tactics, and theatre of operations vary considerably from that of the Army. They have managed because of terrain and their own amphibious capacity to set up three self-sufficient bases which are more easily defended and allow heavier weapons than the Army can normally use in their areas. The Marines and their commander have contrived to make their territory not only a frequent source of good news, but also the most friendly to Americans as far as the Vietnamese civilian population is concerned.

There are several reasons for this. South Vietnam was divided years ago into four military zones, or Corps Areas. The I Corps Area is in the north, closest to Communist North Vietnam and China. Before the Marines arrived, the VC were exerting maximum guerrilla pressure and beginning to conduct larger operations. Important installations including the big French-built air base at Danang were in danger of capture.

Combat units of the Third Marine Division began to come ashore at Danang on 8 March 1965; a battalion landing team took over at Hue/Phu Bai a few days later. The First Marine Air Wing began operating from Danang almost immediately, but another large field

136

was needed; construction at Chu Lai began May 8. Planes were using the field thirty days later. General Walt took command of all this on 4 June 1965. The VC stopped winning shortly after, save in hit-and-run attacks, mostly small. Starlite and Piranha were the first large-scale Marine actions. The confidence the Marines have in themselves and in what they are fighting for seems to have communicated itself to RVNAF units and to the people. Marine perimeters protect a higher percentage of the people here than in any other Corps Area.

General Walt points out that a Communist insurgency war of the modern type cannot be won by military force alone. The power, wealth, and know-how not only of the U.S. but of other anti-Communist countries are being applied to a vast program throughout South Vietnam, including the I Corps Area. Combat Marines are not specialists in this, but are doing their full share under direction of Corps personnel trained in civil affairs. Candy, soap, and small Vietnamese flags are being given away along with protection for harvests, movies, jobs, medical attention, and even machinery. Marines are also building roads, bridges, markets, and schools; they are teaching hygiene and practical living. Most important, the Marines offer friendship.

Civil action, however, is obviously not the primary mission of the Marines. Specific plans to beat the VC in the I Corps Area are, of course, top secret. But from what has already happened, what is presently taking place, and what Marines say and write, it is possible to piece together a kind of general blueprint.

As in the country to the south, air power is extremely important. Conveniently located, well-supplied bases are necessary for both planes and helicopters and are presently functioning. These must be protected from VC ground action, including sneak mortar attacks, so fairly large perimeters are necessary. Furthermore, for maximum efficiency, flying time should be kept to a minimum to any point where air power might frequently be applied. The Marines have three separate but mutually supporting bases. All are supplied from the sea and cover the entire I Corps Area well. They are on the coast about equidistant between the Seventeenth Parallel, each other, and the junction of the I and II Corps Areas more than 200 miles to the southeast.

The airfields at Danang and Chu Lai are capable of accommodating fighter-bombers in considerable numbers and larger aircraft as necessary. Hue/Phu Bai has a smaller field suitable for helicopters and some fixed-wing planes. Because the I Corps Area is narrow, no point in it is more than eighty miles from one of these air bases. All three are stocked with thousands of items needed to keep the planes in operation, staffed by competent mechanics, and provided with bombs, rockets, and ammunition of many types. Fuel is required in staggering quantities, as well as hundreds of tons of other things from Coca-Cola to bulldozers. But it can all be brought in by sea.

Strategic Air Command B-52's sometimes hit targets in the I Corps Area, as they do elsewhere in South Vietnam both strategically and in cooperation with ground forces. In their strategic role the planes are not a part of General Walt's operations, but have proven effective when enemy concentrations can be precisely located. Similar fighter-bomber attacks which hit identified VC targets are even more valuable. As Marine intelligence has improved, these smaller nontactical air strikes have become efficient. From one to several dozen sorties—one flight by one plane is one sortie—can be flown against an enemy concentration quickly.

U.S. air power in the I Corps Area—Marine Air and Air Force units working in close cooperation—are now finding their own targets, at least to some extent, and attacking them quickly when discovered. Two small, fixed-wing aircraft of low speed team up with two powerful jets. One of the little planes flies at tree-top height so as to be practically immune to ground fire. It can spot, however, because of its low altitude and speed, even a single VC soldier. If a worthwhile target is found, the lower pilot throws out a smoke grenade to mark the spot and communicates with his partner in the other small plane, flying at an altitude of about 2000 feet and out of range of ordinary ground fire. The second pilot relays the information to the jet fighter-bombers who may be ten miles away, giving the map coordinates necessary for them to find the smoke markers.

The two jets swoop down at high speed and attack with any

ordnance they have which seems appropriate. They can use up to four large containers of napalm, rockets, high-explosive bombs, and shells from automatic cannon. On occasion, and if alerted to the possibility of special targets, they can also use Bullpup air-to-surface guided missiles, or new top secret shrapnel devices, which have the effect of 800 hand grenades exploded in a fairly even pattern over a target area.

The small planes are sometimes able to bring in their great, powerful, high-speed companions after a delay of seconds only. The whole operation from the spotting of the enemy to the concentration of fire on him seldom takes longer than half a minute. The VC do not have a chance to get away unless they drop what they are doing immediately and rush madly into the jungle. Even this may not work. Casualties produced do not run into the hundreds during any month, but the effect on the morale of the enemy seems to be considerable. One of the innocent little planes can come over at any time during daylight; there is no adequate defense against the thundering infernos of fire, explosives, and bullets which may follow it.

The second general means by which air power finds its own targets is aerial "photography" using new scientific devices, still mostly classified. With these, VC cookfires can be spotted through thick jungle. Positive identification can be made in some instances, particularly in VC base areas, and strikes can be directed fairly precisely. The Marines realize, however, that indiscriminate bombing of VC-controlled territory may not be useful. Napalm and white phosphorus convert neutrals who survive to active enemies.

The more important use of air power in the I Corps Area is to support ground action. Once Marines on operations outside their perimeters discover VC, tactical air support is almost always available. Marine pilots support Marine rifle units superbly. Forward observers can handle both artillery and air strikes. Several different means of target identification are used—for example, smoke delivered in various ways. Even though jet fighter-bombers are not always precisely on target, they deliver an enormous load of ordnance, as much in effectiveness as a heavy bomber in World War

II. They are nearly impervious to VC ground fire. Lower performance aircraft have greater accuracy, but also greater vulnerability to light antiaircraft fire. Armed helicopters are proving to be more useful than Marines expected three years ago. As many as nine in a group of twenty-five ships may be of this type.

Tactical air power can clear a landing zone with bombs, rockets, and bullets so that heliborne Marines can come down in comparative safety complete with support weapons and supplies. Once Marines and their allies are on the ground, combat and logistic support is required. They have an airmobility approaching that of the U.S. First Cavalry Division and a closer relationship with their pilots than the First does.

Marines in the I Corps Area also use their air power for other things, such as supplying friendly forces hard to reach by any other means. Far inland, air power may still be the only reliable means of logistic support as well as the best means of delivering reinforcements in an emergency. But air power so employed is not always effective. It still cannot really operate efficiently at night and in low clouds. Poor visibility means added danger for pilots and extreme difficulty finding targets.

The Communists have had years of experience against enemies who control the air. They can sometimes not only protect themselves, but deliver astonishing offensive operations even in the I Corps Area. An LLDB-U.S. Special Forces post at A Shau was overrun on 9–11 March 1966 by an attack of this type. This light battalion fortification was located two miles from the Laotian border, far too distant from the coast for ground support to reach them. The VC hit the Government-commanded garrison of 375 with heavy firepower including 120-mm mortars when flying conditions were at their worst. The attack came as a surprise and achieved some success initially. Twenty U.S. Special Forces soldiers and some of the men they had trained were able to hold for thirty hours in spite of a notable lack of enthusiasm on the part of some LLDB's for meeting the VC man-to-man.

During this entire period flying conditions were bad. Some tactical air support was achieved, but at considerable cost. The friendly planes that did find their targets had to come in under low clouds. The VC stuck to their dual-purpose machine guns and brought down several U.S. aircraft. The position was lost, although a considerable portion of the garrison was evacuated by helicopter.

Although air operations are important, they cannot achieve a military victory by themselves. General Walt has emphasized from the beginning the necessity of fighting successfully on the ground at all combat levels. These engagements often must be defensive in nature because the Marines have important installations to defend. Air bases and semi-enclosed perimeters around them must be held in depth so that the VC cannot get close enough to cause trouble, even with their 120-mm mortars. Initially, this was an extreme problem because there just were not enough Marines to push perimeters far enough out. The three autonomous bases now seem to be secure; Marines are gradually extending their tactical areas of responsibility. One obvious possible development is that the rough semicircles from each main base may meet. If this happens the entire coast of the I Corps Area will become anti-VC. The roads between the enclaves are now usually open. But General Walt is not trying to hold a de Lattre line, or permanently occupy more territory than he needs. Too much holding would mean too little deployable offensive strike power.

In this same connection, Marines realize that counterguerrilla operations which are defensive on the ground and offensive only in the air are probably doomed to defeat. There is no substitute in guerrilla war for ground victories. Where the guerrillas are able to achieve them, they are magnified in the propaganda carried perhaps by primitive means, but reaching every village and hamlet in the nation and beyond it. News of a guerrilla defeat, such as the one in Starlite, travels just as fast.

The spirit of the Marines from four-man fire teams right up to Walt's headquarters is to go out and hit the enemy on the ground. Big operations are important; victories which destroy VC battalions and regiments are of enormous military and political value. But they are possible in the I Corps Area only if the VC concentrate where they can be hit. Since Starlite and Piranha, the Communists do this very seldom and never in such convenient places as formerly. Even well inland, they avoid gathering in strength, although a dozen or more Marine Corps-ARVN operations have achieved some significant success, particularly Harvest Moon, Texas, Utah, Indiana, New York, and Hastings. But in these the enemy has avoided being trapped tightly because of the ever present jungle and has refused to fight in the same place for any considerable period of time. In March 1965 the VC were approaching Mao's third stage; they and their North Vietnamese allies are now back to the beginning of the second throughout most of the I Corps Area most of the time.

How has this come about? Air strikes, Starlite, and other large actions have helped, but Marine rifle companies, platoon, and even squad operations have been at least equally important. The three base areas have had to be defended, but this has been done in an offensive way. Because of the range of the VC 120-mm mortars—said to be above 8000 yards—perimeters must be at a distance from all vital targets. In actual practice scores of Marine rifle companies are deployed in irregular lines. VC pressure at any point—and this pressure still comes occasionally—is resisted by a variety of units and weapons. The rifle companies have strong points, but these are mostly temporary and small unless an old French bunker happens to be where it can be utilized.

The entire conception of defense remains astonishingly loose. Marine rifle companies sometimes have assigned heavy weapons to give a maximum of fire. Tanks, Ontos, and even 155-mm self-propelled howitzers are ready to add their weight to the Howtars and regular artillery which now includes 8-inch howitzers and some even larger pieces. If big ordnance is available in a static situation, it should certainly be used. But the heart and soul of this defensive system is the offensive strength of rifle companies and platoons in the open assisted by heavier firepower. Patrols, ambushes, and reconnaissance efforts are carried out continuously.

Marines in their billets close behind their rather skimpy perimeters are ready to react quickly and effectively. But they don't want to react if they can help it; they prefer to act first. There is a conscious desire at all levels not to adopt the French system of concrete fortifications and Maginot Line leadership. But practical application of this concept requires offensive jungle experience and good, up-to-the-minute intelligence. Walt's Marines have progressed a long way in both.

The Marine Corps in Vietnam has resolved to fight VC guerrillas in their own territory at night. Anywhere within range of the artillery in the three base areas, the day and the night now belong almost completely to the Marines. Bridges have been increased in strength to take tanks and big self-propelled artillery pieces so that this area is far larger than that enclosed in the perimeters. Heavy armored vehicles as well as troop landing vehicles and Ontos now give supporting fire which the VC cannot hope to match. Both armor and air power are handicapped, however, by darkness. If the war is to be won, Marine riflemen must beat their enemies in small units between dusk and dawn.

Giap, the military head man in North Vietnam, appears to have been basing his predictions of an ultimate VC military victory on the Communists' ability to fight and win small actions at night. He thought he could beat U.S. units of small size with the VC the same way he beat the French with the Viet Minh. But U.S. Marines appear to be well on the road to refuting Giap's theories. Some credit must go to the Marines' unique amphibious and heliborne capabilities and their fire support from ground and air, but a large share remains with their night-fighting riflemen.

Walt and his subordinate commanders send out literally thousands of patrols and sweeps to meet the VC at night; there are often more than 400 in twenty-four hours and 10,000 a month. No unit statistic is as important; commanding officers at all lower levels are graded in part on the basis of how many patrols they send out. The success of these is also important, but a patrol is useful even if VC are not found.

There are two general types of patrols. In the first, rifle-battalion and company commanders in the initial lines of the perimeter defenses continually dispatch small units into their tactical areas of responsibility. The unit which goes out does not risk too much, especially at first; they are not beyond artillery support. With them is an artillery forward observer, and they know their positions precisely. They go out in platoon and company strength either on foot or by helicopter during daylight, or at dusk and establish a base. The commanding officer then sends smaller units to patrol and ambush close to his position. Procedures have been worked out to give U.S. weapons a maximum advantage. Marines do not catch many VC this way, but they have not lost a single platoon-strength patrol either. The vital point is that the Marines and not the Communists usually control the territory even in the total blackness of a monsoon night.

A young captain with whom I discussed this effort pointed out that his company had at least one platoon a night well beyond his actual perimeter. His executive officer told me that the captain himself spends a large portion of his own time beyond his line of strong points. In these operations Marines sometimes encounter what may well be the best guerrillas of all time. In spite of many handicaps—including their cultural background, childhood training, and a sense of fair play—the Marines are doing remarkably well.

This is not always a one-sided affair; the VC can strike and strike hard, as they did on 15 June 1966 against an eighteen-man observation patrol under S/Sgt. James Howard. The patrol occupied the top of a hill out of the range of supporting artillery fire. The VC, probably two rifle companies, stalked them and surrounded their position. About midnight the enemy opened with a hail of 60-mm mortar shells and followed immediately with infantry assaults pressed home so that bayonets were used. The Marines assisted by tactical air—it's used even at night—held out for five hours until reinforcements arrived. The patrol was not overrun, but only two unwounded men remained when help arrived; five Marines were dead. The survivors had only twelve rounds of ammunition between them. The VC left forty-five bodies behind them.

An interesting sidelight of this action was that one Marine used rocks for the last two hours of the fight. These were not thrown primarily to inflict casualties, but to simulate grenades after the unit had none of these left. The sound of one landing would cause VC nearby to move involuntarily. Another Marine could then fire at a definite target. They did not have enough ammunition left to fire at landscape only.

The second type of night operations involves deeper penetrations of jungle and paddy country. Battalion and larger-sized forces execute sweeps of various types which keep them away from the enclaves sometimes for weeks. During the day these task forces move and sometimes fight by companies and battalions with tactical air and artillery support; reinforcements to meet an emergency are always on call. At night platoons are more important. These are sent out beyond the loose perimeters of these temporary bases. The VC have been marching and fighting at night for years, but they are now having their troubles. They blunder into Marine ambushes more often than they used to and suffer more severely.

In both types of night fighting much depends on the civilian population and the intelligence advantage which comes with the friendship the people give to one side or the other. The anti-Communist world cannot expect that people it cannot protect at night will often be useful. But in the tactical areas of responsibility local villagers and their chiefs now give information because they have confidence that the Marines will not only protect them, but ultimately will win the war. Even though there is no de Lattre line, village leaders have been provided with radios and simple plotting boards. They can supplement their own defenses with Marine artillery fire which is on call twenty-four hours a day and arrives precisely where it is needed. The fact that this fire is available and preregistered often means that it will not be required. The VC can find more profitable targets to attack than those with Marine artillery support.

Marines have resolved that the VC will never gain anything, not even possession of useless jungle, by force, if it can possibly be avoided. When necessary, a relatively small Marine or RVNAF unit operating in collaboration with the Marine Corps can be supported by dozens of planes and ground forces as required in an extremely short period of time. If a Marine platoon should be cut off, it will be rescued. Marines say that General Walt will throw in his entire command to rescue one wounded Marine. I was reminded of what Confederate soldiers said of Stonewall Jackson in the valley of Virginia,

"He will fight for a wheelbarrow!" Lew Walt will do the same for the carcass of a downed helicopter already stripped of usable equipment. He will either lift it out or destroy it completely almost regardless of cost.

Marine Corps organization has evolved rapidly with the Vietnamese war. On 1 January 1965, there were three Marine divisions. The Second operated in the Atlantic and Mediterranean with its headquarters at Camp Lejeune in North Carolina. The First was at San Diego and in the Eastern Pacific; the Third was based on Okinawa and operated in the Western Pacific. The Third went to Danang and the First to Okinawa during 1965. The First has now moved to Vietnam also and is under General Walt's command too; he received his third star on 7 March 1966. The First has its headquarters at Chu Lai. Another division, the famous Fifth of World War II, is almost completely trained and is now in part operational. Units of it began to see action in Vietnam in August 1966, but they were attached to the Seventh Fleet, and not in the I Corps Area. Part of this division has now come ashore just south of the Seventeenth Parallel.

U.S. Marine divisions contain a lot of men and a great deal of equipment, but are to some extent variable in composition. Divisions are subdivided into regiments and battalions, but odd battalions from different regiments are often used together as in Starlite. When I visited the Third Division at Danang (August 1965), it consisted of twelve rifle battalions, five artillery battalions, a Recon battalion, an antitank battalion, and a shore-patrol battalion plus engineer, transportation (both regular and troop-landing vehicles), medical, and service units.

A rifle battalion normally contains four rifle companies plus support units. The latter are usually tailored to requirements; a battalion landing team may include armor and artillery. A rifle battalion has eight 81-mm mortars and eight 106-mm recoilless rifles.

A Marine rifle company (6 officers and 210 men) consists of a headquarters (2 and 7) plus a heavy-weapons platoon (1 and 65) with six medium machine guns, six 3.5-inch rocket launchers, and three 60-mm mortars, plus three rifle platoons (1 and 46 each).

Each rifle platoon has a headquarters (1 and 4) and three rifle squads (0 and 14 each). A squad consists of a leader, a grenadier, and three fire teams, each composed of a leader, an automatic rifle gunner, and two riflemen. A rifle company theoretically has 149 rifles, 27 automatic rifles, 40 pistols, and 9 M79 grenade launchers in addition to the heavier weapons.

Weapons are basically the same in the Marine Corps as in the Army; there are only a few variations. But organization, proportion, and present distribution are quite different. Armored vehicles are being used in the I Corps Area to a greater extent than most military men expected. Tanks, troop landing vehicles, Ontos, and self-propelled guns are important. The VC would lose mobility, their second most valuable advantage, if they tried to carry enough effective antitank weapons to protect themselves from these. Where a tank can approach any form of VC fortification, the fortification is almost certainly doomed. A tank-infantry team in suitable terrain and in daylight is almost unbeatable. But armor has many disadvantages in guerrilla war; it has difficulty crossing jungle streams and is vulnerable to mines and antitank weapons on narrow trails and in thick country. A courageous enemy with a Panzerfaust-type grenade launcher—essentially a recoilless smooth-bore weapon and not really a launcher—can sometimes destroy a tank. His chances improve in dense jungle and at night.

Marine conventional artillery is deployed mostly in position to support rifle battalions and companies in the perimeters around air-fields and similar installations. But these installations are self-contained and usually capable of 360-degree fire and local defense. As one moves around inside these areas and on the edges of them, 105- and 155-mm and 8-inch howitzers are firing single rounds or more to register on some target. Then sometimes a short fire mission is poured out. This fire may have been called for by a forward ob-server with a patrol or in a small spotting plane. Less frequently, it will be against VC discovered by infrared photography or reported by friendly villagers. These powerful shells and the fear of them cannot help but decrease the audacity of the VC operating within range of their concentrations.

In mobile operations by light forces General Walt's Marines use the Howtar. It is a unique Marine artillery development which consists essentially of a 4.2-inch mortar tube mounted on the 75-mm pack howitzer carriage. This weapon is more easily and quickly handled and more precise than the 4.2-inch mortar and is much lighter than the 105-mm howitzer, or even the 105-mm pack howitzer used in British Commonwealth armies. The Howtars can be lifted into combat areas by normal Marine (H-34 series) helicopters as in Starlite. They give the Marines a big advantage in operations where other artillery cannot be brought into action.

Another unique piece of Marine weaponry is the Ontos, essentially a light armored vehicle with six 106-mm recoilless rifles mounted outside. This has been an outstanding success because it is light and small enough to travel on most trails and gives a real artillery punch. It is assigned as far down as rifle companies, but is never used as a mobile bunker.

U.S. infantry support weapons have been found adequate except for the 60-mm mortar. By March 1965 this small accurate weapon was gone from both the Army and Marine Corps. But conditions in Vietnam demanded its return. A thirteen-man mortar section has been added to the heavy weapons platoon of each Marine rifle company.

Since the VC has no armor, the antitank potential of the twenty-two-man assault section with six 3.5-inch rocket launchers has not been required. But these arms are still valuable for knocking out bunkers, producing VC casualties in jungle trenches, and eliminating snipers. The personnel of this unit have also not been trained in demolition work including the exploring and destroying of caves and tunnels. Marines prefer the 3.5-inch rocket launcher to the Army's newer 90-mm recoilless rifle because it is lighter and folds in the middle; precision at long range is not necessary in Vietnam. The Energa (M31) rifle grenade is said to be in the hands of Marines in the I Corps Area. One Energa can do a lot of damage to a bunker, but is heavy and difficult to carry.

Marine rifle companies are larger and more lightly armed than those of the U.S. Army, but there is a standard Marine procedure of assigning necessary heavy weapons to rifle company commanders on a semipermanent basis. In the interim before sufficient 60-mm mortars were received, almost all perimeter rifle companies had 81-mm mortars complete with crews from battalion level. But the 81's were mostly for defense. When a rifle company moves in the jungle on foot, medium mortars and ammunition are usually too heavy for even U.S. Marines.

This same procedure is often followed with single 106-mm recoilless rifles from battalion level, flame throwers, Ontos, and even tanks. If a rifle company has a reasonably constant need for a heavy weapon, it will be assigned. These are not only useful militarily, but also politically, as morale builders for the population. The range and precision of a 106 located on a commanding hill reduce VC initiative.

The small-arms situation is confused. In spite of top-level decisions made years ago to abandon the U.S. M1 and M2 carbines, both are back in the hands of combat Marines. So are M1 and M3 submachine guns. All these nonstandard weapons are for personal defense, however, and are not carried as primary arms by combat riflemen. For instance, the rifle company gunnery sergeant is armed according to the table of organization and equipment with a pistol only. But you won't find many gunnery sergeants in combat without something a lot more lethal.

Any Marine who has been able to procure by any means at all a U.S. M16 rifle has been allowed to keep it. Marines in Vietnam are now (Summer, 1967) just being issued these new light rifles to take the place of the M14. I heard no complaints about the lack of killing power for the 55-grain Cal .223-bullets. But a special sniper section (1 officer and 39 men) has been added to each regimental headquarters and is presently using bolt-action Model 70 Winchesters with 8X scopes firing the old Cal. .30-'06 ammunition with 172-grain National Match bullets.

The controversial U.S. M14 rifle has stood up well in Marine combat in Vietnam. Its slight reduction in weight and its twenty-round magazine are real advantages over the M1. Argument still continues as to whether individual riflemen should have the capacity for burst fire. General Walt has allowed rifle-battalion commanders to decide for their entire unit. One battalion has modified every M14 rifle so all can fire bursts. Other commanders are vehemently against this procedure. But it will all be water over the dam soon: the M16's all have a full-automatic capability. Some may be modified to allow two- or three-shot controlled bursts from each trigger pull, but this modification has not yet been made.

The standard M14 Modified, the so-called AR, presently in Marine fire teams, fires bursts and is equipped with a bipod. It is popular with the men who have to carry it, but not with Marines who know the old BAR well. The M14 Modified cannot deliver the same sort of accurate fire as the BAR. The present 7.62 NATO arms are satisfactory in defensive situations where they don't have to be carried, where ammunition can be supplied by mechanical transportation, and where company-level M60 machine guns can take over some of the support fire load from the M14 Modifieds.

Some Marines would like to see the M60 machine gun with bipod mount introduced into each fire team, but the extra weight of the weapon, twenty-three pounds against ten for the M14 Modified, would limit mobility. Further, a belt-fed LMG has obvious disadvantages amid jungle vines and creepers. The belt for the M60, and a webbing bag containing fifty rounds of ammunition, increases its weight to about twenty-six pounds. This is too heavy for mobility; replacing the belt once the first fifty rounds have been expended is difficult and clumsy. Belts can be carried in metal boxes, but most gunners wrap them around their bodies at least part of the time.

The regular issue Model 1911A1 .45-cal. semiautomatic pistol is, of course, the most frequently encountered side arm. As in the U.S. Army, however, there are many others, particularly revolvers which range from single-action Ruger .44-cal. Magnums through Colt and Smith & Wesson .357 Magnums to ordinary .38 Special weapons.

The greatest confusion in the small-arms picture comes from a weapon many Marines would like to have, but don't: the Stoner 63A System of small arms. Marines tested the Stoner rifle, the Stoner AR or LMG (squad or fire-team type), and the Stoner

MMG exhaustively at Parris Island, Camp Lejeune, and Quantico. There is also a Stoner carbine sometimes referred to as a submachine gun. Briefly this system of small arms which fires the 5.56-mm round, the same as the M16, provides four different weapons in which many components are the same. Since the Stoner System includes all direct-fire small arms in a rifle company, only one type of ammunition would be needed. The M1 and M2 carbines and the M1 and M3 submachine guns which have crept back into Marine units would be eliminated. Even though the rifle is slightly heavier than the M16, the whole system would be far lighter than a combination of M16's and M60 MMG's complete with ammunition. Marine tests indicate not only an advantage to the Stoner System in regard to accuracy as a rifle and an AR, but a substantial increase in shooting efficiency at 1000 yards over the tripod-mounted U.S. M60. Limited tests of Stoner arms in Vietnamese combat situations have confirmed the Marine Corps preference and are continuing.

General Walt told me, "If my rifle companies had the Stoner or a similar system of small arms, their effectiveness would be increased 30 per cent." He was the commanding general of the Marine Corps Landing Force Development Center at Quantico, the evaluation and testing section of the Marine Corps, before he took on his present duties. He knows small arms more thoroughly, perhaps, than any other general officer in the world today. His opinions deserve to be weighed carefully in the current small-arms crisis.

Why have two or more types of ammunition at company and platoon level when one would be more effective? One obvious practical solution would be to use M16 rifles and Stoner light and medium machine guns. A company so armed would have better small arms than their enemies, an advantage which at present it does not always enjoy.

Before concluding this chapter, we should look briefly at Marine Operation Hastings, which officially began on 7 July 1966 when the North Vietnamese 324B Division was discovered in South Vietnam just south of the border. This is at the northern end of the I Corps Area opposite the Starlite battlefield. There have been many other similar operations of this type in the past year, but Hastings probably comes closest to Starlite in the success achieved. It is also typical of many others since Starlite in its lack of conclusiveness, even though it lasted almost a month. The combat area extended over about 150 square miles and was 60 miles northwest of the Hue/Phu Bai, well inland. The operation proper was conducted with airborne forces which were supplied by air; although Marine and ARVN units did move inland from the coast, the helicopter-delivered forces did most of the fighting. A total of about 6000 Marines were used in the airborne army; artillery included 155-mm howitzers. These pieces, too heavy for all Marine helicopters in Vietnam, were brought by T-130 transports which landed on a dirt airstrip built near the combat area.

The first severe contact occurred on July 18 when Companies I, K, and L of the Fourth Marines Regiment were carried by helicopters into territory hit by B-52's the day before. A command post was established early on July 18 and defended by two platoons of K Company and an engineering detachment. The rest of the Marines were out on patrol when the port was hit at 1500 hours by heavy mortar fire and about 1000 North Vietnamese. Company I managed to fight its way back during the ensuing battle. Air and artillery support was immediately available and used effectively. But the combat close to the post was almost hand-to-hand and bloody; range was too short for the artillery and tactical air support to do much good. The fighting was extremely favorable to the Marines. Their casualties were heavy for the small number engaged, but the enemy lost 138 counted dead mostly from grenades and small-arms fire close to the command post. An estimated 400 more were killed by heavy support weapons including aircraft farther back in the jungle. The North Vietnamese broke contact.

Fighting continued for more than a week. Small but vicious patrol engagements occurred often, as many as eleven on a single day. The Marines never caught enough of the enemy to force a set-piece battle, but counted dead finally numbered 736; 11 North Vietnamese were captured along with 190 individual and 23 crew-served weapons. There were probably at least 1000 more North Vietnamese buried by their comrades or left dead in pathless jungle during the fighting. The Marines lost about 150 killed and 400 wounded. Many of the latter were evacuated by helicopter in an astonishingly short time to a preliminary medical station ashore and then to one of the finest and most comfortable hospitals in the world, the U.S.S. *Repose,* which is a Navy hospital ship on station in the South China Sea. Less than 1 per cent of the wounded who reached a dressing station alive died; most could fight again a few days or weeks later.

This action was unusual because of the number of improved North Vietnamese camp sites taken; these contained stores of food, clothing, ammunition, medical supplies, and records and documents. The North Vietnamese were trying to play guerrilla but not doing it well because they were essentially regular forces. Their concentration in this area was broken up; their rapid and disorderly disappearance into the uninhabited, inhospitable jungle can hardly have improved their morale.

The action after the battle at the command post on the eighteenth was like many Marine sweeps and searches. There were more contacts and more vicious fighting than usual because Marine intelligence efforts had worked out the location of the enemy carefully and caught them by surprise. But the North Vietnamese, after their single large-scale assault, confined their actions to hitting and running. They would try to fire from cover, use hastily dug fortifications, and then disappear. They were not as good at this as the VC, particularly when the Communists are opposed only by ARVN units. The North Vietnamese organized units finally left the area entirely.

U.S. Marines went into the worst part of an important war that was going badly for the anti-Communist world. After eighteen months of combat, they have not yet won the war even in the I Corps Area. But they have changed the entire complexion of the conflict. The VC and even the North Vietnamese have had to return to Mao's stage two and have lost heavily in civilian support. Although North Vietnamese units are now entering this area from the north across the demilitarized zone, they are soon in poor condition.

There are some indications that these soldiers are not properly indoctrinated. When they are forced to take to the jungle, some of them lose confidence in themselves and even starve to death.

In March 1965 the West was said to be unable to support a non-Communist government successfully in a bargain-basement war. Insurgents were thought to be almost inevitably the winners. This idea is no longer widely held. Some of this optimism stems from Marine Corps victories, from their securely organized bases, and from their system of harassing the VC at all levels. General Walt and his Marines have lived up to their combat records and to the hopes and prayers of Americans who had confidence in them.

10: Thailand

The country formerly known as Siam is the only nation in Southeast Asia that was not the colony of some European power. Thailand managed to retain its independence, in part by playing Britain and France against each other. Both these powers took some Thai territory to add to Indochina, Burma, and Malaya, but the Thais made use of their remarkable diplomatic skill to remain free.

The present Thai government is a monarchy which was essentially absolute until 1932. A constitution was then introduced which has endured, with some changes, until now. Early in World War II, however, the Japanese occupied Thailand after a five-hour fight. There was some guerrilla opposition to the Japanese and some collaboration with them, but most Thais just pointedly ignored their oppressors. With the collapse of Japan, Thailand managed to make peace with the Western Allies without severe penalties, although war had been declared on both Britain and the U.S. in 1942. The Thais reasserted their sovereignty, but were soon caught between the expanding power of Communist China and the West.

Thailand since 1949 has not been entirely stable. Governments which have some aspects of military dictatorships have replaced one another fairly often. These changes have all been bloodless, however, and have not disturbed the country seriously. At one time Thailand collaborated with the Chinese Communists, but more recently the country has been completely anti-Communist. Social and economic conditions are already good and improving. There have been attempts to introduce a truly elective democracy, but this goal has not yet been achieved.

Thailand is presently playing an unusual role in world and Southeast Asia politics. The nation maintains certain aspects of neutrality, but the anti-Communist Southeast Asia Treaty Organization capital is in Bangkok. At least six full squadrons of U.S. fighter-bombers are presently using Thai bases for Vietnamese combat missions. A base for B-52 bombers began to operate in August 1966. Thailand is probably closer to the Free World than even this would indicate. The U.S. military potential in the country is classified, but obviously considerable. All U.S. activities are under brilliant young Maj. Gen. Richard G. Stilwell, former Chief of Staff to Westmoreland in Saigon. They still work together closely and obviously have plans ready if the situation in Southeast Asia should deteriorate further.

Thailand is an extremely important U.S. ally primarily because of those air bases which the Thai Army protects with no drain whatever on U.S. combat forces. Missions flown from them are mainly over friendly territory. If necessary, in-flight refueling is possible at the Thai border. Fighter-bombers serviced in this manner are combat-effective longer than if they are launched from airfields in South Vietnam or carriers in the South China Sea. The big bombers can carry more bombs because they need less fuel. To build bases of similar combat usefulness in Vietnam would take months, tens of millions of dollars, and at least three combat divisions complete with all supporting elements to protect the construction.

Other reasons for Thailand's importance as an ally are its geographic position, its stability, its wholehearted cooperation against Communism, and its relatively high level of education and economic strength. All these and other things are obvious when one flies from Saigon to Bangkok.

What has the U.S. contributed to get these strong and useful allies? First, friendship and moral support. Second, military materiel of many types, including a large stock of surplus U.S. World War II infantry weapons. Third, an undisclosed but large number of U.S. military personnel—there were more than 3500 there in 1965 not including 8000 U.S. Air Force personnel—who serve as advisers and assist with engineering projects. Fourth, certain economic aid that the U.S. would undoubtedly have given anyhow to prevent a Communist take-over.

There is another potentially valuable U.S. contribution to Thailand which is not generally known. Careful investigation by the U.S. and SEATO indicated that conventional military operations are possible in Thailand during at least a part of the year. If the Thais should be attacked by the regular armies of some of their Communist neighbors, they would immediately need conventional force assistance, including armor. The U.S. has all the heavy equipment for an appropriate task force, probably in excess of a division in strength, presently in storage in Thailand. Tanks, self-propelled artillery, heavy guns and howitzers, and vehicles of all types are ready for immediate use. Supplies, including ammunition and gasoline, are in the country. All of this is maintained by skeleton U.S. crews and is properly separated according to the latest U.S. tables of organization and equipment. Troops with only their small arms need be flown in; the entire force could be fighting conventionally in hours.

Thailand is about 1000 miles long by 500 miles wide and contains approximately 30 million people. The country is the cleanest, most prosperous, and most Western-like country on the mainland of Asia. The Thais are rich in natural resources and have a sound, well-run economy. Their gross national product exceeds 3.3 billion dollars per year. The Thai people have more real freedom than in many countries with theoretically more democratic governments. Their tradition of patriotism goes back centuries.

On the debit side Thailand is directly in the path of Communist expansion. China is close with no serious natural barriers between. Communist North Vietnam and Communist-inclined Burma are disturbing; the situations in Laos and Cambodia are not reassuring. The northeast section of Thailand itself is primitive, underdeveloped, and ripe for insurgency of the Communist type. The people are in part non-Thai, already indoctrinated with anti-Government propaganda, and to some extent controlled from North Vietnam. The Chinese publicly claim that Thailand will come next in the line of Communist take-overs after South Vietnam.

A second Communist-infested area in Thailand lies a little over 1000 miles southwest of the first; it is where the few hundred surviving Communist terrorists from the Malayan emergency still hold out. This area in Thailand is so barren and primitive that not much is known about the terrorists. They appear to be beyond civil action, but military reconnaissance and search and destroy missions are occasionally undertaken by both Malaysia and Thailand. The forces of each country are free to use the territory of the other in these operations.

For a while the Thai people and their government were fence-sitters. In spite of charter membership in SEATO in 1954, there were periods of indecision. Since the spring crisis of 1962 in Laos, when U.S. Marines and other forces including units from Britain, Australia, and New Zealand suddenly arrived to bolster the Thai combat potential, however, these people have aligned themselves solidly on the side of the Free World. They have used U.S. arms and aid to produce a strong nation. I was delighted with the Thai military posture in general and their army in particular. The latter presently consists of about 80,000 men divided into four combat divisions, a regimental combat team, and an air defense force. A division consists of three or four rifle regiments plus artillery and armor. Each rifle regiment has three rifle battalions; these are the basic fighting elements of the Thai Army.

Each rifle battalion (34 officers and 846 men) has been armed and organized not only to fight against a conventional force, but also to do the best job possible against guerrillas in Thai terrain. It consists of a battalion headquarters and headquarters company (16 and 231) plus three rifle companies (6 and 205 each). The combat elements of the battalion headquarters company consist of a mortar platoon with three 81-mm mortars, a machine-gun platoon with six U.S. A4's, and a recoilless-rifle platoon with three U.S. 75's. There are also three 3.5-inch rocket launchers in these units. This entire battalion is lightly armed, but contains a larger than normal number of men for Southeast Asia. U.S. Army rifle battalions have less men but more and heavier weapons. U.S. First Cavalry battalions have only 767 personnel, but thirteen 81-mm mortars and eight 106-mm recoilless rifles. But Thailand has no imposing array of helicopters to carry their support arms about; battalions in order to be mobile in a tropical guerrilla war must be light.

Each rifle company contains a company headquarters (2 and 36), a heavy-weapons platoon (1 and 40), and three rifle platoons (1 and 43 each). Personal weapons at company headquarters are thirty M1 carbines and eight M1 rifles (three with grenade launchers). The heavy-weapons platoon has three 60-mm mortars, three 57-mm recoilless rifles, eighteen M1 carbines, seven M1 rifles (four with grenade launchers), and six .45-cal. pistols. Each rifle platoon is divided into a platoon headquarters (1 and 7), and light-machine-gun squad (0 and 9), and three rifle squads (0 and 9 each). The headquarters has a 3.5-inch rocket launcher, four carbines, and four rifles. The machine gun squad has two U.S. A6 machine guns (bipod and buttstock only), five M1 rifles (one equipped with a grenade launcher), and four .45-cal. pistols. Each rifle squad has one BAR and eight M1 rifles (two with grenade launchers).

The basic arm of infantry everywhere is a personal shoulder weapon, usually a rifle. This is particularly true of the U.S. Army and Marine Corps and British Commonwealth forces. It should be remembered, however, that even some Western nations after careful consideration have decided to issue many lighter, handier, and less powerful arms. The Italians still use more submachine guns than rifles; under some circumstances the French do the same. Many U.S. Army units have no M1 or M14 rifles at all; U.S. M16's have only about half the power of 7.62 NATO arms. The Thais are supposed to have more M1 rifles than M1 carbines in their rifle battalions, about a 3 to 2 ratio, but carbines are still thought of as adequate arms for combat.

The most important reason for this is that the average Thai soldier, even though larger than a Vietnamese, is considerably smaller than an American or Australian. The carbine is easier for him to carry, fits him better because of its shorter stock, and recoils less. On the other hand, the Thai Army realizes the importance of the full-power rifle rounds and issues more rifles than carbines in the rifle company, 61 to 117. There are no carbines in the rifle squads at all.

The preponderance of rifles over carbines might change in combat. Casualties, personal preferences, and weapons distributed for special missions could increase the number of carbines. The Thais like the M1 carbine and are presently purchasing them newly manufactured in Japan. They use only the M1 semiautomatic type, however, and show little interest either in converting the weapons they have to M2's (which have a burst-fire capability) or in buying new M2's from Japan.

On the other hand, the Thais appreciate fully the importance of automatic small arms. There is one BAR in each rifle squad and additional medium machine guns at platoon, company, and battalion level. Battalion MMG's are in part still the old reliable water-cooled Brownings (M1917A1). These are better for some situations in irregular warfare than any of the more modern air-cooled GPMG's.

The presence in each rifle company of three U.S. 60-mm mortars is in accordance with American experience in Vietnam and British findings in Malaysia. Mortars are needed, but 81's and their ammunition are too heavy. The 60's and ammunition in adequate quantities can be carried by men on foot. These weapons are capable of accurate, sustained fire at medium range and are real infantry mortars, not glorified grenade launchers. The U.S. 57-mm recoilless rifle is the same weapon that the Viet Cong use so effectively in Vietnam. Battalion level support arms, the 81-mm mortar and the 75-mm recoilless rifle, are the proven veterans of World War II and Korea.

The Thai marines have a different organization and weapons assignment. Because of their possible amphibious role, a Thai marine battalion (36 officers and 927 men) is slightly larger than its army counterpart. It has an extra 75-mm recoilless rifle, three more 81-mm mortars, six flame throwers, and two .50-cal. machine guns. But a marine rifle company is not as heavily armed as an army company; it has no 57-mm recoilless rifles. Each marine rifle platoon is four men stronger than an army platoon, but lacks a weapons squad. As in the U.S. Marine Corps, each Thai marine rifle squad consists of three four-man fire teams plus a squad leader, thirteen men in all. Thai marines use more M1 rifles and fewer carbines.

Thai officers, NCO's, and the older enlisted men are well-trained, well-organized professionals. The rest are National Service and recruited every year for a two-year term. The country is patriotic and respects members of the armed forces. Pay and allowances produce a relatively high standard of living. Military careers are sought after by both officers and enlisted men who can qualify. There are the usual service academies, staff colleges, and other specialized training establishments, all patterned on their U.S. and European counterparts. Many officers and NCO's are trained in U.S. schools, especially at the Special Forces headquarters at Fort Bragg in North Carolina. Educational background is important, but not absolutely required for professional advancement. The army is remarkably free of politics for an Oriental country. Even though there are U.S. advisers at regiment, division, and army headquarters levels, all training is done by Thai personnel.

New soldiers and marines are well taught; they can drill, maneuver, and conduct themselves properly in their normal living environment which is not so cut off from the civilian population as in some countries. But their small-arms marksmanship is not as good as it might be. The basic problem seems to be that the average soldier cannot absorb the recoil of an M1 rifle firing a .30-'06 cartridge and retain sufficient interest in accuracy to become a good shot. Range firing with the M1, particularly in the prone position, is likely to produce flinching and jerking of the trigger. These same faults are present to some extent in the firing of the carbine, although the reason for them has disappeared.

Thai leaders have themselves detected this deficiency and begun appropriate corrective action. They have asked for and received American advice and assistance. A new attitude toward marksmanship is being developed. Padding for the recruit's shoulder has helped, but more real improvement has probably come from demonstrations by U.S. Marines. They have shown the Thais what can be done with the M1 rifle when properly handled. A sniper with a scope-sighted M1 rifle is now a part of each rifle platoon headquarters. He is a long-term professional and has received special training. Some are said to be extremely formidable in Thai terrain.

U.S. advisers in Thailand told me that the tendency toward inaccuracy with personal arms does not carry over to Thai crew-served weapons; these are handled competently and effectively.

Thais, like most Orientals who have the chance, become excellent mortarmen. Crews working together learn quickly and thoroughly, although ammunition for practice is not as plentiful as in U.S. forces.

Formal tactics at battalion level and below are not so important as they might be because the Thai Army does not really expect to have to fight a conventional war. They realize, however, that their country does contain areas where a war of this type would be possible during about half of each year, the dry season. They spend about 25 per cent of their maneuver time practicing the type of tactics that would be used against an enemy operating in conventional fashion. The Royal Thai Marines, because of their amphibious potentialities which could be used away from Thailand, spend about half their time on conventional tactics.

Conventional tactical problems at platoon, company, and battalion level are handled as in similar U.S. units; Thais who fought in Korea were always part of a larger U.S. unit. A relatively large number of officers and NCO's who are veterans of Korea are still on active duty. Even though there was never more than one reinforced battalion active at one time, many men saw service in it because of the Thai policy of fast rotations.

Offensively the Thai infantry would take full advantage of their fine crew-served weapons and their efficient personnel to gain fire superiority. They have coordinated plans for mortar fire and would displace some heavy support weapons, such as their recoilless rifles, medium machine guns, and rocket launchers forward with their maneuver elements in accordance with terrain and opposition.

Defensively Thai soldiers would take full advantage of the real efficiency of their crew-served weapons. Interlocking fields of medium machine gun fire are appreciated and practiced often. Support by other direct and high-angle heavy weapons would be coordinated. Because of the high percentage of regulars with long service, the Thai Army would be able to do well within its logistic and weapons capability on its own terrain, or in similar terrain in Southeast Asia. They are not likely to be asked to fight elsewhere.

The appearance of small Thai combat units in Vietnam benefited both the anti-Communist world and Thailand itself. There is no better place to learn guerrilla war. Thai soldiers and marines will undoubtedly behave well as they always did in Korea. They will work efficiently in cooperation with U.S. units.

The Thai Government, the high command, and all subordinate levels realize that counterinsurgency is their likely combat concern in the immediate future. Basically, a war of this type is to gain the minds of the people. Without knowing the term "civil action," the Thai Army has been engaged in it for years. Civilians have been welcome to receive treatment free at all military medical facilities. Whenever space has been available on military transport, local people have been encouraged to ride. Thai recruits usually serve in the base nearest to their homes; this same procedure is followed where convenient even with senior officers.

Local affairs such as festivals, celebrations, and agricultural exhibitions are always planned jointly by civilian authorities and army post commanders. Large free meals for many people are often given away on appropriate days in rural areas. The Thai Army is popular in regions where there are bases and is a rallying point for all coordinated civil affairs. The recent extending of central Government authority into northeastern Thailand—the area in which the potential Communists are strongest—is basically a projection of the army into this region. All-weather roads have been constructed here for the first time, mostly by the army with U.S. military engineering assistance. So far, the national police have done most of the guerrilla fighting, and the army has been responsible for maintaining civilian good will.

The Thais realize that good works alone won't be successful against Communist aggression led by agents trained and directed by China and North Vietnam. They know that the only way to defeat armed insurgency is by armed, motivated, intelligent, and vicious counterinsurgency. The army has armed, trained, and integrated into the general defense structure numerous units of Territorial Defense Volunteers who still live in their villages, but would defend them when and if necessary. The army and the volunteers train together; they conduct counterinsurgency maneuvers with live ammunition in the northeast, although so far there has been little actual fighting.

Terrain is always important in war. In Thailand it is highly variable. There are large delta areas and rugged mountains similar to Vietnam. The troubled northeastern area has a rainy season, in which the whole country is inundated, and a dry season with severe dust storms. Some of central and eastern Thailand is suitable for armor in the dry season. The wide variations in country and weather are disconcerting to outsiders, but the Thais are used to them.

In a counterinsurgency offensive, infantry plans call for operation both by battalions and by smaller units. Attempts would be made to get intelligence at least equal to that of the guerrillas, move rapidly, and close with the enemy so as to destroy him completely. The Government forces have the advantage of real friends in every area and a system of intelligence already established and based on patriotism, a meaningful term among most Thais. Even though the northeastern section has a population which is predominantly non-Thai—mostly Vietnamese in some localities—these other ethnic groups never constitute a working majority of the total population of any large area. There are numerous Thais in all localities.

Given proper information, the Thais will endeavor to beat their opponents to the punch with ambushes, attacks on enemy base camps, and daring patrols to interfere with communications between local insurgents and their sources of logistic support. The Thai Army has electronic communications equipment and some sophisticated materiel supplied mostly by the U.S., but it will rely more heavily upon its counterinsurgency offensive spirit. In their training the stress is on the importance of tailoring forces from squad patrols to battalion sweeps to fit the actual conditions. Higher echelons can supply reinforcing elements, including tanks, self-propelled artillery, armored personnel carriers, and even quad-mounted .50-cal. machine guns on half-track carriers, if these are needed. Soldiers train often with both tanks and self-propelled weapons.

The Thais realize, however, that guerrilla wars are usually won and lost at platoon level and on foot. The men that fight better under guerrilla conditions with light supporting weapons usually win. The aid of the volunteers as guides and, as units, to protect the people and conduct small offensive operations of their own could be of great value. These men are enthusiastic and intelligent.

Thai patrols will be light enough to retain mobility; they will strive to surprise their enemies as Magsaysay's Philippine units did. Companies and battalions have some extra carbines for issue when necessary to men normally armed with M1 rifles. Even though Thai soldiers are trained and equipped in a modern manner, many of them are serving in areas where they can still act like natives. They can move anywhere swiftly and silently by day or night because they are in friendly country which they themselves often know well. But extensive offensive maneuvers are also being held almost continuously from base camps located in the doubtful northeast. The Thais have the priceless advantage of being forewarned of how the Communists may attack them. They also benefit from having lived in a well-run, prosperous country in time of peace.

In all counterinsurgency operations, defense is necessary. The Government must accept the responsibility and to some extent the handicaps of defending the civilian population in its normal day-to-day activities. Schools, post offices, market places, rural industry, and courts of law must be guarded. The Thais have evolved a system of village fortification which they would coordinate with their offensive plans. These village and hamlet defenses are only partially complete even in troubled areas; further work might solidify a defensive frame of mind. But if necessary, they would consist of sandbag emplacements, bunkers, and trenches protected by wire. Strong points within the system could hold out even when isolated; most would be capable of 360-degree defense.

Thai officers and U.S. advisers close to them give the impression that defensive fortifications are for use as the British use them in Malaysia, not as ARVN often does in Vietnam. They are not overconfident; an explosive situation does exist and they know it. Communist guerrillas like the Viet Minh and VC are organized and in their country. Some small operations of a guerrilla nature and Communist motivation have taken place for some time. If the local

Communists want war, however, and don't have massive Chinese support, they will be hit hard as soon as they declare themselves. The Thai Army and the volunteers are ready to fight them as they enter the very beginning of Mao's second stage, rather than wait almost until the third, as Diem and his forces did in South Vietnam.

Thai soldiers and marines do not have the combat experience, sophisticated weapons, educational background, and high professional competence of U.S., British, and Australian soldiers. But they will not be called on to fight in areas where maximums of these qualities are required. Compared to their neighbors, they have an almost unbelievable military efficiency. They have thought of their probable combat requirements and their strategic position and come to valid conclusions in regard to the infantry weapons they need and the tactics they will employ. With the help of the U.S. Thai rifle battalions and smaller units will make it very difficult for the Chinese Communists to fulfill their boast—"Thailand is next!"—if they stick to bargain-basement war.

Thailand has given the U.S. friendship, full cooperation, and vital bases. The Thai Army is a powerful friend in Southeast Asia, a place of vital importance. If the U.S. should have to send in combat forces, this can be done quickly. Americans would live, move, and fight in an immeasurably better environment politically, economically, and socially than in Vietnam. They would be supported by more virile and dedicated local allies also, people who have done something about a possible emergency before it suddenly explodes into catastrophic proportions.

11: South Korea

The only direct armed conflict between established governments of the Free World and the forces of Communism began in the Far East on 25 June 1950 when the North Koreans drove across the Thirty-eighth Parallel, the artificial boundary between the two Koreas. The long bloody war which followed was fought on conventional lines in the open with World War II weapons. Guerrilla activity in South Korea after the Communist withdrawal did not really present much of a problem. Communist North Koreans have ruthlessly rooted out all opposition to their rule within their borders.

Most people believe the Korean War was over in 1953. This conflict is still going on, however, although on a very small scale. There is a thirteen-year-old armistice, but no peace treaty. A not unusual fire fight occurred just three days before I visited the Republic of Korea Army in the fall of 1965. It took place in the narrow demilitarized zone bordering the original cease-fire line. The talks at Panmunjom no longer make Western newspapers, but they continue. The North Korean and Chinese Communists never admit border infractions, but commit them frequently. Their acrimonious talk is mostly based on falsehood, but is widely circulated throughout their world. The tragedy of the situation is that an accident might snowball into full hostilities. There are safeguards, but the possibility of human error is always present.

Meanwhile, the two Koreas are as separate as East and West. The border is closed tight with no legal crossings whatever, save by the small team of neutral observers from Sweden, Switzerland, Poland, and Czechoslovakia. Both sides are stronger militarily and have more formidable fortifications than in July 1953. The United

Nations command now includes only U.S. and ROK combat troops, but these are ready to hold the entire 145 miles of border. The 2000-meter demilitarized area south of the original cease-fire line—two strands of barbed wire on small wooden posts called the center tape—is patrolled almost continuously by U.S. and South Korean rifle units. Total forces from the two nations available in this area number about 50,000 and 500,000 men respectively. The forward elements of a dozen divisions are on a twenty-four-hour alert. Entire units could be in defensive positions within fifteen minutes. To the north there is a similar situation; a 2000-meter demilitarized zone adjoins the center tape on the North Korean side, too, with an uninhabited area and fortifications beyond. The North Korean fortifications are said to be 40 to 50 miles broad and as much as 100 feet deep.

South Korea is about the size of Kentucky and has a population of 25 million. The strain on the country of maintaining armed forces of nearly 650,000 on a full war footing for more than sixteen years has been terrific, but the army itself has benefited greatly. During the three years of the Korean War, individuals and units fought bravely, but not always efficiently. The army was new and sometimes lacked discipline, training, and motivation; effective articulation at higher levels was also conspiciously missing on occasions. This has all changed. The army today appears to be one of the best in the world. No other national force, save that of North Korea, has had as much experience working together at full strength in the immediate presence of an enemy. South Korea's soldiers are now well armed, professionally competent, and efficiently organized, even by U.S. and British standards. Officers and men are loyal, alert, and in good physical condition. The South Korean Army is more than twice the size of the British; Korean marines are second to the U.S. Marines in strength and in fighting potential for all marine organizations.

The association between the U.S. and South Korean armies is close and efficient. More than 700,000 Americans fought in Korea; 33,729 died there. Tens of thousands of South Koreans entered the U.S. Army and remained an effective part of it as individuals for years, both in active war and during the long armistice. These men have proven their worth and are now a valuable increment to American forces in the area. U.S. servicemen get on well in Korea; the people are friendly and appear to appreciate what America has done and is continuing to do for their country.

The top U.S. commander is still the top United Nations commander in South Korea. He commands, therefore, all South Korean units, also. But the formal lines of responsibility, where two separate national armies are concerned, can mean little if the will to cooperate for the common good is not present. In South Korea this desire is apparent on both sides. A strong, vicious, and intensely hostile enemy is only 4000 meters away. As is apparent in Vietnam, full efficiency is possible only with a unified command.

The South Korean Army has been organized and trained primarily to fight a Korean-type war for obvious reasons. It is divided into triangular army corps and divisions similar to those used by the U.S. Army in the later stages of the 1950–53 war. These larger units contain artillery, armor, and aircraft, but not quite so much of each as is now found in comparable U.S. units.

The backbone of each South Korean infantry division is its riflemen. There are three regiments in each division, along with artillery and tanks. Each regiment has three rifle battalions; each battalion (32 officers and 777 men) consists of a headquarters and headquarters company (9 and 86), a heavy-weapons company (5 and 145) with eight medium machine guns and six 81-mm mortars, and three rifle companies (6 and 182 each).

Each rifle company has a headquarters (2 and 18), a heavy-weapons platoon (1 and 41), and three rifle platoons (1 and 41 each). The heavy-weapons platoon has three 60-mm mortars and two 57-mm recoilless rifles. Each rifle platoon has a headquarters (1 and 5), a heavy-weapons squad (0 and 9), and three rifle squads (0 and 9 each). The heavy-weapons squad has a medium machine gun and a 3.5-inch rocket launcher. Each rifle squad has an automatic rifle and eight infantry rifles; two of the latter are equipped with grenade launchers.

Korean infantry, like that of the Philippines, Thailand, and

South Vietnam, is mostly armed with U.S. World War II weapons. The U.S. .30-'06 small arms are important in the South Korean Army. The M1 rifle, the BAR, and the two air-cooled Browning medium machine guns all fire .30-'06 rounds. An A6 is issued to the heavy-weapons squad of each rifle platoon to make a total of nine in a battalion. Four A4's are issued to each of two machine gun sections in the heavy-weapons company.

The army also uses a number of U.S. M1 carbines to arm men not fighting primarily with their personal arms; gunners, assistant gunners, and ammunition bearers in support weapons crews have these lighter weapons. Officers and headquarters personnel also usually carry carbines; there are 303 of them in each rifle battalion against 477 M1 rifles and 27 BAR's. But there are only two pistols in the entire battalion; the Koreans do not think much of pistols, not even the powerful U.S. .45-cal. 1911A1 which they issue more liberally in nonrifle units.

Infantry support weapons are standard U.S. models, but these are normally found one level higher than in the U.S. Army. Wire-guided antitank missiles, 106-mm recoilless rifles, and 4.2-inch mortars are not organic to rifle battalions, but are found at regimental level. This relative lightness for rifle battalions increases foot-mobility in rugged country, and is made possible by the intimate knowledge which all field officers and higher commanders have of the border terrain. Regiment and division commanders know where antitank and similar heavy weapons will be required and want to place them personally on the basis of their own wartime experience.

The Korean marines have the same arms, but issue them in a slightly different way, in part because their organization differs from the army's. The marines officially have no carbines at all in their rifle battalions. The .45-cal. M1911A1 pistol is issued to gunners and assistant gunners of crew-served weapons; most of the rest have M1 rifles. The marines have six 106-mm recoilless rifles per battalion (38 officers and 908 men), but no smaller recoilless rifles at all; there are eight rather than six 81-mm mortars. Both these types of weapons are located in the headquarters and headquarters company (17 and 269); there is no separate heavy-weapons company.

Each rifle company (7 and 213) has three 60-mm mortars, three 3.5-inch rocket launchers, and *eight* A4's; a U.S. Marine rifle company is normally assigned only six medium machine guns. Each rifle platoon (1 and 43) consists of a headquarters (1 and 4) and three rifle squads (0 and 13 each). A rifle squad, as in the U.S. Marines, is composed of three four-man fire teams each armed with a BAR and three M1's.

The difference between Korean soldiers and marines in their thinking about M1 carbines and the .45-cal. pistols is astonishing. The army is primarily concerned with the kind of war they experienced the last time; such a war could break out easily almost any morning. Everyone in each rifle battalion must have the capability of fighting in rugged border terrain to protect all support positions and command posts on a 360-degree basis. The carbine, even though a poor shoulder weapon, is better for actual fighting than any pistol. The marines contend, however, that the carbine is heavier and clumsier to carry than a pistol. The army accepts this in order to get a better secondary weapon in their rifle units. Korean soldiers are fully capable physically of absorbing the recoil of an M1 rifle without discomfort, although it is a little long in the stock for some of them.

The marines are primarily interested in amphibious operations. Isolation of small units is perhaps not so likely. They feel that if a man really needs a shoulder weapon at all, he should have a real rifle. But the M1 rifle is too heavy and bulky for any man to carry around who is not primarily fighting with it. Where a marine is part of the crew of a support weapon, he can do a more valuable service for his unit in keeping this weapon in action than by fighting individually. He is less inconvenienced by a pistol than by a carbine.

During the Korean War all South Korean weapons and ammunition were brought in by sea from America and replaced when seriously defective. This situation had many obvious disadvantages. Today these same arms are kept in good shape in arsenals established for the purpose. All weapons can be rebuilt and new parts added as necessary. Completely new weapons can be assembled in some instances from components made in Korea. South Korean industry is presently producing ammunition for them all. The army is not entirely independent of American weapons support, but could now fight for several months without it.

Our allies in South Korea like those in the Philippines know about all the recent small-arms developments around the world. They have tested particularly the new American and British arms, but have no intention of trying to adopt any 7.62 NATO round weapons. They believe that any new cartridge of about the same power and weight as the .30-'06 may be an interim expedient only. They also have seen the fumbling that has occurred in connection with anything radically different like the U.S. M16's, the Stoners, the AR-18's, and the new special-purpose infantry weapon (SPIW). In summer 1966 they were not convinced of the military value of 5.56-mm ammunition. Unlike Vietnam, much of their border country is wide-open, bare mountains where ranges are likely to be long. Based on limited tests, they preferred the Russian 7.62 Intermediate to the U.S. 5.56-mm round. They do like, however, and are now receiving, M79 grenade launchers and high-explosive ammunition for them.

There are some other weapons which might be used by South Korean rifle battalions. Flame throwers and demolition explosives are presently available throughout the border area. Ground .50-cal. machine guns (M2's) can be issued where needed. I was told that there are still some water-cooled Model 1917A1 Brownings in fixed installations. These arms are heavy, of course, but reliable; they can deliver more useful fire than any modern air-cooled medium machine gun.

The Army has many motor vehicles, but has not forgotten how to move on foot. All rifle-company weapons including the 60-mm mortars, 57-mm recoilless rifles, and the medium machine guns with plenty of ammunition can be carried by Korean soldiers over the steepest kind of mountainous terrain. The amount which they can carry, even up a mountain, astonishes all foreigners. But they need this ability; their country is extremely rugged.

In order to understand the desires and to some extent the unconscious aims of South Korean military leaders today, we must know something of their recent history. All Koreans are intensely nationalistic. They still resent domination by the Japanese before 1945, even though several of their present senior commanders received their early training and advancement in the Imperial Japanese Army. South Koreans have now been cut off from their brothers to the north for almost twenty years, but blame Communism for separating the country. They feel certain if all on both sides of the border could vote freely there would be but one Korea, and that one non-Communist. They consider this goal to be worthy of extreme effort.

As the armed forces have grown stronger with more training, new weapons, and better organization, military leaders have begun to think in terms of reunifying their homeland by force. They would like to drive the Chinese Communists and their followers out of North Korea. The South Koreans will not be the aggressors; they realize their obligations to the United Nations and the U.S. But they are confident that they could retake the North, if given the chance, and if outside powers refrained from intervening on either side.

The army has had a great deal of combat experience. All present field and general officers and many senior NCO's first demonstrated their efficiency in combat, mostly in their 1950–53 war, but some in World War II.

General Chung In Won, the young commanding general of the Eighth Division, is an example. He is only thirty-nine years old. He rose during the war to become a full colonel in 1952 at twenty-four. He is a good organizer, a good trainer and teacher, and a fine natural leader. The enthusiasm of his entire command is apparent. His men are proud of themselves, their unit, and their commanding general. They do things quickly and precisely because of good training, but I saw them also adjust efficiently to changes in maneuver plans. Working together at full war strength, but in a peaceful condition for more than thirteen years under good commanders, appears to have produced fine units.

So long as there is no peace, but only a most imperfect armistice, the South Korean Army is ready to resume hostilities at any time. If faced with superior force, they would give ground slowly and grudgingly in defense of their own country to the south. With massive Chinese assistance for the North Koreans, the South Koreans would have to do this while awaiting U.S. and allied assistance. If badly outnumbered, they would retreat to the mountaintops and hold them.

As one flies over the area south of the border today, old bunkers and trenches can be seen at the top of almost every eminence. This terrain would be easy for good troops to defend. South Korean soldiers are astonishingly physically fit and know the whole area like the back of their hands. But they have the training and the morale to fight efficiently anywhere. Every division wanted to be the one chosen to join the U.S. combat forces in Vietnam in the fall of 1965.

Battalion and company offensive tactics in Korea would take full advantage of all available support. If terrain was suitable, tanks might be assigned temporarily to rifle battalions, or even companies. I observed a company attack-and-hold maneuver in which two tanks were in support, but armor is normally used at a higher level. Battalions and companies generally have to rely on their own organic heavy weapons. The high-angle fire of the battalion 81-mm mortars would be coordinated where ranges allowed with the company 60-mm mortars in an over-all fire plan, perhaps with the support of higher echelon artillery and tactical air power. This could be of several types with a series of objectives for various units, or a single concentration for all weapons. Forward observers would direct this fire on targets as required, even if it meant changing the original plan. There are so many good observation situations in Korea and such good military maps of the border area that all mortars could frequently be employed precisely, or dispositions made to cover areas with fire from other units when one set of company 60-mm mortars is displaced forward.

Rifle units of small size would still rely more heavily on their own direct (flat trajectory) firepower from medium machine guns, recoilless rifles, automatic rifles, and individual rifles. They would take advantage of whatever surprise was possible offensively, but would plan to gain fire superiority once their intentions were known to the

Dept. of Defense (USMC)

General Walt (right), a Marine Ontos, and its crew.

General Walt addressing newly arrived Marines. The general makes a point of seeing all units personally and welcoming them to his command. Note that all troops have retained their weapons.

Dept. of Defense (USMC)

A Marine self-propelled 155-mm howitzer with part of the sprawling
Danang base behind it. These vehicles have enormous punch in either
direct or high-angle fire. Able to withstand enemy HMG fire, they
have been extremely useful in the I Corps Area.

An M48M2 tank in support of a Marine rifle battalion outside the Danang base. A VC spotted within 1500 yards can be destroyed, usually with a single round. The canopy protects the crew from the sun.

Joint maneuvers conducted by U.S. Marines and the Royal Thai Marines in Thailand. Bottom photo shows a BAR in the foreground and U.S. M1 rifles behind it.

Thai infantrymen supported by an M41 light tank. A patrol of this type is highly effective because the tank can clobber opposition while the infantry protects the tank.

A U.S.-South Korean Army position just south of the demilitarized zone in South Korea. This is known as Charlie Block and is said to contain some of the most powerful American weapons deployed anywhere outside the United States. The photograph was taken from as close as security rules allow.

Two South Korean infantrymen with their 60-mm mortar. This weapon is a favorite in the Korean Army because of its portability, accuracy, and surprising power for its weight.

Two Japanese soldiers with a Type 62 GPMG. The weapon can be fired from its bipod, or mounted on a tripod as shown here. It is more accurate in burst fire than any other modern GPMG.

A Japanese officer firing a twenty-round burst from a type 64 infantry rifle. No other rifle which fires a full rifle power round can be shot so accurately. Even though several cartridges have already been fired (see blurs at right), the barrel is still directed precisely on the target.

Australian soldiers in an alert position on an Australian 6 x 6 truck. Identifiable weapons are the U.S. M60 MG, Owen SMG's, and SLR's.

Practice firing in the Australian Army with the Energa antitank rifle grenade from the SLR. This combination has reasonable accuracy and power, but its range is only about 100 yards and the recoil is heavy.

Two New Zealanders demonstrating their British 2-inch mortar. This mortar is the lightest and weakest of those presently in regular use anywhere in the world, but is more easily carried in the jungle than any other. Its bombs are small, but more powerful than hand grenades and can be fired to a much greater range with more accuracy.

General Wallace M. Greene, Jr., Commandant, U.S. Marine Corps, fires a Stoner 63 rifle on the Quantico range while the inventor, Eugene Stoner (in dark suit), looks on.

A U.S. Air Force B-57 jet bomber at the Danang air base.

A U.S. Air Force C-123 Transport at the Bien Hoa air base. This plane is the workhorse of the U.S. in-country transportation system where fixed-wing operation is possible from reasonably good fields.

The black aircraft, an EC-121K, is a remodeled Superconstellation whose exact functions are secret. These planes are used over North Vietnam perhaps to confound the relatively simple guidance systems of the Russian ground-to-air missiles used by the North Vietnamese. The white plane is a USN A3 fighter-bomber which is normally carrier-based.

Marines escape from a crashed helicopter during Operation Hastings, at the landing zone, forty miles north of Hue, Vietnam.

Marines move through burned rice paddies after leaving their forward drop zone during Operation Hastings.

Weapons of the Stoner System of small arms.

The most recent 63A carbine or SMG.

The standard rifle with a new jungle strap which allows a soldier to keep the weapon ready for action.

The Bren-type LMG.

The belt-fed type of LMG with a plastic box containing 150 rounds attached.

Top: the M16 rifle being used in Vietnam with a twenty-round magazine attached. Middle: the M16 with an M79 grenade-launcher type attachment mounted below the barrel. The attachment supplies additional weight to make the weapon more accurate in burst fire. Bottom: the new Colt Commando SMG. It is built with the same basic action as the M16, but has a shorter barrel, a telescoping stock, and a thirty-round magazine.

Captain James Mimbs explaining the new launching system for M-3 rockets attached to armed helicopters. Third from left is former All-American lonely end Bill Carpenter from West Point.

Four pistols in use in Vietnam. The small hammerless Cal .38 Special revolver and holster weigh less than half the G.I. weapon and shoulder holster and less than a third the Cal .44 Magnum and Cal .45 Long Colt with their carrying rigs.

The author on his private range holding his Stoner 63 LMG (top) and his U.S. M16 rifle (bottom).

enemy before moving in the open. They would displace forward direct-fire support weapons at short intervals so as to provide nearly continuous cover.

Army tacticians have been doing a lot of thinking about night fighting. They have attacked at night and under cover of smoke and bad weather in their training maneuvers, but these have not been conclusive. If night offensives worked early in a new conventional war, South Korean units would certainly continue them. But veterans recall some rather painful disappointments in darkness in the 1950–53 war.

I also gathered that commanders are not sure of the efficiency of assaults using marching fire. If they were shown to be successful, they would be continued, but the commanders expect that movement of a part of a unit preceded and supported by fire from the rest would be more useful.

Korean rifle-unit commanding officers realize the extreme effectiveness of enemy crew-served weapons against all forms of attacks and would try to knock them out as soon as they can be located. Forward observers controlling mortars and artillery would aid in this; one reason for the popularity of the light 60-mm mortar is that it is truly accurate, as well as mobile. A shell from one of these can dispose of any enemy automatic weapon, save in a bunker. Ranging-in is usually possible without revealing the position of the mortar. They can also keep up with an attack better than the 81's. A 60-mm shell delivered precisely and on time from short range is superior to more powerful 81-mm rounds fired from a long way back.

If the enemy has overhead protection for crew-served weapons, mortars of any size are generally useless. But bunkers are vulnerable to recoilless rifles and even rocket launchers when range is short. The former are superbly accurate when properly zeroed in and can destroy all but the heaviest fortifications, although they do give away their positions with the first shot. The South Korean infantry prefers the 57-mm recoilless to heavier weapons of the same type because it is light and can keep up. The marines have 106's because they hope to have mechanical transport available most of the time. The Koreans, because of their knowledge of their country and their years of field maneuvers, will be able to handle their support weapons well and take maximum advantage of them.

Infantry units have perfected a technique of coordinating platoons and companies as well as larger units so that a continuous offensive pressure can be exerted. Breaking through the wide band of North Korean defenses, particularly in the area around their famous Iron Triangle of the earlier war, will be a long process. There is no question, however, that the South Korean troops have the desire to tackle the job, the know-how to support their offensives at all levels, and the bayonet and grenade potential to carry it through.

Defensively, the South Korean Army is presently in a better posture along the south side of the cease-fire line than ever before. Within the last eighteen months, new installations involving large quantities of concrete and 360-degree defenses on the tops of key mountains have been added. Some of these, like the one called Charlie Block, are classified and cannot be discussed for publication. They could contain the most powerful type of U.S. weapons installed in very heavily fortified sites. The presence of even one is a guarantee to the Korean people of continued American support.

The defense of South Korea does not rest, however, solely on massive retaliation, nor is it overdependent upon fixed defenses. There are fortifications, but they are not continuous; mobile combat units of several sizes are required to make them effective. Artillery, armor, and tactical air power are all important, but infantry was the key in the old war and will be in any renewal of it.

At battalion and company level South Korean infantry would rely heavily in defense on their organic support weapons. All mortars, both 60's and 81's, could be controlled from a central command post, or the 60's could be left under company control. In some situations a rifle company commander might have a pair of 81's responding to his orders also. Because of terrain and good forward-observer positions, mortars would be unusually valuable; so would recoilless rifles because of their wide fields of fire. The 3.5-inch rocket launchers are probably at a disadvantage, save against enemy armor at relatively short range.

The most powerful defensive weapons in South Korean battalions are its organic medium machine guns. A total of nine A6's and eight A4's is unusually large for a personnel strength of 809. In the Korean war MMG's were extremely important; toward the end of it, defensive positions were held mainly by these weapons in bunkers. The trenches between them initially occupied by riflemen and BAR gunners were often abandoned. South Korean positions are not now so obvious as they were in the old war; there is more flexibility even in defense. Perimeters would be stressed instead of lines. But the fine .30-'06 Brownings are still the arms with which dedicated crews can inflict maximum casualties on an attacking enemy. These weapons can reach out effectively to at least 2000 yards. At closer ranges Koreans with BAR's and M1's could be as tough as any soldiers in the world. They now have a spirit of unit loyalty that will hold up through the last vital few inches, the length of their bayonets.

These are all tactics in so-called conventional war, the kind fought in Korea in 1950–53. In Vietnam, South Korean infantrymen and marines have taken over U.S. combat tactics to a considerable extent, but seem to be evolving some new and effective variations. Many Koreans presently fighting in Vietnam—the Capital Division of the army and a full brigade of marines, 45,000 in all—are long-term professionals with a great deal of active duty experience. Being Orientals themselves, they have the priceless advantage of understanding Vietnamese mental processes, if not their languages, better than Americans. The Koreans, however, look like wrestlers, weight-lifters, and professional football players compared with the local people. They are larger and have better muscular development than the Vietnamese. Some can break four bricks with a single blow of a bare hand.

The South Korean armed forces were young and untried in their tragic war of 1950–53; they grew enormously in size, but irregularly in dedication. This appears now to be changed. Almost every soldier knows what Communist domination is actually like. Most senior officers and NCO's were in the armies that were forced back into the Pusan beachhead and then advanced again to the Yalu. The younger men were only boys then, but most of them saw Communist brutality at close range. The army would not be fighting Communism on the basis of theory alone; they know what would actually happen to their country if they lost a war.

The two U.S. divisions plus more than twenty South Korean divisions have the equipment, training, leadership, and desire to take care of any North Korean land or amphibious attack that has only moderate Chinese assistance. The joint U.S. and South Korean navies and air forces would also do their full share. In my opinion the U.S. would not again allow the real enemy, the Chinese Communists, to take advantage of sanctuaries just beyond the North Korean borders. If the Chinese attacked in full strength, the fat would be in the fire, perhaps for most of the world.

The Koreans are a proud, courageous, physically strong, and hard-working people that can go far. They appreciate what the U.S. has done for them, but have themselves made much the larger contribution to joint efforts to bring security to South Korea. They have also sent their best and most efficient fighting men to help Americans in Vietnam.

12: Japan

The Japanese armed forces were astonishingly successful in World War II. They conquered all of Southeast Asia down to Australia and fought successfully for a time in Burma. They controlled what is now Malaysia and most of Indonesia. They captured many of the Pacific islands and were in uneasy possession of the Philippines. Then U.S. industrial production and the combat efficiency of various joint commands under MacArthur, Nimitz, and Mountbatten turned the tide. The crowning blows were, of course, the atomic bombs on Hiroshima and Nagasaki. The individual Japanese soldier was efficient in combat and almost always displayed unusual bravery.

This final disastrous defeat of Japan not only destroyed the military power of the nation, but also appears to have put an end to the collective psychological capacity of the people to make war. The country has recovered commercially, industrially, and financially to an astonishing extent. It is stronger today than ever before and has a higher standard of living and gross national product. But the idea of national expansion by war is now incomprehensible. The Imperial Japanese Army and Navy practically ruled the country for many years before World War II. Each of them had a seat in the Cabinet with the right to veto any decision; they could bring down any civilian government at any time. The virtues of the old samurai, the warrior class, were extolled; all soldiers occupied privileged positions.

All this has changed. Defeat in World War II brought vast material damage and civilian casualties; it killed militarism in Japan, at least for the foreseeable future. The people resented their leaders who had cost them so many lives and left the country literally in ruins. They placed military men so low in popular favor as to refuse them the right to wear World War II decorations. The new constitution adopted in 1946 specifically outlawed any capability whatever to make war of any type at all. For more than four years there was not even a national police force. By degrees, starting with the Korean war, the Japanese began to form small military units for internal security. Even today all the Japanese Self Defense Forces together contain only about 300,000 men. The Ground Self Defense Force, what would be the army in another nation, has just under 190,000 men; equipment runs no heavier than light tanks and 155-mm howitzers.

The post-World War II Japanese soldiers were at first poorly paid and housed and treated with contempt by most civilians. They were forced to give up their seats in trains to farmers and industrial workers. Even though considerable strides have been made in improving the standards of living of officers and men, the public image of the military profession is only just beginning to recover. Soldiers have gained the respect of the people more by their efforts in helping in earthquake emergencies, youth training, and similar programs than because civilians appreciate the security that their new armed forces give them.

The army, navy, and air force are not important politically; they receive together less than 1.1 per cent of the Japanese gross national product. About 8.9 per cent of the budget is appropriated for all defense activities. These figures compare with about 10 and 50 per cent for the U.S. Within these limitations, however, the Japanese are again efficient, well trained, and well armed.

The Japanese Army consists presently of thirteen divisions plus support troops and some extra brigades. One division is partly mechanized; it has some tanks and sufficient armored personnel carriers for most of its rifle units. The other divisions usually have a minimum of armor, but plenty of new first-quality trucks. The five divisions of the Northern Army, which face the Russians only twenty miles away, have four brigades each; the rest have three. Each brigade consists of three or four battle groups. Each battle group contains five rifle companies, one mortar company with 4.2-inch mortars, and a battle group headquarters company that includes a reconnaissance platoon and a combat engineers platoon. The battle group at full strength consists of between 1500 and 1700 men.

A rifle company (8 officers and 205 men) contains a company headquarters (2 and 15), a mortar platoon with four 81-mm mortars (1 and 29), an antitank platoon with four 106-mm recoilless rifles (1 and 13), and four rifle platoons (1 and 37 each). Additional company heavy weapons outside the rifle platoons consist of three .50-cal. machine guns, two in company headquarters and one in the mortar platoon headquarters. There are four extra 3.5-inch rocket launchers, two in company headquarters and two with the mortar platoon. Each of the four rifle platoons consists of a headquarters (1 and 4) and three eleven-man squads. The platoon headquarters has two 3.5-inch rocket launchers, three rifles, and two pistols. Each squad has seven rifles, one rifle equipped with a telescope sight for a sniper, two automatic rifles, and one tripod-mounted medium machine gun. The Japanese rifle squad, platoon, and company are all very heavily armed. Mobility as a result cannot help but suffer.

After the end of World War II in 1945, practically all weapons, including even antique swords and civilian sporting arms, were destroyed. Japan has fewer licensed pistol owners today than any other large nation; there are said to be only about fifty legitimate civilian owners of pistols throughout Japan. While criminals do occasionally use them, they cost several hundred dollars on the black market in Tokyo.

When the Korean war caused General Douglas MacArthur to suggest that Japan rearm, weapons and the capacity to produce them were lacking. The Japanese Land Defense Force received mostly U.S. materiel, although some old Japanese World War II small arms were bought from the Philippines. The new Japanese armed forces are still partly equipped with U.S. weapons, but the divisions facing the Russians are now completely supplied with small arms designed and produced in Japan since 1961.

First and most important, they have a new infantry rifle known as Type 64; 1964 was the year of adoption. In my opinion it is the best weapon of its type in the world today. I was able to fire tighter bursts, both prone and offhand, with it than with any other full-rifle-power, rifle-weight weapon I have ever tested. It can also deliver accurate single shots at all practical military ranges with a minimum of sight adjustments and recruit training. All these features are inherent in the excellent and original design. This weapon is not a copy of anything produced elsewhere and contains no more than the normal amount of proven World War II small-arms principles from other countries.

The weapon weighs 10.0 pounds unloaded and is 39.0 inches long over-all without a bayonet. It has a truly in-line stock in which the force of recoil acts through the middle of the butt. Gen. K. Iwashita, the principal designer of this new arm, achieved this result not only by placing the barrel under the gas cylinder, but also by installing simple, strong folding sights. The rifle is, of course, gas-operated and fires at the abnormally low cyclic rate of 450 to 500 rpm. Magazines hold twenty 7.62 NATO cartridges.

The new arm is four inches shorter than the U.S. M1, five inches shorter than the U.S. M14, and two inches shorter than the British self-loading rifle. Even though heavier than all three, it balances and handles well. Its compact weight, its low cyclic rate, and its low line of recoil give it high burst-fire accuracy. The integral bipod is often used in Japan even for single shots when firing from a prone position. This bipod does not change the point of impact appreciably, perhaps because of the heavy eighteen-inch barrel. Muzzle velocity with full power loads is 2640 fps. The weapon has an unusual feature of firing both full- and semi-automatic from a closed bolt until the action is warm. It then fires bursts from an open bolt.

The second important new Japanese weapon is their general purpose machine gun Type 62; it is also chambered for the 7.62 NATO round. This weapon is gas-operated, weighs slightly more than 23 pounds, and is 47.25 inches long. It has an integral bipod, but can be mounted on a tripod which has a built-in recoil-absorbing device.

Cyclic rate is about 500 rpm and cannot be varied by the gunner. Accuracy in burst fire is astonishingly good, particularly for the light machine gun (bipod mounted) conformation. I fired a single forty-round burst into 3⅝ inches at 35 meters. Barrels can be changed quickly and easily.

Both these new NATO round arms, Type 64 and Type 62, can handle the full-power loads used in the U.S., British, and most other NATO and Commonwealth services. But they can also effectively shoot a special reduced-power Japanese load in the same cartridge case. This ammunition gives a 150 grain about 2400 fps at the muzzle and has several advantages, notably in burst accuracy and reduction of recoil felt by the shooter. Young Japanese soldiers today are taller and heavier than their fathers, but not as big as most Westerners. Recruits are more easily trained with reduced-power ammunition which appears to be just as accurate out to 600 yards.

Pistols and submachine guns are not as important in Japan as in some other armies. Presently the Japanese use the U.S. Model 1911A1 pistol and U.S. Model M1 and M3 submachine guns. They have designed and field-tested, however, two new pistols which are now available for mass production. They are both modern Browning-type military semiautomatics of different weights, bulks, and powers. The Type 57A fires the 9-mm Parabellum cartridge and resembles the U.S. .45, but is shorter and a half-pound lighter—total weight, 32 ounces. The Type 57B fires the .32 ACP (7.65 mm) cartridge; it resembles some of the Browning pocket pistols, weighs 21 ounces, and is only six inches over-all. These two weapons are not revolutionary in design, but have all modern improvements and are capable of being manufactured quickly, easily, and cheaply.

The Japanese also have a new submachine gun; it weighs 7.4 pounds and is 19.75 inches long with the stock folded; it resembles the current Swedish submachine gun slightly. It has a selector which allows either single shots or burst fire and is chambered for the universally popular 9-mm Parabellum cartridge. The cyclic rate is about 600 rpm, or slightly lower in some specimens. The arm is simple in design, easy to manufacture, and appears to be rugged. Its weight and low cyclic rate mean that even long bursts can be held precisely.

Infantry support weapons at battle-group level and below, save for the general purpose machine gun, are presently standard U.S. types. These consist of the .50-cal. machine guns, 81-mm and 4.2-inch mortars, 3.5-inch rocket launchers, and 106-mm recoilless rifles. But some of these weapons are presently being produced in Japan. The Japanese are using U.S. artillery and tanks, but have designed and manufactured an armored personnel carrier of their own which has several modern, desirable features. Infantrymen carried inside are able to fight without dismounting. It carries a high-velocity 20-mm automatic cannon which can penetrate the armor of other armored personnel carriers and some tanks. There are also semiturrets for two general purpose machine guns which can be dismounted and carried on foot as required.

Japanese military leaders do not presently contemplate fighting outside their own country; the only offensive strategy currently thought of is in relation to counterattacks. This means that their army is organized, equipped, and trained for Japanese terrain. These beautiful islands are mostly mountains, valleys of no great width, and coastal plains which can usually be controlled by artillery and even recoilless rifles from the mountains nearby. There are strong defensive positions almost everywhere. Transportation and communications facilities are excellent, however, so that logistic support will not be a serious problem.

Another factor which appears to have shaped modern Japanese tactics is their experience during World War II. Even though no officer with a 1945 rank of colonel or above has been allowed in the new army, the younger men recall the staggering firepower of U.S. Army and Marine units. Japanese soldiers on defense were often literally smothered in fire of all kinds; they were seldom able to see what movements their enemies were making until too late. When the Japanese counterattacked, they again met a hail of fire. Heavy weapons actually used against them were often double or triple what

U.S. tables of organization and equipment then required. Almost every U.S. soldier and Marine, according to the few Japanese survivors of some of the island battles, had at least a BAR. Many U.S. platoon-sized groups had medium machine guns, rocket launchers, and recoilless rifles. Ammunition for all weapons was available and was used in large quantities.

The Japanese have copied what U.S. units actually had, or perhaps what the Japanese thought they had, rather than what U.S. tables of organization and equipment called for in 1945. Another legacy from World War II is an appreciation in the new army of accurate aimed fire at long range. From time to time in World War II, American Marines and soldiers picked off Japanese personnel at 400 to 700 yards. This is why one man in each rifle squad now has a scope-sighted weapon; the Type 62 is excellent for this purpose. The sniper is usually the best shot in the group and has some special training.

The new Japanese organization and weapons emphasize firepower and more firepower. Mobility has to suffer. This would indicate a reliance on defensive tactics in most areas. But when the concept of fighting in Japan only is also explored, one sees that this is not a bad idea. The Japanese have not built concrete and steel forts which they could now easily afford. They will rely on some fortifications, but these will be extemporized and defended with fair flexibility. They realize the heavy expenditure of ammunition which would occur in combat with their weapons and organization, but feel they can replace it as required all the way from factory to rifle squad.

The idea of firepower regardless of weight is new. No other rifle squad anywhere in the world is capable of delivering as many bullets accurately in a given time. For eleven men to have three general purpose machine guns, one tripod-mounted and two bipod-mounted Type 62's, plus eight Type 64 rifles, all capable of accurate burst fire, seems fantastic. But the probable use to which these squads will be put is also unusual. The Japanese Army is professionally competent. If they imagined that they would fight again in the East Indies, they would not be organized and armed as they are now. If foot-mobile offensive war over a considerable area or in jungles were likely, there would be quick changes. But the Japanese are not preparing for such combat.

Japan is now ready to defend her home islands. The nation would not even consider this limited commitment to use force a few years ago. The Japanese can rely on U.S. naval and air strength to supplement her own at sea and in the air, but the army must carry the entire load on the ground. The Russians, and more remotely the Chinese Communists, might invade Japan. The former still occupy many small Japanese islands and all of the big island of Sakhalin, half of which was Japanese before World War II.

In the event of amphibious landings on Japan an enormous amount of firepower of all kinds would be concentrated on and immediately behind the beaches. Shoreline defenses would be doomed, as they were in the Southwest Pacific in World War II. But troops in less obvious positions in the rugged mountains not far away would have a better chance of surviving and fighting effectively. The primary mission of the new battle groups appears to be to occupy in fair depth more or less fluid lines of defense against amphibious attacks. There are no concrete and steel fortifications, but the Japanese demonstrated in World War II an unusual capacity to construct strong works quickly, mostly from materials found locally. They were masters of camouflage and concealment.

The Japanese will adopt different types of defense based on whether or not they have air superiority. They are now spending money on some high-performance aircraft. If they can maintain air superiority, as would be likely against the Chinese, but perhaps not against the Russians, they would endeavor to defend the top of the forward slopes of their hills and mountains (in technical language, the military crests). This gives a maximum of forward-observer control for artillery and battle-group support weapons—presently mostly 4.2-inch mortars—and perhaps tactical aircraft.

If the air were lost, the Japanese would concentrate particularly on using reverse slopes and holding the actual crests of ridges above them where possible. Positions on the very top of mountains are not as efficient, but are more easily concealed and often just as strong.

A reverse-slope deployment and support area is relatively immune to damage by enemy artillery, tactical aircraft, and mortars. The Japanese have also been doing some thinking and testing in maneuvers of quickly installed forward slope positions such as the Viet Minh used at Dien Bien Phu. If ground fire superiority and camouflage against enemy air can be maintained, these appear to be surprisingly effective.

At company, platoon, and squad level the Japanese would take full advantage of their massive defensive firepower. Ammunition could be brought close to combat areas in vehicles and would be available in extemporized bunkers and trenches as required. They know how to place and conceal medium machine guns for maximum tactical advantage; the two additional light machine guns in each squad plus eight fine automatic rifles give enormous burst-fire capability. The low cyclic rates of both general purpose machine guns and automatic rifles ensure unusual accuracy in burst fire and, most likely, ammunition economy as well.

The Japanese cannot presently imagine fighting an offensive war. They don't even plan attacks on a large scale in their staff schools. They realize the folly of a static defense, however, and do include small offensives in all their maneuvers. At battle-group and company level they would attack and plan to use quick thrusts forward as an important part of their over-all defense. They would support an offensive of this type with artillery, mortars, recoilless rifles, and other arms. Their heavily armed rifle platoons could deliver more direct fire of their own to protect their movements than in any other army. They have the weapons to gain and hold fire superiority. Their maneuver elements could then displace forward to form a new line to be reinforced eventually by the fire components.

The Japanese are good soldiers; some men who fought against them in World War II say this is a considerable understatement. Their personnel weaknesses, if they had any, were at above battalion level. The new tactics would surely work as long as ammunition held out. But three even slow-firing general purpose machine guns per rifle squad can consume ammunition voraciously. So do the eight-burst firing rifles. Strict fire discipline would be required to prevent running out of cartridges. Even then low-level rifle units in combat would need large supplies to function in the manner desired.

The modern Japanese soldier is well armed, well organized, and well trained for the fighting that he may be called upon to do. Every one is a volunteer. Many of the NCO's and most of the officers have irrevocably adopted the army as their life's work. Their professional competence is considerable. In the immediate future the Japanese are prevented by memories of World War II from helping fight the battles against Communism outside Japan. But their present Ground Self Defense Force can hold their home islands against any nonnuclear attack that is even remotely probable. Japan is the strongest nation in the Orient industrially, politically, and logistically. It is a superb bastion of strength against Communist aggression and won't need even one U.S. combat soldier or Marine. A few days with their army and their industry left me convinced of their total friendship to the U.S., their efficiency, and their reliability.

13: Australia and New Zealand

Australia and New Zealand were remote from Southeast Asia as recently as forty years ago. The people and their governments not only ignored the existence of Asia in general, but removed the internal problem created by Chinese immigrants in their Gold Rush days by sending them all back to China. The Australians and New Zealanders were more British ethnically than the British are themselves today. The British Navy seemed even in 1941 to ensure their continuing insular existence.

The Japanese expansion in World War II changed all this. These Anglo-Saxon peoples were a part of Southeast Asia whether they liked it or not. They rose magnificently to the Japanese challenge and did their full share to defeat it. But they also realize that their future security now depends upon the Free World. They are doing their level best to support not only the U.S. and Britain, but all the anti-Communist governments in the countries to the north of them.

Australians are much like Americans. They work, play, and elect their political leaders in the same way. Their country is slightly larger than the continental U.S.; both nations started out as British colonies. But the U.S. had a big head start; the first white settlers did not move into Australia until 1770. Even today there are only about 12 million Australians, but almost all, save for about 75,000 aborigines and mixed bloods, are Anglo-Saxons. There are only a few Chinese and other Orientals, but qualified European emigrants from many nations are being sought actively.

Australians have essentially the same ambitions, language, customs, and laws as Americans. They have been coming even closer to the U.S. recently because of mutual concern about Communist expansion in Southeast Asia. The armed forces of the two nations collaborate at all levels. Australians fought remarkably well in World War II, Korea, and Malaya. They are presently doing a good combat job in Vietnam.

Australia has enormous agricultural potential, modern industry with fine plants and precision machine tools, and increasing know-how. Its natural resources are comparable to those of Communist China. But there are now more than 700 million Chinese with a continuing population increase said to be as much as 30 million per year—an annual gain approximately two and one-half times the total population of Australia.

New Zealand is a small country compared with Australia, the U.S., and Canada; it has only 2.7 million people. But it is larger in area than the British Isles, rich in natural resources, and as progressive and democratic as any country on earth. While truly independent, New Zealand has a very strong tradition of loyalty to Britain and the British way of life. Battle casualties in World War I and World War II were greater in the New Zealand Army on a per capita basis than in the British, the U.S., or in other armies where accurate records were kept.

New Zealand was once remote, far from foreign danger. Her nearest neighbor, Australia, was a thousand long steamship miles away and friendly. But the world grew smaller; New Zealand has benefited enormously economically. Large quantities of her refrigerated foodstuffs are now sold in Western Europe. High-quality meat, dairy products, and wool are easily and cheaply produced in New Zealand and transported to world markets.

Both Australia and New Zealand realize that they lie next in China's path after Vietnam, Thailand, and the East Indies. Japan in World War II showed in her successful island-hopping campaigns that a combination of land, air, and naval power in narrow seas can move rapidly.

The gallant peoples of Australia and New Zealand are determined to resist to the limit of their considerable resources any domination from the outside, particularly by the Chinese Communists. But they realize fully that action by them alone will not constitute an adequate defense. Both are members of the United Nations, the British Commonwealth, SEATO, and ANZUS (Australia, New Zealand, and the U.S.). Australia and New Zealand depend particularly on Britain and the U.S. militarily, politically, and economically.

These two nations spend a large portion of their considerable annual gross national products on defense. Their armed forces are in good condition, well trained, and amply and efficiently armed. Their armies are particularly effective in the areas where they may have to fight, but inevitably small. They have about 30,000 and 6,000 combat troops respectively. Both have organized reserves so that these totals could be increased rapidly, but ultimate size is always limited by total population. Both armies, however, in recent years have become well-rounded forces with all conventional arms. Infantry, armor, and artillery are equally combat effective. If tanks are needed in future, these armies will have them manned by their own crews and under their own command.

Australians pioneered jungle warfare training. Their Jungle Warfare Center at Canungra taught many Americans during World War I; U.S., British, New Zealand, and other allied officers still go there. Many Australian and New Zealand officers and enlisted men are veterans with actual combat experience in World War II, Korea, Malaya, Borneo, and now Vietnam. They have none of the defensive-mindedness about fighting in the jungle which the French often displayed. Both nations want the fighting, if fighting is necessary, to take place in Malaya, Borneo, and Vietnam rather than in Australia. They want to take the fight to the enemy at all levels. These men are proud of their country, themselves, and their fighting ability, either with or without weapons. If you are young, strong, and surly, you can get beaten in a fair fight easily Down Under.

The Aussie army was at one time organized into divisions with five battle groups each. They adapted these to climate and terrain where they would have had to fight and called them Pentropic divisions, a name similar to U.S. Pentomic divisions. Their five-unit formation at division level was found, however, to be unwieldy and difficult to control. A battle-group commanding officer had trouble handling the five units under him and still maintaining close contact with his commanding general, who also had difficulties.

They have recently reorganized their army on a three- and five-unit basis which bears some similarity to the new U.S. ROAD table of organization and equipment. The Aussies have retained the same sort of flexibility as the U.S. has at divisional level. They can change a subordinate unit in regard to personnel and weapons so as to perform any task assigned to it with maximum efficiency. A division presently contains nine rifle battalions, three battalions of 105-mm artillery, and a battalion of tanks. Each division contains also three task-force headquarters capable of controlling from two to six battalions of any type in action as required. Normally, however, a task-force headquarters would administer three infantry battalions, one battalion of three batteries of 105 pack howitzers, and one squadron of three troops of tanks.

The rifle battalion (52 officers and 1252 men) is the basic unit of the Australian Army. It is administered by a battalion headquarters and headquarters company (15 and 151) which includes command, medical, and service units, but no support weapons. There is a heavy-weapons company (7 and 191) which contains a mortar platoon (2 and 79) with twelve 81-mm mortars, and an antitank platoon (1 and 18) with either four 106-mm recoilless rifles or eight of the new Carl Gustav 84-mm recoilless rifles, and an assault pioneer unit (1 and 40) which has flame throwers, mines, demolition devices, and equipment necessary for constructing fortifications. There is also a signals platoon (1 and 39); all these support units have a total of thirteen medium machine guns.

A battalion also has five rifle companies (6 and 182 each). A company contains a headquarters (2 and 26)—this includes an organic support section with two medium machine guns and three 3.5-inch rocket launchers—and four rifle platoons (1 and 39 each). Each platoon consists of a headquarters (1 and 3) armed with submachine guns and three rifles, plus four rifle squads of nine men each. Each rifle squad has a light machine gun with bipod, one or two submachine guns, and seven or six rifles.

An Australian rifle battalion is very strong in numbers and to a lesser extent in weapons. This change should not be misunderstood; it does not mean ponderousness, but rather the reverse. There are twenty rifle platoons rather than the standard nine in each battalion. Each platoon can operate independently supported as necessary with temporarily attached weapons from company and battalion level. They have deliberately planned to sacrifice sheer power for mobility.

Organization of the New Zealand Army in theory must be above battalion level because of the small size of the force under arms. This is even more necessary when one considers that New Zealand presently has a reinforced battalion in the Twenty-eighth Commonwealth Division under British leadership in Malaysia and some combat forces in Vietnam operating under U.S. and Australian command. The battalion is presently the largest active New Zealand unit.

A New Zealand rifle battalion (44 officers and 892 men) has a battalion headquarters and headquarters company (14 and 250), a support weapons company (6 and 122), and four rifle companies (6 and 130 each). The headquarters company is mainly involved with command, administrative, and logistic support duties. It is unusually large because in this army it usually has to handle also high level quartermaster and supply functions. The support weapons company (6 and 122) consists of a headquarters (1 and 20), a reconnaissance platoon (1 and 19), a mortar platoon (1 and 53), an antitank platoon (1 and 20), and an assault pioneer platoon (1 and 24). The reconnaissance platoon has four medium machine guns, and four medium antitank weapons and can function as a medium machine gun support unit. There are eight 81-mm mortars in the mortar platoon as well as two medium machine guns and four medium antitank weapons. The antitank platoon has four heavy antitank weapons plus four medium machine guns and four 2-inch mortars.

Each rifle company (6 and 130) consists of a headquarters (2 and 10) with one 2-inch mortar and one medium machine gun plus four rifle platoons (1 and 30 each). Each rifle platoon as a headquarters (1 and 5) with one 2-inch mortar and one medium anti-tank weapon plus three rifle squads of eight men each. Each squad has a light machine gun, a submachine gun, and six rifles (two with grenade launchers). The number of rifle platoons per battalion, sixteen to Australia's twenty, is still very high considering total personnel. Both armies have great flexibility.

The Australian and New Zealand armies use the British self-loading rifle. They are delighted with it and don't want a full-automatic capability, even though this rifle can be provided with one easily. At present, they do not feel that 5.56-mm weapons such as the AR-15 and the Stoner are practical for them, although both have experimental programs testing these arms. The Australians in combat in Vietnam are using some AR-15's practically identical with U.S. M16's. They also have some West German (Heckler and Koch) G3's adapted to the 5.56-mm round.

Both armies have adopted the 1935 FN Browning as their issue pistol. This weapon is reasonably light, powerful, and capable of firing fourteen shots without reloading. It is, of course, chambered for the 9-mm Parabellum cartridge. But since neither army considers the pistol as a suitable weapon for combat, it has been issued only sparingly. There are six per company in the Australian Army and even fewer in similar New Zealand units.

The Australian submachine gun is the Owen, a weapon designed and made in Australia. It's a bit inconvenient to carry and looks clumsy because the long magazine extends vertically, Bren fashion; the sights have to be set off to the side. It cannot be used conveniently by a left-handed shooter, but is capable of taking a bayonet. It has a switch so that it can be fired either in bursts, or one shot for each pull of the trigger.

The acid test of any weapon is combat. In Malaya, Borneo, and Vietnam the Owen is the favorite submachine gun of all troops who have used it against enemies. It is strong, reliable, and accurate. When a man's life is at stake, he does not mind the unusual appearance and clumsy lines, or even the inconvenience of carrying a heavy arm.

My burst-fire tests of the Owen were extremely satisfactory. My first full-automatic string, thirty shots fired continuously with a single trigger pull from a standing position at twenty-five yards, placed all bullets in a silhouette target. Twenty-nine were in the chest area with the thirtieth—probably the second shot in the string—in the lower right abdomen. This accuracy is unusually good for any submachine gun, but is about normal for the Owen. The weapon is accurate because of its relatively heavy weight (slightly more than ten pounds with a loaded magazine), its low cyclic rate (below 600 rpm), and the two-handle configuration which aids steady holding.

The Australians also have a new submachine gun that may eventually take the place of the Owen. I found it not quite so accurate in full-automatic fire, but lighter and less clumsy. The new weapon is still not as easily carried as some European types, but it will score more hits. It retains the capacity to take a bayonet and a switch which allows single shots or bursts. Limited issue to combat Aussie infantrymen, however, has been met with resistance; most of them prefer the Owen.

The submachine gun situation in the New Zealand Army is complicated; two different weapons are presently in use. The British Patchett (L2A3) is one of the best in the world for reliability, accuracy, and general handiness, but the Australian Owen is even more accurate in bursts and is preferred by most New Zealand soldiers who have used it in combat. The New Zealand table of organization and equipment calls for 221 submachine guns per rifle battalion; there are usually some of each weapon in this total.

In rifles and submachine guns Australians and New Zealanders have stayed close to each other. In machine guns, however, they have split radically. In the New Zealand Army, the new British general purpose machine gun is being used both as the squad light machine gun with bipod and as the support MMG when mounted on its special recoil-absorbing tripod. This single weapon with two types of mounting has replaced the Bren LMG and the Vickers water-cooled MMG more completely in New Zealand than in any other Commonwealth country, or even in the British Army itself. New Zealand soldiers accepted the new weapons as soon as the official decisions were made to adopt them. They then set out to learn to use them, without wasting time regretting the passing of the two old friends which were rich in memories and traditions, but at best obsolescent in terms of ammunition.

The Australians have not followed the British and New Zealand lead in regard to the new general purpose machine gun. To some extent this decision was based on a desire to adopt a U.S. rather than a British weapon. The Aussies are not as pro-British as the New Zealanders. They also wanted to have the best available and ran extensive tests comparing all available light machine guns. These consisted of the old .303 Bren, the new British GPMG with bipod, the Canadian C2 (a heavy-barreled, burst-firing SLR), the M14 Modified, the new 7.62 NATO Bren, and the U.S. M60 GPMG. Some Australians liked the new 7.62 NATO Bren, but the official decision was to adopt the U.S. M60. These weapons are presently in all Australian combat infantry units including those in Vietnam. The Aussies are particularly pleased with the accuracy of the M60 and its ability to deliver large quantities of fire for short periods, more than can be delivered with any magazine-fed light machine guns.

The Australians have placed M60 machine guns in their rifle squads, something that many weapons experts in the U.S. Army and Marine Corps have long wanted to do because of the undesirable features of the M14 Modified. But the Australians have only one light machine gun per rifle squad, not two as in the U.S. Army, or three as in the U.S. Marine Corps.

As a result of these same tests, however, some Australians developed an admiration for the Canadian C2. They have redesigned this weapon to improve its capacity for accurate burst fire in the hands of the average soldier and are manufacturing some of them in Australia for use in their armor, engineer, and artillery units. They are nine pounds lighter than the M60's and use thirty-round box magazines instead of belts which have a tendency to catch in vines and creepers in the jungle. These modified C2's also have a three-pound weight advantage over the new 7.62 NATO Bren's and are similar in many respects to the SLR; training is simplified. Australian C2's might replace the M60's in their rifle squads under some circumstances in the future. They are lighter, but not so accurate or capable of providing as much support fire.

The U.S. M60 is also being used on its tripod as the Australian infantry medium machine gun. It is not perfect in the opinion of some officers, who remember fondly the old .303 Vickers, but the era of heavy water-cooled MMG's is probably past. Other Australians who have served in Malaya and Borneo would have preferred to have seen the British GPMG adopted at this level because of its better tripod and superior sighting equipment for use in darkness, fog, and smoke. But men making the final decision did not want another roughly similar weapon in their army. They prefer to have one only, and to be equipped with the same machine guns as U.S. combat units.

Support weapons other than machine guns in Australian and New Zealand rifle battalions consist at present of standard NATO 81-mm mortars with the new ammunition, 3.5-inch rocket launchers, and three recoilless rifles. Both nations currently have the U.S. 106-mm recoilless rifle. They have also experimented with the two new British models, the 120-mm Wambat and the 84-mm Carl Gustav. Both armies like the latter especially. The Australians are substituting it on a 2-for-1 basis for the 106-mm recoilless rifle. The saving in weight is great and the loss in range not serious in their probable theatre of operations. The Carl Gustavs are said to be as good against bunkers and even enemy personnel in the open out to medium range. They and their ammunition can probably be considered foot-mobile; neither the 106-mm nor the British 120-mm recoilless rifles are. Australian tests indicated the 84-mm recoilless rifle is superior to the new U.S. 90-mm in short-range accuracy, weight of ammunition, and length. The Carl Gustav is slightly lighter and equally powerful, but apparently not quite so effective at long range.

The discussion of recoilless rifles, both large and medium, is mostly theoretical at the moment. Aussie and New Zealand units in Borneo and Vietnam don't have any of them. They prefer 3.5-inch rocket launchers or the new U.S. M72 disposable rocket launcher when they can get it. Both armies have 4.2-inch mortars, but they have followed the British practice of considering them as artillery rather than infantry weapons.

Both Australian and New Zealand armies were composed until four years ago of 100 per cent professional soldiers enlisted for long terms. But these two nations now have full employment. There are more jobs than employable applicants. Civilian concerns are particularly anxious to attract young men with the same qualities that make good soldiers. Even though men in both armies are well paid and have considerable prestige, recruiting for a minimum of six years has run into difficulties. National Service has had to be reintroduced, although it is different in the two countries.

In Australia men who qualify mentally, physically, and morally are drafted for two years and serve in the same units with the professionals. In New Zealand National Service personnel are not drafted into the Regular Army, but receive fourteen weeks of basic training with twenty days additional each year for three years. They become trained reservists and are organized into easily mobilized units. It should be borne clearly in mind, however, that in both countries the army is popular. Young men who really do not want to serve in Aussie units can generally avoid it, although at the expense of some pride. In New Zealand many National Servicemen volunteer for the Regular Army after their fourteen weeks of basic training.

The men responsible for Australian and New Zealand organization, weapons, tactics, and advanced training have analyzed their geographical and political situations carefully. If they must fight in defense of their homelands, they would prefer to do it closer to Communist China, the real enemy. They will take full advantage of tactical air support, modern air transport, land vehicles including armor, heavy support weapons, and electronic communications equipment. They remember, however, that jungle and guerrilla wars are ultimately won and lost by men with their personal arms fighting on foot.

At the present time both armies have combat units in Malaysia and Vietnam. Although the Chinese might begin a bargain-basement war in another area almost overnight, all likely theatres of conflict are tropical; jungle often covers both mountains and swamps. Rice paddies are more frequent than territory fit for tanks. As a result, both the Australians and New Zealanders spend between 70 and 80 per cent of their training time on jungle warfare. They appreciate the possibilities of using armor and similar weapons in parts of Thailand during the dry season, but feel that such an operation would be special. Hot, wet jungle is far more likely. They learn to live in rain forest, navigate in mangrove swamps, and create strong bases in mountainous areas where supply is by air only. They emphasize the great value of surprise on offense and twenty-four-hour alertness to prevent it on defense. They also appreciate proper intelligence at all levels as well as how to fight with maximum viciousness. Base defense is tolerated only as a necessary requirement for continuing efficient offensive action.

Both Australia and New Zealand benefit from two types of pre-induction activity of their young men. These two nations are extremely sports conscious. The physical condition of almost all inductees is good; many of them are trained athletes with extensive experience in physical contact sports. Furthermore, the recruits in both nations have a high preinduction acquaintanceship with rifle marksmanship. In New Zealand some varieties of deer have become so numerous that bounties are paid for their ears. Both hides and meat can be sold in the open market. Kangaroos are in almost the same category throughout a large part of Australia. Range rifle competition is more common in New Zealand, but Australians have more open, unpopulated country where the ability to shoot a rifle accurately is often acquired at a young age.

Even though these countries cannot count on 100 per cent preinduction marksmanship ability, they are able to modify their rifle training plans to some extent because of it. The high proportion of recruits who do have some rifle skill aids all. The presence of a few real marksmen and hunters appears to inspire entire units. Current instruction in both armies is along U.S. Trainfire lines with emphasis on target identification, recognition, and fairly quick shooting from several different nonstandard positions. Slings of the American type are not used. Recruits in each army normally fire about three hundred rounds with their rifles, but may fire many more, if they do not qualify at various stages during their courses. Instructors are skillful and catch tendencies to develop common faults quickly. Where required, the old "known distance, bull's-eye target" techniques are still stressed.

Submachine-gun training is not so thorough as that with the rifle, but every recruit fires about 125 rounds to get the feel of a weapon of this type. Marksmanship proficiency with the light machine gun is not a basic requirement either, but every soldier must be able to handle a machine gun reasonably satisfactorily in case of an emergency. Recruits fire a minimum of about two hundred rounds; if a man has a natural flair for the weapon, he will get a lot more specialized instruction and fire hundreds of additional rounds later.

Advanced training is far more thorough and more specific than in most other armies because of long-term regular enlistments and the relatively high educational level of all personnel. Combat exercises and maneuvers are based largely on the supposition that Australians and New Zealanders will fight in Southeast Asia. Even though New Zealand is temperate in climate throughout, these islands have so little hard freezing in winter that their forests are not significantly different from those in Vietnam. Patrolling squads, platoons, and even companies lose themselves among enormous trees as much as eighteen feet in diameter at the base; fern-type bush rises twenty feet from the jungle floor.

There are five exercises, three in the Australian and two in the New Zealand Army, which typify their elaborate training. First, an Aussie advanced rifle marksmanship course. All men who take this have already completed their bull's-eye firing and done some shooting at pop-up silhouette targets in unexpected places under simulated jungle conditions. The setting is mountainous jungle only slightly cleared; there is a single firing point with four groups of targets placed in different directions, both horizontally and vertically, at ranges varying from 50 to 150 yards. The targets in each group are of the same type and in line, but of different colors. There are sometimes two targets of the same color in the same group. All targets are reasonably visible continuously, but the firer receives instructions to shoot one target only.

"Shoot the blue balloon on the right," the instructor says. The firer has first to remember which group of targets is composed of balloons, check his memory by looking at the group, survey this particular row of targets to locate the blue balloons, and then shoot the blue one on the right. The same procedure is followed if a firer is told, "Shoot the red star on the left." The targets either vanish when struck like balloons, or ring like steel bells. A man continues to fire until he hits his target.

This course leads not only to quick target identification, but also to positive reaction to orders. Since some targets are partially obscured by brush, conditions of jungle warfare are approached. Each soldier also learns to adjust his speed of fire to range. The targets at 50 yards are much easier and take less time to hit than those at 150 yards, but all are considerably smaller than normal U.S. Trainfire targets. If a man desires, he can take another position, although he receives all his orders while standing. The course of fire also helps in regard to fire discipline; men who have had it are not so likely to blast away at empty jungle.

While in New Zealand, I saw the beginning of a weekend of volunteer extra-duty jungle training for four men, three recruits and a young NCO. This was made possible by the surplus of deer. Several varieties of deer imported within the last hundred years have multiplied so rapidly that they harm crops and gardens, as well as sheep and cattle ranges. These soldiers were going out to spend two days and three nights stalking these animals for training, pleasure, profit, and to rid the country of pests. A large red stag nets a hunter for meat and hide as much as twenty dollars.

It would be hard to imagine a better way to produce jungle know-how; only actual combat is more beneficial. Soldiers who engage in this sport not only take with them their regular service rifle and ammunition, but also their military equipment necessary to live comfortably in the bush. Different parties will often play tricks on each other so that all are cautioned to identify targets positively before firing. The various hunting parties have a good time and often more than double their week's pay, but remain under some discipline.

An Australian jungle-training course that impressed me most

favorably was their patrolling practice. This comes early for all recruits and has the dual purposes of making surprise by the enemy
difficult and teaching immediate vicious reaction to it, if it does
come. A fairly large group attends a lecture and then watches a
demonstration. Small groups then practice under careful super-
vision. The usual diamond or arrowhead patrol formation is used in
open country, but is not adaptable to a narrow jungle trail. Here
men must learn to move forward more or less in single file, but with
considerable intervals between them. If possible a staggered file—
two lines close together with the men in each opposite spaces in the
other—is used. If not, a single line has to be employed; in dense
jungle there often isn't any other practical formation.

Each man is taught to twist his body slowly from side to side
while keeping both his eyes and his rifle continuously pointing toward where he is facing. This is said to be the best means of keeping a soldier's attention concentrated on observing jungle thoroughly, a small bit at a time. Tests indicate that a man, at least a
civilized white man, does not pick up visual evidence of the enemy
intuitively, but has to search systematically.

As soon as a patrolling recruit spots something unusual, he alerts
his patrol leader by stopping and motioning. If he sees an "enemy,"
he reacts immediately with fire; blanks, of course, in this training.
The whole patrol moves quickly and without orders to concentrate
either in a firing line, or a perimeter according to previous instructions. The acting commander sizes up the situation and gives his
orders, usually for fire by the whole patrol and then movement by
part of it on one flank. In small meeting actions in the jungle the
side that first takes a positive vicious offensive action usually wins.
Even when a patrol is ambushed, it can often beat the enemy, if it
can capture the initiative. I saw also an antiambush exercise to
teach the same general principles learned by the foot patrols earlier.
This training exercise—it was not a special demonstration—was for
two squads of more experienced troops, each mounted in an
Australian six-by-six truck. All soldiers were facing outward with
their weapons ready to fire from where they were. They didn't know
if and when they would be ambushed. They were prepared to open

fire from the trucks, or to jump out according to orders if an "enemy" showed himself at any time. An ambush was simulated by the explosion of a mine between the two vehicles and some blank full-automatic fire from one side. An NCO in each vehicle shouted an order. I was astonished at the speed with which the two trucks were emptied and the precision of what followed.

A sergeant threw a smoke grenade to indicate the apparent direction from which the enemy fire was coming. In a twinkling all men were in position opposite the column of smoke, and laying down a heavy volume of fire. Instead of forming a defense perimeter, however, the two squad M60's supported by a 3.5-inch rocket launcher and about half the total personnel formed a base of fire. The rest under the senior NCO moved to one flank, concentrated, and then swept down on the ambush itself as indicated by the smoke grenade. The entire exercise was completed in less than five minutes; the attack from the flank was certainly convincing in its power and coordination.

Both armies spend a great deal of time on physical fitness; some field officers are still active in sports. I met a New Zealand major who nearly crushed my hand when he shook it; I found out later he was still one of the top rugger players in a football-mad country. But something that made an even greater impression was an exercise by a ten-man tug-of-war team from a training platoon. These recruits were only incidentally preparing for competition. They were also exercising together and finding out what men can accomplish by cooperation.

A big rope from the team out in the field extended over a limb of a tree and down to a block of concrete with an iron ring in it. Weight had been adjusted so that only a few top teams could just raise the weight to the limb by a steady, coordinated pull. The men I watched were not the best, but were average, strong, callus-handed New Zealanders. They had to work for about four minutes, alternately exerting their maximum strength together and seeing the rope stretch, but slowly lift the block a few inches. Then they would half rest, get a new footing, and pull again. The block never moved far at any one pull, but it was finally all the way up.

One gathers from talking to Australian and New Zealand infantry officers that their basic combat unit for the jungle is the platoon. This may be an oversimplification, but both armies emphasize operations at this level and are obviously organized with this in mind. Their rifle platoons are lighter than in most armies; they contain no heavy-weapons squad like that in the U.S. Army which has theoretically two medium machine guns and two 90-mm recoilless rifles. An Australian rifle platoon has no organic support weapons at all, although a similar New Zealand unit does have a 2-inch mortar and a 3.5-inch rocket launcher in its headquarters.

This difference is more theoretical than real. An Australian unit which needed weapons of this type would have them assigned from a higher level. A New Zealand platoon which probably would not need the two headquarters support weapons might not carry them on a jungle patrol. We should remember, however, that light support weapons have proven of considerable value in counterinsurgency war. High-explosive bombs for the little 2-inch mortar were still used in Borneo; they are considerably more powerful than grenades from the U.S. M79. The 3.5-inch rocket launcher has proven its worth in Vietnam. These support arms are light enough to be carried easily through most terrain.

There are three types of missions in which Australian and New Zealand platoons specialize. First, there are conventional attacks, even in jungle terrain. A platoon would move forward with its squads either in line, in column, in a V, or in a modified diamond. These would vary slightly because the Aussies have four rifle squads and a small headquarters; a New Zealand platoon has three squads and a large headquarters. "In line" would be with all squads abreast and the platoon headquarters in close support. "In column" would be as the term indicates; this is often necessary on jungle trails. The platoon headquarters would generally be in the second position. The V (or square in the case of a four-rifle-squad unit) is formed by two squads of the platoon forward with the headquarters and the others in support. A diamond or arrowhead formation is formed by one squad leading with two more in the middle and the fourth or the platoon headquarters to the rear. In all these offensive formations the individual squads could operate in a variety of ways, but would always use both fire and movement once the enemy was located. Both rifle platoons would take full advantage of concealment and mobility and their heavy direct firepower from light machine guns and rifles.

The second type of platoon mission would be a more or less standard defense depending on terrain. The most important platoon defensive weapons are the light machine guns. When necessary, a platoon commander can request one or more conversion kits (tripods and heavy barrels) from company or battalion headquarters to convert an LMG to an MMG. An MMG is much more effective in sustained fire at long range because of its greater stability. Fire by riflemen in defensive situations is not usually allowed in either army, if the enemy cannot be seen.

Australian and New Zealand infantry tacticians do not approve reconnaissance by fire. If this sort of thing is necessary at all, light and medium machine guns deliver it. Riflemen are taught to shoot only at enemies they actually see, or have real reason to believe are in a relatively small area as in an ambush. But these soldiers are remarkably capable with their personal weapons when they do have visible targets. Hunting of kangaroo and deer is wonderful practice for shooting at guerrillas briefly seen in the jungle.

The third type of mission for rifle platoons is patrolling, the most important of all tactics in bargain-basement war. An army that cannot patrol with audacity on a twenty-four-hour basis at platoon level will not win. The Australian and New Zealand manuals do not burden their platoon commanders with too much theory; the emphasis is on going out and practicing. So much depends on terrain, the anticipated opposition, climate, and the composition and morale of the platoon. These units on patrol do not stop for a smoke or smoke at all on the march. But they do carry four quarts of water and food for three days. They understand darkness better than soldiers from other Free World nations. Regardless of formation and circumstances, the moment of contact with an enemy must be the beginning of explosive counteractivity. Fire must be delivered or returned, but there must also be controlled movement. Initiative by squad leaders and even individual riflemen can be of extreme importance.

No discussion of these two armies would be complete without mention of their forces presently in Vietnam. An Australian rifle battalion (the First of the Royal Australian Infantry Regiment) was attached along with a four-gun New Zealand artillery battery of 105-mm pack howitzers to the U.S. 173rd Airborne Brigade. Both these units earned an enviable reputation where it means most, with the hard-core Communist units who opposed them. A VC directive is said to have been sent out to their commanders which says in essence, "Watch out for the Australians. They don't attack the way they should, but hit you on your flank and rear without warning."

The New Zealand artillerymen can fly in with their pieces slung under even the relatively low-powered H-34 series of helicopters and be in action in five minutes. Their professional excellence as gunners—strictly in the fine British Royal Artillery tradition—is equaled only by their remarkable ability to defend their pieces at the closest ranges with small arms. The Aussies say their New Zealand gunners are "fair diggers," high praise for anyone not born where the kangaroos are.

The Australian forces in Vietnam have been more than doubled. A task force consisting of the Fifth and Sixth battalions plus some small ranger-type units and other supporting arms has replaced the First Battalion which has returned home. The New Zealand forces have also augmented, but are still associated with the Aussies. This joint force is now operating more independently of U.S. control and has received some light armored vehicles. Australian Air Force units are also now operational in this area.

The Australian and New Zealand armies are small; even in wartime, their capabilities would be limited by population. But their quality is excellent. Their thinking in connection with jungle weapons and tactics appears to be flawless. Their present training and actual combat experience in both Malaysia and Vietnam could hardly be improved.

These soldiers, from young riflemen to general officers, are skilled professionals doing something that they like to do. If they are called on for maximum effort in a large war, they will achieve unusual results. They can adjust to limited guerrilla war also, as they are doing now. Their abundant game, widespread competitive rifle shooting, natural fighting ability, and good physical training has led to great combat effectiveness. The British Commonwealth and the U.S. are fortunate in having them for allies.

14: Weapons and Tactics of the Future

‖‖

Bargain-basement wars are likely to continue. In Southeast Asia in particular and in other underdeveloped portions of the world they are the logical final resort for all sorts of discontent. Inevitably, Communism and the Free World will take sides. In some ways this could be good. If the two conflicting ideologies can have an outlet for violence at this level, civilization may not be blasted into nothingness by nuclear explosives. Life for many of the world's people may continue to be reasonably normal.

Active bargain-basement conflicts do not, of course, prevent larger conventional and even nuclear wars. The first could escalate into the second and third. But at present there is reason to hope that this will not happen. The nuclear stalemate could continue for the rest of the century, but several old and new insurgency situations are sure to flare into violence.

What will these small wars be like? Some future developments in weapons and tactics appear reasonably clear based on what is being done now. The anti-Communist world has obvious advantages because of professional armed forces of high efficiency, economic power, industrial systems, and scientific knowledge and inventiveness. The extreme pessimism of even two years ago has been replaced by a limited optimism. Guerrillas can be beaten. The U.S. in particular is trying to develop new ways of defeating them more easily through scientific research involving materiel, organization, and combat procedures.

On the other hand, Communist insurgents are also improving

their techniques not only in providing internal motivation and gaining popular support, but also by utilizing their better knowledge and control of familiar terrain, vital low-level support from outside, and experience gained in many ways. Their political and military organization, strategy, and tactics have all improved and will continue to do so. Scientific know-how will be used by the other side, although necessarily at a lower and lighter level. Communist guerrilla procedures are obviously different from those of the West, but they also will change and surely become more effective.

What specifically will be the nature of these changes in the immediate future? Perhaps the best way to discuss this broad question is to start with the enemy, what the insurgents are likely to do. Bear in mind that political action is more important to them than military action. They will continue to strive for power in the minds of the people they try to control. Their techniques are beyond the scope of this book, but the Communists will probably increase their reliance on terror against a part of the people while continuing to rely on the patriotism and self-interest of the rest.

The VC are presently masters of the proper use of terror; all who read newspapers have heard too much of their cruelty. Men and families are kept under strict discipline in this way, but terror is even more important when some village people can be persuaded to use it themselves against those they consider their enemies.

The VC and insurgents who may come after them will also, of course, improve in their mass appeals and tailor them more logically to the people they are trying to win. The guerrillas will be closer than the Government to those sections of the population where there is hardship, frustration, and need. The Communists are becoming masters of blending the soft sell with viciousness. Where they have something real to exploit, they will do it well.

Militarily, insurgents, including the VC, are in a more difficult situation, at least where the Government they fight has massive outside support. It may not be possible for them to advance to Mao's third stage and win there as they did in China and against the French in Indochina. To choose a level below this, but still use regiments, or at least several battalions, in an operation may be difficult.

Concentrations of soldiers throughout history have posed supply problems. Regiments in order to operate efficiently need some heavy weapons, but these bring even heavier logistic loads.

The VC will probably receive not only more materiel like antiaircraft weapons that are effective but light, but also pharmaceuticals and other equipment that is important for human efficiency in the jungle. Some devices from simple claymore mines and cheap infrared detection to light electronic antiaircraft fire-control equipment will also help. The combat capability of hard-core VC units is directly related to supply of small arms and ammunition, dual-purpose .50-cal. machine guns, and 120-mm mortars they receive. So long as these things do not hurt guerrilla mobility, they are beneficial to them. But these require support which means concentrations of supplies that appear to be vulnerable to airmobile attacks.

Specifically in South Vietnam, the VC probably will improve even further their fortification. Bunkers, tunnels, and caves will become better, more numerous, and practically tear-gas-proof. The VC can afford the labor to build a hundred of these for every one that will ever be used. They will learn even more tricks and procedures to minimize the U.S. and RVNAF advantage in expensive and complicated equipment. Their already remarkable knowledge of their own strengths and weaknesses will probably improve. Their combat efficiency and leadership will get better because soldiers employed continuously become experienced veterans, a priceless asset in all kinds of war.

It would appear safe to prophesy that the VC will not try to duplicate the Viet Minh victory at Dien Bien Phu. If they should hazard so much in the face of U.S. tactical and strategic air power and airmobility, they would be taking an extreme chance. But U.S. commanders all had nightmares about this possibility. Perhaps their realization that it did occur to the French when Navarre and his advisers thought that the Viet Minh could not possibly win a set-piece battle was the major cause that led to the heavy, continuing U.S. build-up in South Vietnam.

Predictions about changes in weapons and tactics of the U.S. and its allies are more difficult because of classification of much that is being developed. But some of the best American brains are working on these problems. Counterinsurgency materiel—gadgets and hardware—is now being invented and manufactured in astonishing variety and complexity. Never in the history of the world has science and industry had so much to do with a small war. Old procedures and devices are being beefed up; new ones are being devised.

The new means of taking advantage of air are perhaps the most dramatic. Tactical air support of combat infantry is already good; it is sure to get better. Both fixed-wing aircraft and helicopters now carry a variety of arms including rockets and automatic weapons of various calibers. The Minigun designed and produced by General Electric fires up to 6000 7.62 NATO cartridges per minute and weighs thirty-six pounds. It is being made in both 5.56-mm and 20-mm and uses the old Gatling six-barrel mechanical system of operation invented by a country doctor during the American Civil War. But an electric motor has replaced the old hand crank. M60 medium machine guns used in helicopters now often use piggyback ammunition—two bullets in one cartridge case—which doubles the number of bullets from any given burst.

This direct fire from close-support aircraft using nonexplosive bullets is extremely valuable. Better weapons can make it better still. A .50-cal. machine gun fitted with a special shotgun barrel and firing thirty-six 00 Buck pellets per discharge has been tried experimentally; various packets of arrows have also been shot from it.

Even more promising are various types of weapons that can deliver large numbers of explosive shells or rockets, such as the automatic cannon, which delivers M79 grenades fast and at close to 2000 fps. The CBU (cluster bomb unit) idea can also be used. In one form 800 projectiles, each more powerful than the best hand grenade, can be thrust out at the enemy at once by compressed air. An even pattern is said to be possible over a fairly wide area. Napalm can also be delivered by this system.

Nontactical bombing in Vietnam will probably improve. As intelligence becomes more accurate and up to date, strikes against VC and North Vietnamese units will be more effective. Finding the enemy is the problem; ordnance to work against any defenses he may have can probably be provided. Air-to-ground missiles like the Bullpup are sometimes useful; they can be rigged so as to seek out VC campfires. Ways may be found to make the Ho Chi Minh trails less easily used. Tiny air-dropped booby traps are said to be operational. Other unpleasant things for the VC will be ready soon in this area.

The concept of airmobility may prove even more valuable than all direct damage to the enemy by airborne weapons. Where rifle battalions and regiments can move into enemy territory suddenly with artillery and tactical air support, guerrilla advantages are reduced. In the Central Highlands, VC and North Vietnamese units have had two alternatives when an airborne attack catches them by surprise. They can stand and fight at a time and place not of their own choosing or they can abandon materiel and installations and disappear into the jungle. Even if they defend their powerful defensive systems successfully for a time as in Operation Hawthorne, the remarkable new tactic of pulling out U.S. rifle units, plastering the area with bombs from B-52's, and then returning the combat infantry to mop up can be used. The military advantages of airmobility for infantry, artillery, and even light armor—not yet employed in this war—are likely to increase with experience.

This airmobility could counter the guerrilla advantage over Western forces in regard to casualties. VC leaders appreciate that a fight in which they can kill one Western soldier for three of theirs is desirable from their point of view. Casualties really mean little to them; human life is cheap in Southeast Asia. Even their unit morale may be improved if they hold bunkers for a time against G.I.'s before being driven out. U.S. soldiers and Marines killed in action are individually reported lost by an average of half a dozen U.S. stateside newspapers. This situation is extremely serious; public reactions against the war could be more fatal than the enemy. If airmobility contributes, however, to finding, fixing, and defeating the enemy often and decisively, the VC will lose utterly. This technique has not yet been perfected, but it may be in the future.

The airmobile concept does not apply just to the U.S. First

Cavalry. All other U.S. combat units and on occasion allied forces use it. There will soon be enough helicopters in Vietnam for three divisions to be moved at once without undue disjointing of other airborne operations. Helicopters for transportation of combat units, fire support, and resupply are presently valuable. They may become even more important. The helicopter casualty rate is around one machine per twelve to eighteen thousand missions. If the VC bring in more antiaircraft weapons, they will become heavier and more easily caught by airmobility in their base areas and elsewhere.

The inherent danger of relying too greatly on air power must be recognized. Really bad weather with thick clouds down to the tree-tops prevents aircraft of all types from finding the ground unit that they are trying to help. Heavy bombers can attack reasonably small VC targets through thousands of feet of clouds, but a helicopter cannot find a U.S. rifle platoon under the same conditions. This problem appears unsolvable.

Changes are also likely to be made in the weapons men carry in their hands. Full-rifle-power NATO ammunition and small arms to fire it are too heavy for use in Vietnam and other similar areas of tropical jungle and paddy. Fighters in Southeast Asia cannot continue to be burdened with the weight of double ammunition and weapons only because the NATO round is suitable for conditions in Western Europe.

Which rifle is best for firing the new 5.56-mm ammunition is a matter of opinion, but the answer may not be important. The U.S. M16 as made by Colt has an enormous head start with 480,000 actually in service. It may soon be the dominant rifle in Vietnam. It is not the perfect weapon, but it is a real step forward. Some changes not affecting the basic design may be made such as shortening the barrel, lowering the cyclic rate, and partially telescoping the stock. All are possible and would be desirable, but the M16 eventually will become the U.S. standard for Southeast Asia, even if no changes at all are made in it.

If the Marine Corps can get the Stoner 63A system, there are obvious advantages. The Stoner rifle is more accurate and more nearly what most Marines like to look at and handle. Limited use by the

Marines in Vietnam has led to improvements, but the interchange-ability of parts and the uniformity of ammunition for all company direct-fire arms are even more important. The cyclic rate should be reduced; the automatic-rifle and light-machine-gun conformations should be able to fire simple shots. But even if these changes are not made, the Stoner light and medium machine guns should be issued to units with M16 rifles. One light-rifle ammunition would replace at least two.

Small arms that fire a single projectile from each cartridge will probably be with us for some time, but multiple discharges are almost sure to be used eventually, either in place of or in addition to the present type of arms. Multiple-projectile weapons have obvious advantages in bargain-basement war. Simple pump-action shotguns do work, but combat weapons of this type got off to an unfortunate start in Vietnam because of the irregular dispersion pattern of pellets in the ammunition that was issued initially. It remains to be seen whether the same size cartridges—12-gauge—loaded with a cluster of small steel arrows presently being used particularly in river boat operations by the U.S. Navy will restore shotgun prestige. If the pattern can be fairly even and closely controlled, this ammunition would seem to have a considerable advantage. Short range is relatively unimportant; most casualties in guerrilla war are inflicted at seventy-five yards or closer.

For more than a century infantry soldiers have been armed either with a single-projectile rifle, or much less frequently a multiple-projectile (shotgun) type of weapon. We may be on the threshold of a new concept in weapons. The SPIW was hailed enthusiastically several years ago, but has not yet materialized. It is said to be a combination of an accurate single-projectile weapon, a multiple-projectile arm, and a grenade launcher. It does not fire bullets, but little steel arrows about Cal .10 for both its single and multiple capability. Even in its single projectile role it is now said to fire a flight of three of these small flechettes, one after another. One tends to disbelieve the efficiency of the entire concept, however, because nothing militarily useful has been developed after almost ten years of varying publicity and semiclassified development.

In the foreseeable future some M16 or Stoner rifles will have a second barrel assembly mounted beneath the regular barrel which will fire M79 grenade launcher ammunition. These are already available. If M79 ammunition can include not only high-explosive bombs as at present, but also a packet-of-arrows round, the combination of 5.56 rifle and grenade launchers would be ideal for use in the jungle. It need not weigh more than the M1 or M14 does now. The Stoner 63A with a GL attachment would be more accurate in burst single projectile fire than any other similar arm in the world. It would do most of what the proponents of the SPIW claim for their elusive contraption.

Combat in Malaya, the Philippines, and Vietnam has proved the importance of automatic weapons. LMG's appear to be necessary at squad level; MMG's give maximum efficiency to larger units. The Vietnam fighting has emphasized, however, characteristics which are different from weapons for conventional war in temperate climates. Reliability in hot, humid jungle is necessary and difficult to achieve. Everything may be wet or covered with dust alternately. Belt-fed weapons can deliver longer bursts which are important, but are inconvenient to carry, slow to get into action, and subject to stoppages because of dirty ammunition. The Stoner 63A light machine gun with 150 rounds in a sealed drum may be one answer. It weighs about thirteen pounds; with the new ejection port cover closed, it appears to be dust- and water-proof. For offensive action, patrolling, and the like, this weapon would be almost perfect. Additional sealed magazines could be carried up to as many as three. A master sergeant of the First Cavalry has carried 580 rounds for his M16 regularly. Most U.S. Marines who have used Stoner arms in training maneuvers are high in their praise.

Another important factor in automatic weapons for the future is logical consideration of cyclic rate. Fast-firing arms make noise and aid the morale of friendly soldiers while hurting that of the enemy. High cyclic rate accomplishes nothing else beneficial. Ammunition is wasted; target efficiency is drastically reduced. The time saved in firing a practical number of rounds in any one burst is infinitesimal. Ammunition consumption in combat situations in the jungle is so extremely important that one wonders why cyclic rates above 600 rpm are tolerated.

But there is a lot of honest difference of opinion here, as well as false information. The worst of the latter is that any weapon which fires very fast tends to produce a tight pattern on a target. In theory, a weapon firing at a rate of 2500 rpm or above would stay in position for short bursts because of weapon inertia. This just isn't true for any practical hand-held automatic arm. The new German MG42-59 has the highest cyclic rate of any weapon issued to rifle units, above 1500 rpm if assembled for maximum speed of fire. Because of this and in spite of excellent design features and heavy weight, this weapon is the most inaccurate of any that I have ever fired. Only the first round of each burst is on the target.

It is unfortunate that something akin to mass hypnotism has created a desire for high cyclic rate. Weapons designers like Gene Stoner—he is the genius behind the M16 and AR-18, as well as the Stoner and other arms—have been forced against their better judgment to produce arms which shoot at rates about twice what they should be. Both the Stoner 63 and the M16 as originally produced fired about 750 rpm. But when the 5.56-mm ammunition was increased in power, actual cyclic rates went over 1000 rpm for many specimens. These fine weapons not only fire inaccurately compared to what they could do at 500 rpm, but waste ammunition and wear out many times as fast. Fatigue deterioration in some moving parts is said to go up as the third power of the cyclic rate.

A recent experimental development has been the mechanically controlled burst of two or three rounds from almost any weapon capable of full-automatic fire. If a soldier must fire full-automatic, a switch which allows only a predetermined number of rounds is useful. But with the old BAR on low cyclic rate even an inexperienced gunner could count his rounds as he fired them and control the number precisely.

Counterguerrilla operations have sometimes led to the reintroduction of the slow-firing, water-cooled medium machine guns. But this has occurred only when mobility is not important. Special weapons useful only for defensive operations mostly in bunkers are not likely to be manufactured even though many officers of several nationalities in Southeast Asia would like to have the old medium machine guns available.

I fired an intriguing weapon recently (June 1966) on a farm outside Godwin, North Carolina. David Marshall Williams, the inventor of the U.S. M1 and M2 carbines, the Williams floating chamber, and several sporting arms, has produced a Cal .22 medium machine gun that fires rimfire ammunition. The same action could be adapted to a ten-pound light machine gun. It has two rates of fire, 1000 and 2000 rpm, but it is extremely accurate at both because of the low recoil energy of the cartridge. For guerrilla war lightweight ammunition would be an extreme advantage; 1000 rounds for this arm in 2 sealed magazines would weigh about 10 pounds. The same number of 5.56-mm rounds in Stoner light machine gun magazines—belts inside plastic boxes—weigh 23.2 pounds, while 1000 7.62 NATO cartridges in M14 Modified magazines weigh about 65 pounds.

There are many disadvantages to the Cal .22 rimfire machine guns, most of them psychological. Small boys shoot .22 rimfires at cans and rabbits. But in guerrilla war, an insurgent hit anywhere with a plated lead bullet likely to infect if not removed may do more damage to the morale of his side than if killed by a slug from a Cal .50 heavy machine gun. A weapon firing subsonic Cal .22 rimfire ammunition can be made nearly impossible to locate by sound.

A Williams light machine gun, because of the floating chamber, would have the capability in spite of the low power of the cartridge to pull out long belts from a magazine. Four bullets from it would be as deadly as any full-power-rifle slug. It's the only practical weapon that can take advantage of the high cyclic rate accuracy principle. A burst attachment set for, say, five rounds would have real advantages because the gun would be almost completely silent. But at this writing, the Williams light and medium machine guns do not appear to have much chance of becoming operational. They do stir the military imagination, however, and might have real usefulness.

The American soldier in Vietnam emphasizes weapons for personal defense. U.S. soldiers and Marines are loaded down with pistols and knives. Not many VC have been killed with these weapons. Similar combat in Malaya, the Philippines, and Borneo did not lead to the same result; British antiguerrilla patrols wanted no pistols and no more than enough machetes to cut a path. There is at least a suspicion that U.S. movies and TV shows may have implanted this desire for side arms in Americans when they were young. But it is surely there and important.

Almost all the pistols presently in use in Vietnam including the G.I. .45 are too heavy and too bulky. If a pistol is required, and it obviously is at least psychologically, the wealthiest nation in the world should certainly arm its soldiers with something better than a 2.25-pound monstrosity in a one-pound holster adopted fifty-six years ago. It may have been good for horse cavalry, but just cannot be carried conveniently by anyone today. A five-shot aluminum frame .38 Special revolver would be easier to carry, quicker to fire in an emergency, safer, and about two pounds lighter. The bayonets for the M14 and the M16 rifles are not ideal knives, but could be improved with hollow handles for survival items and better shaped blades for normal cutting.

In an attempt to determine scientifically which weapons actually are best, the U.S. has conducted a semiclassified but extensive program called SAWS (small arms weapons systems). A team of scientists and soldiers have tried to evaluate all available low-level infantry weapons including those of our allies and our actual or potential enemies. Millions have been spent on ranges; the latest research procedures have been employed. Teams of average soldiers and picked marksmen have fired different weapons under careful direction and the results have been carefully recorded. Even the distance from a target of each miss has been measured electronically and fed automatically into computers. An analysis of this data has been made in the same way as if it pertained to space flight; every man involved in this research is professionally competent.

SAWS conclusions are secret, but one that has appeared in print is that U.S. 7.62 NATO ammunition weapons as a class scored lower than Russian Intermediate cartridge arms. There is also a comparison of the M16–M60 combination against the Stoners and against other systems. But one hears that useful conclusions are difficult to reach. Scientists are wonderful, but Army and Marine riflemen who spend their lives with small arms also know a lot. Sometimes arbitrary decisions based on practical procurement make evaluations of this sort useless. One hopes for the best.

Support arms organic to battalions in bargain-basement war will change in the foreseeable future. New types of mortars are likely to be used soon, among them the U.S. 107-mm, which has been bogged down in red tape for several years. More powerful explosives like tetryl for bursting charges may make mortars even more important than in the past.

Vietnam has produced a mixed reaction to rocket launchers and recoilless rifles. Obviously enemy armor is not important, but these pieces all have a secondary role. The lighter types which can be taken on foot into rough country and on patrols in the jungle at night are valuable and will be more so with cluster-of-arrows ammunition. The 3.5-inch rocket launcher can be replaced with advantage by the LAW, the light antitank weapon, but single 106-mm recoilless rifles are surprisingly useful in Marine company perimeters.

A considerable change has already occurred in connection with armor. The U.S. First Infantry Division left all its tanks behind when it went to Vietnam. But the Marines used Ontos, troop-landing vehicles, and M48A2's so effectively in Starlite that most Army units including the First Infantry now have some armor. This does not yet apply, however, to the First Cavalry. ARVN experience with M41 light tanks and M113 armored personnel carriers has been mixed, but on the whole more satisfactory than that of the French in their war in the same area. Armored vehicles are useful where they can move. U.S. tanks and armored personnel carriers are not so easily ambushed as similar French vehicles. An armored car and perhaps the new light Sheridan tank with its 150-mm howitzer capable of firing both regular ammunition and guided missiles may be operational in Vietnam soon.

Several other devices which are not actually weapons deserve mention. So much has been tried; some of it shows real promise. Most important for low-level combat are the things which aid reconnaissance. There are two types: first, the hardware which aids soldiers to see the enemy at night, and second, devices which alert friendly troops to the presence of the enemy without actually seeing him. High on the first list comes artificial white-light illumination. Searchlights are still sometimes used, but these draw enemy fire. All sorts of parachute illumination devices, 81-mm mortar rounds to 155 howitzer projectiles, and air-dropped flares of large size have been used effectively. Darkness may be even more completely banished from future battlefields by artificial light than at present, but there are disadvantages to this procedure.

For several years U.S. forces used successfully infrared "searchlights" of various sizes from sniper-scopes on an M1 carbine to powerful beams mounted on tanks. A special optical arrangement allowed a U.S. soldier to see by means of this invisible light and fire at targets so revealed. These are no longer effective against North Vietnamese and hard-core VC units because they have simple devices known as metascopes which reveal infrared light sources as clearly as if emitting white light.

A new development along this line is a device which concentrates the light already present. Illumination from faint stars suitably amplified is said to reveal a man at 200 yards and a truck at 1000. This device cannot be detected because it only collects and does not give out energy. A refinement of this principle is said to intensify an image inside the telescope for even greater effectiveness.

Radar-type devices are also being made more sensitive and lighter. Some of these can, with proper topographical conditions and with good operators, see through darkness, fog, and light vegetation to detect human movement. One of these, weighing two pounds and developed by RCA, can be mounted on a light machine gun; it allows the gunner to fire precisely at an enemy 200 yards away through reeds or during darkness. Heavier, but even more astonishing, a radar-sound-flash artillery fire-control system has been developed which will under some conditions locate and fire 105-mm howitzers at a VC mortar before the mortar's first round has arrived.

Extremely sensitive seismic devices also have been developed. These record tiny movements in the surface of the earth. They take time to install and are subject to enemy interference, but suitable heads properly placed can pick up ground vibrations from a single man walking as far away as fifty yards. A system of this type can do even more exact surveillance than the most alert sentries and does not get tired or sleepy.

The gadgets discussed hardly start the long list of what is being tried. Only a few will be practical and of real value, but some may shorten the war considerably and prevent many U.S. casualties. All of them including the very best have one major disadvantage. They tend to move major emphasis from men to hardware. Guerrilla war like all other types of war is won and lost when soldiers with weapons in their hands meet face-to-face in anger. Science and industry can help enormously, but they can also hinder if men rely too heavily on their gadgets and too little on themselves. As the brilliant young lieutenant colonel, quoted in Chapter 8 said, men are the real problem and the final and complete answer.

The foremost lesson that thousands of U.S. servicemen have learned in Vietnam is the continuing importance of the individual. If the U.S. is to win, American fighting men must believe in their cause and be willing to give their lives for it if necessary. Combat infantrymen of the future must be soundly and professionally trained, mentally ready, and confident even while living in the jungle and meeting indigenous guerrillas on a man-to-man basis with individual weapons at night. This is a large order, but both the U.S. Army and the Marine Corps are presently preparing their fighting men for this before they arrive in Vietnam and doing more on-the-job training once they get there. The situation is not perfect, but it's better than in 1965 and will improve even further in the future.

Americans are not naturally attuned to the jungle nor to the taking of human life, but if the motivation is present they can overcome their inhibitions. In my opinion, the two best groups of fighters of this type in the world today are the Communist VC and the British Gurkhas. The natural tendency of a Vietnamese village boy is to fear the jungle and avoid it as much as possible, even though living near it all his life. Indoctrination, jungle and night training, and finally confidence born of successful experience have changed the VC entirely. By using the jungle, darkness, and better foot-mobility, they have mastered large areas which give them bases and an intelligence system. The low-level advantages of the VC are making up for vast deficiencies in air power, materiel, and logistic support.

The development of British Gurkha soldiers into jungle night fighters has been similar. These young men grow up in Nepal, a high rocky area between India and China with about as much jungle as can be found in the Teton Mountains of Wyoming. But since 1946 they have been trained in Malaya. Both body and mind have been acclimatized to a new, unfamiliar area. Good organization and weapons, unit discipline and morale, and their great individual military desire have produced jungle war specialists of a high order.

U.S. officers who are expert in jungle fighting confidently predict that Americans also can succeed in this area. Young men will have to make adjustments in their patterns of life, including temporary living without electric light, air conditioning, balanced diets, and even cleanliness. This development is of enormous future importance; ultimate victory probably rests more heavily on this than any other single factor.

If U.S. jungle fighters of the future can learn to carry an efficient fifty-pound jungle kit, including weapons, ammunition, and all clothing, and use it properly, they will gain a real advantage over their Communist enemies. Health is of extreme importance in all war. The VC are as much subject to their diseases as Americans. Science and experience will probably produce an assortment of items within this weight limit that will allow a man to live in reasonable comfort and health even in the jungle. For top performance he will continue to use items of hardware which help him. But he won't let them interfere with his mobility or his offensive spirit.

Some men in several U.S. units have already demonstrated a proficiency of this type. A sergeant major of the First Cavalry is said to have gone out many times on individual missions and returned with VC weapons and more gruesome trophies. Some Americans once learned to beat the Indians at their own type of war. Soldiers and Marines can do the same again against the VC.

Methods of organization are likely to change along with weapons. Both the U.S. Army and Marine Corps still have official tables of organization and equipment which call for essentially conventional-war rifle battalions. These units in both organizations are not ideal for bargain-basement war. The Marine Corps has adopted a special Vietnam setup and made liberal use of their established procedure of assigning support weapons including armored vehicles on a semi-permanent basis to rifle companies in accordance with special needs. The U.S. Ninth Infantry Division, the first one tailored for Vietnam, has a rifle battalion of six companies not including administration and supply. There is a headquarters with some heavy weapons, a combat support or heavy-weapons company, and four rifle companies. No changes have been announced below company level, but it appears probable that there are some.

U.S. Army rifle platoons unaltered are not able to move effectively on foot because of their heavy-weapons squad. Antitank sections in both the Army and the Marines have already become lighter, but have developed into demolition and perhaps tear gas experts. A trend toward four uniform platoons has been observed. More but lighter rifle platoons modeled after the Australian and New Zealand pattern appear to be desirable. Vehicles and support weapons that cannot be usefully employed have been eliminated, but where terrain permits, armored vehicles may be added.

A more important organizational idea is presently widespread among Americans who know Vietnam. They want to introduce indigenous personnel right into U.S. units. If the U.S. really has something to sell the Vietnamese, the very best way to achieve success is to get qualified Vietnamese personnel into U.S. combat units and let them sell themselves as did the Katusas in Korea. The U.S. would not only convince an important minority of Vietnamese firsthand of the advantages of the American way of doing things, but would also augment its forces with personnel who know some of the local languages and many other essentials in regard to the civilian population. U.S. soldiers and Marines of Vietnamese origin would improve the public image of America and benefit enormously the U.S. systems of intelligence which presently suffer from a near total ignorance of the civilian population. Only a few U.S. servicemen with an unusual flair for languages and anthropology can achieve any proficiency in this area soon enough to be of much service during a twelve-month tour. Language training before going to Vietnam has not been an unqualified success.

The best potential Vietnamese recruits for U.S. forces would come from rural areas. If carefully selected and then thoroughly trained, they would be able to establish a real rapport with the villagers, something that most ARVN officers do not achieve, or perhaps don't want to achieve. These G.I.'s would not have to be rotated every year; they would be available continuously and perhaps develop something of the Gurkha pride, ambition, and professional dedication. Soldiers of this type could form a kind of permanent nucleus in all platoons and larger units, if this war drags on. U.S. Marines enlisted in the West Indies and Central America early in the twentieth century were often a credit to the Corps. Some retired with considerable rank after long, effective, and faithful service. Perhaps of even greater pertinence, French Indochinese units were sometimes as brave as the Foreign Legion.

Future strategy and tactics are shrouded in secrecy. Almost surely the U.S. Administration in Washington, General Westmoreland, General Walt, and other American leaders have decided that since American combat forces are committed they should win as quickly and as conclusively as possible. They all caution the public and each other that this will take a long time, but do their best to make their own predictions untrue. The air bombings of North Vietnam are to isolate the VC as much as possible. The massive U.S. build-up in combat forces is to control more territory, protect more local people, and restore Government control of roads, rail lines, and local administrations outside U.S. and RVNAF perimeters.

All this is important, but the VC must also be beaten in hundreds of small actions, mostly at night. No one, not even the enemy, can actually operate efficiently in deep jungle. The Communists stay in it during the day, but come out at dusk to use the roads for political and military action. So far, U.S. night patrols and ambushes have been numerous, but have stayed close to U.S. perimeters. If the VC can be denied the use of the roads over considerable areas on a twenty-four-hour basis, their control will slip.

Daytime control of much of South Vietnam now rests with the U.S. and its allies by virtue of air power. If this can be extended to the hours of darkness, a sudden change with a snowball effect is not impossible. If the small U.S. combat units composed in part of soldiers recruited in South Vietnam can begin to operate at a distance from their perimeters in the manner of similar Philippine forces under Magsaysay, the VC will lose their superiority in morale and become the hunted rather than the hunters. A large number of small patrols which are competent, intercommunicating, and capable of taking advantage of the terrain in which they are operating would not only weaken the VC where they are presently strongest, but would also make a deep impression on the civilian population. Better relations with the village people would lead to better intelligence. Larger U.S.–RVNAF operations would then be more productive.

15: Summing Up

|||||||||||||||||||||||||||||||||||||||||||||||||||||||||||||||||||||||||||||||||||||

The major conflict in Vietnam receives most of the headlines, though forces allied to the Free World are fighting those supported by the Chinese Communists in at least five other places in the Far East. The situation in each of these areas is potentially dangerous. Korea and Thailand could explode at almost any time; the enormous potential of the Chinese Army operating on the mainland of Asia is sobering. At present, the Chinese Communists do not appear to want another Korea, or to be involved directly in any war with the West. But they are masters in the art of escalating to a point most satisfactory to them and then relying on world opinion to keep the conflict at that level.

Outbreak of a major war between Indonesia and Malaysia appears less likely following the partial eclipse of Sukarno, but the danger may still exist. There may be enough internal Communist strength in both Malaya and the Philippines to erupt again into active war. Nationalist China which now controls only Formosa and the offshore islands so coveted by the Chinese Communists is also a potential trouble spot. There are so many possibilities that the future is unknowable. But continued Communist aggression seems almost certain, particularly in the areas of Southeast Asia where the socioeconomic and political structure is weakest.

There are two ways of meeting this challenge; essentially, the U.S. and its allies can oppose the Chinese Communists or give them virtually a free hand to conquer weaker neighbors both politically and militarily. Four successive U.S. administrations with approval of most of the Free World have chosen the former course. Perhaps inevitably, decisions have led cumulatively to the use of force. U.S. combat infantry as well as air and sea power are now engaged. South Korean, Australian, New Zealand, and Filipino units are also fighting.

On the other hand, some leaders of the Free World, especially De Gaulle, have become critical in their public utterances of the use of force by the U.S. in Vietnam. In my opinion they oppose escalation essentially because their countries are not suffering the casualties that can be held to a minimum only by using some, at least, of U.S. strengths. America is pressing the war in spite of the opposition. The U.S., which is suffering losses, has had to escalate in order to save the lives of its troops.

Is this the right decision? I traveled more than 45,000 miles in the Far East and spent time with the armies of all U.S. allies out there. I visited all the trouble spots discussed in the previous chapters including, of course, Vietnam. I talked to hundreds of U.S. and other servicemen. I had U.S. Department of Defense accreditation, but paid all my own expenses. I am not employed by the U.S. or any other government; I am not an active member of any political party. Here is what I found.

The case for pulling out of Vietnam is a strong one. The best argument for it in my opinion is that young Americans are being asked to risk sudden, violent death and to spend a considerable portion of their lives in a place that could hardly be less attractive to most of them. The climate is terrible; living conditions are unusually poor. U.S. servicemen are deprived of practically everything that they really desire in life. They have no dependents in the country and few congenial associations with the local civilian population. The people that most G.I.'s meet appear to be the least attractive that American soldiers and Marines know anywhere in the world. U.S. forces are not only in danger twenty-four hours a day, but also incredibly bored and lonely.

Americans stationed in Vietnam rarely feel welcome. They realize that most disinterested Vietnamese don't really want them; civilians there do not want the Communists either, but a bargain-basement war in their country is least attractive of all. The Government of South Vietnam does not appeal to many Americans. It is not a democracy and is not efficient. ARVN sometimes has serious faults, including poor discipline under fire, a high rate of desertion, and cruelty to its own people.

Most Americans in Vietnam work hard, often unbelievably hard, seven days a week. In some places and at some levels the same men work all day and are subject to a full 50 per cent alert—half of each unit under arms continuously—against the VC at night. Not many can feel a normal sense of accomplishment, however, because of conditions beyond their control. If it were not for patriotism and duty, it would be difficult to hire men at any price to do what they are doing.

A second argument for pulling out is the danger that this fighting will escalate into a conventional war against the Chinese Communists or large "volunteer" units of them on the mainland of Asia. Many who know geography, military strategy, and the strength of the Chinese armed forces deplore this drift closer to fighting them again as in Korea. But U.S. combat soldiers are now being committed where the Chinese could walk to battle. America must transport every man, every pound of equipment, and every round of ammunition over 8000 miles of ocean. The United States sacrifices the advantages of offensive sea power once its ground forces are tied down to one battle area.

Third, the terrain, geographical position, and economic development of South Vietnam could hardly be worse from the American point of view. The country is jungle, mountain, and delta—90 per cent-plus favorable to guerrillas. Communications on land are almost impossible to maintain. There are presently only a few places where the U.S. can use efficiently its heavy equipment; targets of value for the magnificent U.S. Air Force are not abundant. The VC are still supplied from sanctuaries across international borders. Their system of transportation is primitive, but adequate for the short distances and relatively light weights involved. The VC use a large number of jungle trails which so far have been almost impervious to attacks from the air.

Fourth, the South Vietnamese socioeconomic and political situations are regrettable from the U.S. point of view. Some men in power are selfish, if not actually dishonest; almost all of them come from a city-bred aristocracy which does not want to understand the rural villagers. The latter are frequently illiterate, sometimes distrust white men, and don't understand what Americans and their allies are trying to do for them. Communism, capitalism, and democracy are all just incomprehensible words. Even to the educated Vietnamese, real democracy is only what they have read about, mostly in foreign languages.

The people outside the cities have a way of life more compatible with the VC than with the Government. In a popularity contest some experienced observers believe the RVNAF would surely lose to the VC. The first choice of the hamlets which still contain the bulk of the Vietnamese population would be to be let alone. Most VC agents are peasants themselves, sincere, honest, and usually unselfish. They have a simple message and a lot of experience putting it across. They understand the efficient use of terror, but normally don't go too far. They are masters of several Big Lies, including, "Everything will be right, prosperous, and fair in your village when the VC take over."

They have also attached to Americans all the bad qualities of the French and then branded the Government as "lackeys of U.S. imperialism." The fact that this is not true is practically impossible for a man in a Vietnamese hamlet to determine. Americans and French look about the same to a Vietnamese and employ the same weapons: armored vehicles, artillery, and above all air power. Bombing appears to the Vietnamese villagers to be indiscriminate and cruel. In the villages, words by the million mean less than a few napalm and high explosive bombs, rockets, and shells. Even when a village is predominantly VC in sentiment, the blasting of it by planes or cannon—the U.S. is always blamed by the VC, even if the planes and artillery units are South Vietnamese—does not help the situation.

The VC "reasonings" and "explainings" to the villagers are long, devious, and clever. The men and women who preside know their audience; neither those who talk nor those who listen have any place to go or anything more interesting to do. Neither the Government nor well-trained U.S. civil-action workers are likely to win an argument against them. In some areas at least, the VC have roused a crusading spirit against Americans which transcends all selfish personal interests.

Another reason for leaving Vietnam is that the U.S. may lose the shooting war. With roughly the same advantages the U.S. has now, the French lost in Indochina. The U.S. and its allies are more powerful than the French were in 1954 and have less territory to defend. But the Chinese and North Vietnamese allies of the VC are far more powerful than the friendly countries supplying logistic support to the Viet Minh were twelve years ago. To some extent, sentiment in the U.S. duplicates the feelings of the French people during the unpopular Indochinese war. Soldiers who feel they are not supported fully at home cannot do their best. History is full of wars which were not won by the stronger side. Britain and France did not win against Egypt in the Suez Canal flare-up in 1956.

Potentially the most compelling reason for leaving Vietnam is that further combat there directly by U.S. forces could lead to uncontrollable escalation and nuclear war. For the first time in history the world is faced with a situation where at least two nations, the U.S. and Russia, cannot go to war because they would both be destroyed. But it could happen unintentionally. The U.S. is probably in Vietnam now only because the Chinese and the Russians have their differences, but they are still both Communist and the prospect of a clear win for the U.S. might persuade them to end their feuding.

The U.S. is at a considerable disadvantage because of the military characteristics of RVNAF. Perhaps this is another reason for getting out. America is giving the Government everything it needs including pay for its armed forces, enormous quantities of military equipment, and economic aid. Americans are unable to control the way their local allies use anything. ARVN soldiers sometimes ruin new small arms in less than a week, mishandle armored vehicles in combat so that they are destroyed, and calmly give up the hours of darkness to the enemy without a real fight. Money for economic aid and civil action often ends in the pockets or foreign bank accounts of Government officials. Although the RVNAF accept everything and clamor for more, individual Vietnamese commanders often behave like spoiled children. Some of their Government leaders have been so jealous of Americans that they won't do what Americans suggest even when the advice is obviously right. Even now that U.S. combat forces have been in action there for two years, a joint command along U.S.–British lines in World War II seems impossible.

There are dozens, perhaps hundreds, of other reasons not to stay in Vietnam. Every U.S. serviceman who has been there can add a few personal and military frustrations. The whole situation is diabolical; the war has already cost so much in blood, money, and unhappiness. It is certain to cost more of all these if Americans stay. The U.S. is not supporting a way of life compatible with its ideals, nor always fighting in a way of which it can be proud. There is the risk of losing a small war, or building it into a mass nuclear suicide for the whole world.

The principal reason why the U.S. must fight on in Vietnam, or obtain an honorable and secure peace, is geographical. Southeast Asia is like a curving, two-pronged line of dominoes stretching away from China, with Burma and India at the end of one prong and Australia and New Zealand at the end of the other. The stakes are enormous. If the Chinese Communists should control this area, they would be potentially much the most powerful amalgamation of productive capacity and peoples the world has ever seen. Australia alone is larger than continental United States. The natural, agricultural, and industrial resources of the whole area are tremendous; in a few years, it will contain a population of more than two billion.

The ghastly consequences of Chinese Communist domination of this area should be obvious to everyone. All non-Communists appreciate their ambition and ruthlessness, but few realize just how little opposition there is to China's expansion. Neutral nations like Burma and India are not yet strong. The presently pro-Western forces in Thailand, the Philippines, South Korea, Nationalist China, Malaysia, and even Japan depend materially and spiritually on the U.S., Britain, Australia, and New Zealand. The U.S. just cannot disappoint—actually betray—its allies in Southeast Asia.

An American retreat from Vietnam would surely be considered

tantamount to a desertion of Thailand in Bangkok, a broken promise to the Filipinos in Manila, and a faithless casting adrift of a non-Communist ally like South Korea in Seoul. These nations might have to make their separate peace with a victorious, aggressive, and cruel Chinese Communism. If the U.S. left Vietnam, it is unlikely that its allies in this area would feel justified in making battlegrounds of their countries. They all realize they can hope to win only with American support. If that support cannot be relied upon, any type of national degradation to Communism may be better than fighting and losing a bargain-basement war in their own country.

Even breaking all American pledges and covenants and giving up the mainland of Asia completely would not get the U.S. out of trouble. China would expand quickly. The free nations would surely find themselves fighting again soon under even less favorable conditions. The Chinese war machine would increase in power as their areas and resources increased. Chinese nuclear weapons would not be far away; targets offered to similar U.S. weapons would remain relatively poor.

The only probable stopping point between retiring from Vietnam and the loss of all of Southeast Asia might be between Indonesia and Australia to the south and the Philippines to the east. The U.S. and the allies who still remained would certainly try to hold these lines; perhaps they could for a time. But if the Communists were in control of the mainland, and most of the Indies, the task would be difficult. Almost surely the U.S. and its allies have a better chance of holding Vietnam now than of stopping a raging forest fire of Communism after it has swept a thousand miles almost into Australia.

The Chinese have said that Thailand is next on their agenda after Vietnam. This country was once perilously close to becoming neutral, or even entering the Communist camp. President Johnson's decision of March 1965 to commit U.S. combat troops to Vietnam finally bolstered Thai civilian and military morale to a high level. Their government is more popular even in the northeast area where conditions are almost ideal for Communist insurgency than it was four years ago. All this would vanish, however, if the Thais and the

Chinese Communists believed that the U.S. could be forced to withdraw from the mainland of Asia. If Americans left Vietnam, or lost the war there, Thailand would be faced with an impossible situation. She has only 30 million people; there are 700 million mainland Chinese.

If Vietnam only were lost, defending the Philippines would still be theoretically simple from a military point of view. The U.S. Seventh Fleet is the most powerful naval force the world has ever known and controls all the approaches to these islands. But this is not really important; China has no amphibious landing capacity from the high seas against any modern Western-aligned nation. Their threat against the Philippines would be in the twilight zone of "national liberation," where the convictions of people are more important than even the most powerful weapons. If the U.S. abandons Vietnam, it loses face in the Philippines. The islands would surely be aflame again with Communist insurgency as they were from 1948 to 1954.

Americans cannot rearrange the people and geography of Asia to fit their ideas of what is right and desirable. They cannot even change decisions made by U.S. leaders on too little knowledge soon after the end of World War II. But friends of the U.S. in Southeast Asia have a right to expect pledges to be kept, even if they should not have been made. If Americans do not prove their integrity, power, and resolution when the chips are down in Vietnam, they have only wealth, soft living, and political slogans to recommend them. Asians may not have television or even indoor plumbing, but they are not stupid. If they are to stand up to the Chinese Communists, they want an ally they can trust.

Malaysia, the Philippines, and South Korea have fought Communism and emerged victorious since World War II; Nationalist China has built a new anti-Communist nation on Taiwan. The U.S. has supported all and supplied them collectively with enormous quantities of military and economic aid. Americans helped Japan rebuild industrially, economically, and militarily. All these U.S. allies are now staunchly anti-Communist and appear able to maintain their governments by civil and military action so long as they are not subject to a catastrophe such as the American withdrawal from Vietnam.

Assuming the U.S. will stay in Vietnam, can it win the type of war it is presently fighting? This depends essentially on the Vietnamese and how they perform in both civil and military action. It is fashionable now to say that civil action is more important than military action. This may not be literally true, but both are necessary for victory in a bargain-basement war. U.S. combat forces can win actions which approach battles in size with little or no aid from ARVN, but only the Vietnamese Government can win in civil action. It should not be forgotten, however, that in guerrilla warfare a civilian population will not often side with those they believe are going to lose.

The American public cannot help but be wary of announced changes in the Vietnamese Government's approach to civil action and reform. Statements of this kind have been made before and turned out to be premature. On the average, Vietnamese civil servants do not have the integrity, honesty, and industry of Western counterparts. There are indications, however, that the Government is improving its public image with the rural population. Both personnel and organizations for use in the hamlets are better than they were. There are various programs headed by men of real intelligence and experience, all operating together in something like harmony.

One of the most promising current civil-action programs is headed by retired U.S. Maj. Gen. Edward Lansdale who was asked to return by Ambassador Henry Cabot Lodge. Under Lansdale's direction small areas are being given maximum attention and guidance as well as protection. Solid anti-Communist life is to be set up and matured before his teams move to other areas. This plan certainly appears first-rate in theory. It worked in Malaya, but failed in Vietnam when applied under Diem because of too much speed and too little real support.

U.S. combat forces can help in this type of civil action by providing security in the areas they occupy. This is particularly true of the Marines in the I Corps Area where their present bases are almost perfectly situated. These contain the most friendly group of Vietnamese civilians in the country so far as Government and U.S. forces are concerned. Their perimeters give real continuous security to the people inside them. Even in the tactical areas of responsibility beyond the perimeters, the civil action programs have unusual advantages.

The RVNAF are certainly stronger and more efficient than they were militarily. The commission of U.S. combat troops in the spring of 1965 proved to them that Americans were willing to support them with blood as well as money and materiel. The Vietnamese have faults, but they learn from the actions that they fight, even their defeats. Where rifle units have good officers, they are at least satisfactory. As officers improve, their units will get better. ARVN could improve as much during the next few years as the South Korean Army has over the past few.

There are more than 120 Chinese regular divisions plus 30 million organized and armed militia who could all walk to South Vietnam. The U.S. has about twenty divisions including the Marines deployed around the world. Australian, Korean, New Zealand, and Filipino combat units are available, but in extremely limited strength compared with that of China. Regardless of the superiority of Western divisions in tanks, heavy artillery, vehicles, and logistics, the anti-Communist nations involved could not now deploy enough men in Southeast Asia to take on the Chinese army in a Korea-type war.

U.S. leaders must have considered this possibility before beginning to send in combat troops in March 1965. Why did they go ahead with this course? The answer seems to have two parts. First, a large Chinese or even a "volunteer" expeditionary force operating in North and South Vietnam would be extremely difficult to support logistically from China because of terrain in the border area and the present limited transportation facilities. Second, the U.S. would presumably not again give them sanctuary behind their border as it did in Korea. The U.S. has presently, and is likely to continue to have for some years to come, an overwhelming advantage in nuclear weapons. The mountainous zone between China and North Vietnam has been said to be an ideal place to use this advantage. Some believe that this natural barrier could be made impenetrable by atomic explosions which would do relatively little damage to people. The U.S. would be spared the unfortunate world publicity which would surely come if population and industrial centers were attacked. If this border closing by bombs were not possible, the U.S. might be forced to use nuclear power directly.

No one can visit U.S. Army and Marine units without feeling confidence in their ultimate efforts to learn to fight in the jungle. The best young military brains in America are presently working on new weapons, new tactics, and new combinations of old weapons and tactics. The ability, ambition, and bravery of these men is extremely encouraging. The equipment that they have to work with is the best that any nation has ever provided; Americans have not yet lost a single war since they won their independence.

The Vietnam conflict is not now limited to jungle guerrilla actions. In some places Americans have just removed the jungle. Modern ports such as Cam Ranh Bay are surrounded by relatively easily defended perimeters in cleared areas of great size. The longer Americans stay, the more they change the face of the country. They may or may not be potentially the finest jungle fighters, but they are surely by far the best in the world at getting rid of the jungle itself.

Perhaps U.S. commanders cannot control their Vietnamese allies as they did the South Koreans, or have the type of joint command that worked out so efficiently with the British in World War II. This is unfortunate; Allied armed forces would operate more efficiently under a unified command. It would be desirable also for the RVNAF to be less cruel to their own civilian population. But the U.S. cannot interfere too much. Joint command would lead to an American commander, at least in the larger units. To the Vietnamese, this might be considered a return to colonialism. As soon as this word enters a discussion, logical thought by Asians becomes impossible.

Westerners must resist the temptation to be critical of the Vietnamese. They have obvious disadvantages, but are not one bit less intelligent. They are capable of extreme bravery and patriotism.

Those who have studied the American Revolution have found many similarities between the patriots of that era and ARVN today. French military comments about the early U.S. Army sound surprisingly like those American advisers sometimes make about ARVN today.

The U.S. must continue its adviser teams down to battalion level in ARVN and in most subsectors. The system is not perfect, but it is improving. American officers in their second or third tours of duty in Vietnam do better jobs than they did at first. The Vietnamese are more receptive and less personally jealous now that U.S. combat forces are in action. This is particularly true in ARVN units which have collaborated with American fighting men to win victories in the field. All these things are going to get better.

Additional reasons for optimism can be found, perhaps too many. As a nation, the U.S. is prone to believe that they will succeed. Wars can be lost; there is always a first time. But Americans certainly have a good chance so long as they hold to their present strategy and tactics, and the Chinese do not openly enter the conflict in great strength. If the Chinese do come in, they may lose so disastrously that they will cease to be a threat to Russia, India, or the West for a long time. All this is conjecture with no solid basis in fact; no one knows much about nuclear battles and wars. Circumstances which may appear trivial now could build up into a defeat for the stronger side.

Staying in Vietnam is extremely costly. But the U.S. and its allies are buying time for the Free World. Western effort in Vietnam is absorbing Communist strength and pressure that might otherwise be used elsewhere. Democracies do work, if they are given a fair chance. Time is being gained for the Vietnamese and other new countries throughout the world to mature, learn to govern themselves, and grow stronger.

The presence of U.S. armed forces in Vietnam is of direct benefit to anti-Communist governments in that section of Asia and elsewhere. Some of our allies make disparaging remarks, but all are more secure. The fighting efficiency of the Western-aligned nations is improving; Communist guerrillas do not always win. The units engaged against them will become better; this applies not only to the Americans, but also the RVNAF, Australians, New Zealanders, South Koreans, and Filipinos. Even one casualty is deplorable, but nothing improves a combat unit like actual fighting. Experience in fighting one bargain-basement war will be of great value in others. If the West wins this one, others may be avoided.

America can afford the money, the risks, and even the loss of life because the alternatives are worse. But those who don't fight or serve in Vietnam owe an eternal debt to those who do. Their contributions are of incalculable value. Conditions are indeed almost intolerable, but a continuing U.S. presence seems absolutely necessary.

Of the scores of Americans I talked to, not a single man wanted to pull out. They are fighting in a purgatory 8000 miles from home, but they know the reasons why. At the end of Starlite, Marine General Lew Walt said, "I'm so proud of my Marines, I can hardly talk!" These sentiments apply to other U.S. servicemen also. They are all doing a tough job well, and the nation is in their debt.

ABBREVIATIONS

ammo	ammunition	LLDB	South Vietnamese Special Forces
AR	automatic rifle		
ARVN	Army of South Vietnam	LMG	light machine gun
		MG	machine gun
BAR	Browning Automatic Rifle	MMG	medium machine gun
CT	Communist terrorist	NATO	North Atlantic Treaty Organization
GL	grenade launcher		
GPMG	general purpose machine gun	NCO	noncommissioned officer
HMG	heavy machine gun	PAVN	Peoples Army of North Vietnam
HQ	headquarters		
HUK	Hukbalahap	ROK	Republic of Korea

RVNAF	Republic of Vietnam Armed Forces	TDV	Territorial Defense Volunteer
SEATO	Southeast Asia Treaty Organization	TO&E	table of organization and equipment
SLR	self-loading rifle	VC	Viet Cong

TABLE I: STATISTICS FOR NATIONS CONCERNED WITH SOUTHEAST ASIA

NATION	AREA (THOUSAND SQUARE MILES)	POPULATION (MILLIONS)	ARMED FORCES (THOUSANDS)	ANNUAL DEFENSE COST (MILLIONS OF DOLLARS)	NATIONAL ECONOMY RATING	POLITICAL STABILITY RATING	MILITARY ADVANCEMENT RATING	TYPE OF GOVERNMENT [1]
Australia	2971	12	70	900	A	AAA	AA	Democracy
Britain	94	54	440	5937	AA	AAA	AAA	Democracy
Burma	261	24	50	...	C	A	D	Republic
Cambodia	88	6	32	...	D	C	D	Constitutional Monarchy
China Communist	3800	700+	2500	...	AA	AA	A	Communist Republic
Nationalist	13	12	525	147	B	AA	C	Republic
India	1261	480+	900	2100	A	A	A	Neutral Republic
Indonesia	736	100+	420	1000	B	C	B	Republic
Japan	143	100+	250	1000	AA	AA	B	Democracy
Korea (North)	48	12+	350	...	C	A	C	Communist Republic
Korea (South)	37	28+	600	183	B	AA	C	Republic
Laos	91	3	60	...	D	D	D	Constitutional Monarchy

							Government
Malaysia	130	10	30	150	A	A	D	Federation, democracy
New Zealand	104	2.7	13	115	A	AAA	B	Democracy
Pakistan	365	100+	200	300	B	B	A	Republic
Philippines	116	31+	50	75	B	AA	B	Democracy
Russia	8656	230+	3150	40,000	AAA	AAA	AAA	Communist Republic
Thailand	200	30+	140	95	B	A	C	Constitutional Monarchy
U.S.	3542	195+	3000	55,000	AAA	AAA	AAA	Democracy
Vietnam (North)	62	17	250	...	D	C	D	Communist Republic
Vietnam (South)	65	15	700	...	D	D	C	Republic

NOTE: Ratings—AAA, very strong and powerful; AA, strong and powerful; A, powerful; B, good; C, fair; D, poor

[1] Classification is difficult; Japan and Britain are in theory constitutional monarchies. Most nations called republics here are actually dictatorships.

TABLE II: SMALL ARMS BY COUNTRIES

COUNTRY	MMG's	AR or LMG's	RIFLES	SMG's or CARBINES	PISTOLS	AMMO REQUIRED
Australia	U.S. M60	U.S. M60	SLR, AR-15 (experimentally)	Owen	1935 Browning	7.62 NATO, 9-mm Parabellum, 5.56-mm (experimentally)
Britain	GPMG Vickers	GPMG Bren } 2 calibers	SLR, AR-15	L2A3 (Sterling or Patchett)[1]	1935 Browning	7.62 NATO, .303 British, 9-mm Parabellum, 5.56-mm
Japan[2]	Type 62	Type 62	Type 64	U.S. M1 carbines U.S. M1 & M3 SMG's	U.S. 1911A1	7.62 NATO, .30-cal. carbine, .45-cal. ACP
Korea (South)	U.S. M1919A4 U.S. M1919A6	BAR	U.S. M1	U.S. M1 carbine U.S. M1 SMG	U.S. 1911A1	.30-'06, .30-cal. carbine, .45-cal. ACP
New Zealand	GPMG	GPMG	SLR	L2A3 (Sterling or Patchett)[1] Owen	1935 Browning	7.62 NATO, 9-mm Parabellum
Philippines	U.S. M1919A4 U.S. M1919A6 U.S. M1917A1	BAR	U.S. M1	U.S. M1 carbine U.S. M1 SMG	U.S. 1911A1	.30-'06, .30-cal. carbine, .45-cal. ACP

	Machine Guns	Automatic Rifle	Rifle	Carbine & SMG	Pistol	Cartridges
RVNAF (South Vietnam)	U.S. M1919A4 U.S. M1919A6	BAR	U.S. M1	U.S. M1 carbine U.S. M1 SMG[3]	U.S. 1911A1[3]	.30-'06, .30-cal. carbine, .45-cal. ACP
Thailand	U.S. M1919A4 U.S. M1919A6 U.S. M1917A1	BAR	U.S. M1	U.S. M1 carbine U.S. M1 SMG	U.S. 1911A1	.30-'06, .30-cal. carbine, .45-cal. ACP
U.S.	M60	M14 Modified	M14, M16 (AR-15)	M1 & M2 carbines M1 & M3 SMG's	1911A1[3]	7.62 NATO, .30-cal. carbine, .45-cal. ACP, 5.56-mm
VC and PAVN[4]	DP DPM	RPD (Degtyarev)	Russian M44 carbine SKS (Simonov)	AK (Kalashikov) Toharev Some Chinese SMG's		7.62 Russian, 7.62 Intermediate, 7.62 Russian pistol

1 All three designations refer to the same weapon.
2 Japan still has some U.S. World War II MMG's, AR's and rifles, but these are being replaced. This country also has a new SMG and two pistols of its own, but these are not yet being introduced into their armed forces (as of summer 1966).

3 A wide variety of arms are actually in use by troops in these categories, but those listed here are most common.
4 These units have examples of almost all small arms used in Asia in the twentieth century, but it would appear that those shown here would replace all others if a sufficient quantity of them were available.

TABLE III: DETAILS OF MMG's

COUNTRY	WEAPONS	WEIGHT [1] (LB)	CYCLIC RATE RPM	TYPE OF ACTION	TYPE OF FEED	COOL-ING	AMMO	ACCU-RACY RATING
Britain	GPMG	46.0	700 to 1100	Gas	Disintegrating link belt	Air	7.62 NATO	Medium
	Vickers	100+	500 or below	Recoil assisted by gas at muzzle	Fabric belt	Water	.303 British	Good
Japan	Type 62	37.5	600	Gas	Disintegrating link belt	Air	7.62 NATO	Good
U.S. World War II	M1917A1	86.2	400	Recoil	Fabric or disintegrating link belt	Water	.30-'06	Good
	M1919A4	45.0	500	Recoil	Same	Air	.30-'06	Medium
	M1919A6	46.5 [2]	500	Recoil	Same	Air	.30-'06	Medium
U.S. Modern	M60	36.4	550	Gas	Disintegrating link belt	Air	7.62 NATO	Medium
	Stoner 63	29.0	1050	Gas	Disintegrating link belt	Air	5.56-mm	Good
VC and PAVN	DP, DPM, DS [3]	27 to about 150	550 to 1000	Gas	Belts and magazines of various types	Air	7.62 Russian	Medium

1 Includes tripod, but not ammo.
2 Includes weight of buttstock.
3 Several different Russian and Chinese weapons used. Dual-purpose carriages increase total weight to above 100 pounds.

$$\text{TABLE IV: DETAILS OF AR's OR LMG's}$$

COUNTRY	WEAPON	WEIGHT (LB)	LENGTH (IN)	CYCLIC RATE RPM	TYPE OF ACTION	MAGAZINE OR FEED	AMMO	ACCURACY RATING
Australia	Special C2	14.5	41.5	600	Gas	20- or 30-round box	7.62 NATO	Poor
Britain	GPMG	24.0 (no ammo)	49.2	700 to 1100	Gas	Belt [1]	7.62 NATO	Poor
	Bren (7.62 NATO)	18.8	47.0	500	Gas	30-round box	7.62 NATO	Medium
Japan	Type 62	23.5 (no ammo)	45.2	600	Gas	Belt [1]	7.62 NATO	Good
U.S. World War II	BAR	21.5	47.0	340 or 600	Gas	20-round box	.30'06	Medium
	M1919A6 [2]	32.5 (no ammo)	53.0	600	Recoil	Belt	.30'06	Good
U.S. Modern	M14 Modified	10.5 [3]	44.6	750	Gas	20-round box	7.62 NATO	Poor
	M60	23.2 (no ammo)	43.5	550	Gas	Belt [1]	7.62 NATO	Medium
	Stoner 63 [4]	16.5	1050.0	1050	Gas	Plastic box with 150 rounds in a disintegrating link belt	5.56-mm	Good
VC and PAVN	RPD [5]	19.4	40.8	600	Gas	Belts in drums Boxes	7.62 Intermediate	Medium

[1] The British GPMG, the U.S. M60, and the Japanese Type 62 use the same disintegrating link belts. Sections of both can be put in fabric "magazines," but this is not often satisfactory.
[2] A bipod-mounted weapon, but not really light.
[3] There is a further modification which adds 1.25 lbs.
[4] This data is for the belt-fed, bipod-mounted conformation.
[5] There are, of course, others.

245

TABLE V: DETAILS OF RIFLES

COUNTRY	WEAPON	WEIGHT LOADED (LB)	CYCLIC RATE RPM [1]	LENGTH (IN)	TYPE OF ACTION [2]	MAGAZINE CAPACITY	AMMO
Britain	SLR	10.4	Single shots only	41.4	Gas	20	7.62 NATO
Japan	Type 64	10.7	550	38.6	Gas	20	7.62 NATO
U.S. World War II	M1	10.5	Single shots only	43.0	Gas	8	.30-'06
	M1 carbine [3]	6.1	Single shots only	36.0	Gas	15	.30-cal. carbine
U.S. Modern	M14	9.2	Single shots only [4]	44.1	Gas	20	7.62 NATO
	M16	6.8	1000	38.7	Gas	20-30	5.56-mm
	Stoner 63	8.8	1000	40.4	Gas	30	5.56-mm
VC and PAVN [5]	M44 carbine	9.2	Single shots only	40.0	Bolt	5	7.62 Russian
	SKS	8.8	Single shots only	40.2	Gas	10	7.62 Intermediate

[1] All weapons can deliver single shots; cyclic rates shown for those with burst capability also.
[2] Not including bayonet.
[3] The U.S. M1 carbine is sometimes issued as a rifle in Southeast Asia.
[4] Sometimes modified to deliver bursts even in infantry rifle role.
[5] VC units have many other arms also; the AK is also used as a rifle, but see SMG's and carbines for details.

TABLE VI: DETAILS OF SMG's AND CARBINES

COUNTRY	WEAPON	WEIGHT LOADED (LB)	CYCLIC RATE RPM	LENGTH (IN) [1]	NUMBER OF ROUNDS IN MAGAZINE	AMMO	ACCU- RACY RATING	TAKES BAYONET
Australia	Owen	11.5	550	24–32	33	9-mm Parabellum	Excellent	Yes
Britain	L2A3	7.8	550	19–28	32	9-mm Parabellum	Good	Yes
Japan	Nambu [2]	8.8	600	19.7–30.0	30	9-mm Parabellum	Good	No
U.S. World War II	M1 (Thompson)	11.0	650	31–31	20 [3]	.45 ACP	Medium	No
	M3	9.9	450	22–30	30 [3]	.45 ACP	Good	No
	M2 carbine	6.1	750	36–36	15 [3]	.30 carbine	Poor	Yes
U.S. Modern	Colt Commando SMG [4]	6.3	1000	28.0–31.25	20 [3]	5.56-mm	Poor	Yes
	Stoner carbine	8.6	1000	26.6–35.9	30	5.56-mm	Medium	Yes
VC and PAVN	AK	11.7	600	34–34 [5]	30	7.62 Intermediate	Medium	Yes

[1] Length with stock folded given first.
[2] This weapon is not actually in production (summer 1966), but the old Nambu factory could make it quickly.
[3] These are the most common magazines; there are others.
[4] Essentially the M16 with a shorter barrel and telescoping stock.
[5] The AK usually has wood stock; sometimes it is found with a folding stock.

247

TABLE VII: RIFLE COMPANY ORGANIZATION

COUNTRY	PERSONNEL IN COMPANY HQ	PERSONNEL IN H.W. PLATOON	NUMBER OF RIFLE PLATOONS	PERSONNEL IN EACH RIFLE PLATOON	TOTAL PERSONNEL IN RIFLE PLATOONS	TOTAL PERSONNEL IN COMPANY
Australia	2 officers + 26 men	None	4	1 officer + 39 men	4 officers + 156 men	6 officers + 182 men
Britain	2 officers + 10 men	1 officer + 23 men	3	1 officer + 31 men	1 officer + 95 men	4 officers + 128 men
Japan [1]	2 officers + 15 men	1 officer + 29 men (Mortar platoon) 1 officer + 13 men (AT platoon)	4	1 officer + 37 men	4 officers + 148 men	8 officers + 205 men
Korea—Army (South)	2 officers + 18 men	1 officer + 41 men	3	1 officer + 41 men	3 officers + 123 men	6 officers + 182 men
Korea—Marines (South)	4 officers + 84 men [2]	None	3	1 officer + 43 men	3 officers + 129 men	7 officers + 213 men
New Zealand	2 officers + 10 men	None	4	1 officer + 30 men	4 officers + 120 men	6 officers + 130 men
Philippines	2 officers + 17 men	1 officer + 35 men	3	1 officer + 38 men	3 officers + 104 men	6 officers + 166 men

RVNAF[3]	2 officers + 8 men	1 officer + 24 men	3	1 officer + 25 men	3 officers + 75 men	6 officers + 107 men[4]
Thailand—Army	2 officers + 36 men	1 officer + 40 men	3	1 officer + 43 men	3 officers + 129 men	6 officers + 205 men
Thailand—Marines	3 officers + 36 men	1 officer + 37 men	3	1 officer + 44 men	3 officers + 132 men	7 officers + 205 men
U.S.—Army	2 officers + 10 men	1 officer + 35 men	3	1 officer + 43 men	3 officers + 129 men	6 officers + 174 men
USMC	2 officers + 7 men	1 officer + 52 men	3	1 officer + 46 men	3 officers + 138 men	6 officers + 197 men
U.S. Special Forces[5]	16	Probably none	3	38	114	130
VC and PAVN[6]	25	40	3	35	105	170

[1] A Japanese rifle company has uniquely a HQ and six platoons.

[2] The company HQ includes a mortar and MMG, and an AT section, but these are not classified as independent platoons.

[3] There are several different forces included here. TO&E's vary somewhat between organizations and are classified. Field units are often under-strength. But the organization shown here is said to be about what is now used as an objective (summer 1966).

[4] Not many companies have all six officers present for duty at the same time.

[5] This is the TO&E of mercenaries raised, trained, and sometimes commanded by U.S. Special Forces. Ratio of officers to men varies widely.

[6] This is an approximation only of these units at full strength. Breakdown into officers and men is not known.

TABLE VIII: RIFLE PLATOON ORGANIZATION

COUNTRY	PERSONNEL IN PLATOON HEADQUARTERS	PERSONNEL IN H.W. SQUAD	NUMBER OF RIFLE SQUADS	PERSONNEL IN EACH RIFLE SQUAD	TOTAL PERSONNEL IN RIFLE SQUADS	TOTAL PERSONNEL IN RIFLE PLATOON
Australia	1 officer + 3 men	None	4	9	36 men	1 officer + 39 men
Britain	1 officer + 7 men	None	3	8	24 men	1 officer + 31 men
Japan	1 officer + 4 men	None	3	11	33 men	1 officer + 37 men
Korea—Army (South)	1 officer + 5 men	9 men	3	9	27 men	1 officer + 41 men
Korea—Marines (South)	1 officer + 5 men	None	3	13	39 men	1 officer + 44 men
New Zealand	1 officer + 6 men	None	3	8	24 men	1 officer + 30 men
Philippines	1 officer + 2 men	9 men	3	9	27 men	1 officer + 38 men
RVNAF	1 officer + 1 man	None	3 [1]	8	24 men	1 officer + 25 men
Thailand—Army	1 officer + 7 men	9 men	3	9	27 men	1 officer + 43 men
Thailand—Marines	1 officer + 8 men	None	3	13	39 men	1 officer + 47 men
U.S.—Army	1 officer + 2 men	11 men	3	10	30 men	1 officer + 43 men
USMC	1 officer + 4 men	None	3	14	42 men	1 officer + 46 men
U.S. Special Forces	4 officers + 0 men	10 officers	3	8	24 officers	38 officers + 0 men
VC and PAVN	This is variable and changing; there are probably two or three rifle squads and an LMG squad in each platoon.					

[1] There are two rifle fire squads and one rifle maneuver squad in each platoon; see Table XII for composition of these.

TABLE IX: RIFLE COMPANY INDIVIDUAL WEAPONS

COUNTRY	TOTAL PERSONNEL	AR's or LMG's	RIFLES	CARBINES	SMG's	PISTOLS	TOTAL WEAPONS	GRENADE LAUNCHERS[1]
Australia	188	16	133	None	33	6	188	32+
Britain	132	9	122	None	None	1	132	As required
Japan	213	36[2]	152[3]	None	None	25	213	152
Korea—Army (South)	188	12	105	61	None	None	188	24
Korea—Marines (South)	220	27	134	None	None	59	220	31
New Zealand	136	12[4]	96	None	12	None	136	26
Philippines	172	18	136	None	None	18	172	23
RVNAF	113	6	52	40	15	10	113	Variable
Thailand—Army	211	9	117[5]	61	None	24	211	30
Thailand—Marines	212	27	105	59	None	21	212	31
U.S.—Army[6]	180	18	104	None	None	58	108[7]	18
USMC[6]	203	27	150	None	None	26	203[7]	9
U.S. Special Forces	130	9	As required and available; units of this type generally have more M1 rifles and fewer carbines than ARVN.					
VC and PAVN	170	10	About 150 in these 3 classes			10	170	3[8]

[1] In U.S. Army and USMC these are separate weapons (M79 GL's); in most other armies they attach to rifles. All Japanese rifles can launch grenades without modification.

[2] Includes 12 MMG's.

[3] Includes 12 rifles with scope sights for snipers.

[4] This does not include the GPMG in company HQ.

[5] One of these in each rifle platoon HQ has a scope sight for a sniper.

[6] These are theoretical; in Vietnam most of the men who are supposed to have a pistol only have another weapon, often a shotgun, SMG, or carbine.

[7] Not including the M79 GL's which are carried by grenadiers who also have pistols.

[8] This is a separate weapon which launches Panzerfaust fashion a 40-mm projectile with an 82-mm warhead.

TABLE X: RIFLE COMPANY SUPPORT WEAPONS

COUNTRY	IN COMPANY HEADQUARTERS	IN H.W. PLATOON	IN EACH RIFLE PLATOON
Australia	3 3.5-inch RL's 2 MMG's	None	None
Britain	None permanently assigned	2 81-mm mortars 2 MAT weapons	1 MAT weapon 1 2-inch mortar
Japan	1 .50-cal. HMG 2 3.5-inch RL's	4 81-mm mortars 4 106-mm RR's 1 .50-cal. HMG 2 3.5-inch RL's	2 3.5-inch RL's
Korea—Army (South)	None	3 60-mm mortars 2 57-mm RR's	1 MMG (A6) 1 3.5-inch RL
Korea—Marines (South)	3 60-mm mortars 3 3.5-inch RL's 8 MMG's (A4's)	None	None
New Zealand	1 MMG 1 2-inch mortar	None	1 3.5-inch RL 1 2-inch mortar
Philippines	2 3.5-inch RL's	3 81-mm mortars 2 75-mm RR's 2 3.5-inch RL's	2 MMG's 1 3.5-inch RL

RVNAF[1]	2 3.5-inch RL's	2 MMG's (A4-6) 2 60-mm mortars	None
Thailand—Army	None	3 60-mm mortars 3 57-mm RR's	1 3.5-inch RL 2 MMG's (A6's)
Thailand—Marines	3 60-mm mortars 2 3.5-inch RL's	6 MMG's (A4's)	None
U.S.—Army	2 3.5-inch RL's	2 106-mm RR's 3 81-mm mortars 1 3.5-inch RL	2 MMG's 2 90-mm RR's
USMC	None	3 MMG's 3 3.5-inch RL's	None
U.S. Special Forces	2 60-mm mortars sometimes	None	2 MMG's 1 3.5-inch RL's sometimes
VC and PAVN	3 3.5-inch RL's or 3 57-mm RR's	3 60-mm mortars 3 MMG's	1 40-mm AT GL

[1] Not all units have these weapons. Some RVNAF companies have weapons and organizations which vary considerably from those given in tables.

TABLE XI: RIFLE PLATOON PERSONAL WEAPONS

COUNTRY	TOTAL PERSONNEL	AR's or LMG's	RIFLES	CARBINES	SMG's	PISTOLS	TOTAL WEAPONS	GRENADE LAUNCHERS
Australia	40	4	29	None	7	None	40	As required
Britain	32	3	29	None	None	None	32	As required
Japan	38	9[1]	27	None	None	2	38	27[2]
Korea—Army (South)	42	4	32	6	None	None	42	7
Korea—Marines (South)	45	9	36	None	None	None	45	10
New Zealand	31	3	22	None	6	None	31	6
Philippines	39	6	30	0	0	3[3]	39	7
RVNAF	26	2	15	5	4	None		Variable
Thailand—Army	44	3	33[4]	4	None	4	44	8
Thailand—Marines	45	9	30	6	None	0	45	10
U.S.—Army	44	6	28	None	None	10	50	6
USMC	47	9	33	None	None	5	50	3
U.S. Special Forces	38	3	As available and required by personnel.			1	38	Variable[5]
VC and PAVN		In better units AK's, SKS, and M1944 carbines predominantly in that order. AR's now seem to be in these units at least the Chinese RPD's.						

[1] Three of these are MMG's.
[2] The type 64 rifle can fire grenades without an attachment.
[3] Carried by the three gunners in the H.W. squad.

[4] One of these is equipped with a scope for a sniper who is in platoon HQ.
[5] These units sometimes have an M79 GL.

254

TABLE XII: RIFLE SQUAD WEAPONS

COUNTRY	TOTAL PERSONNEL	WEAPONS
Australia	9	1 M60, 1 SMG, 7 SLR's.
Britain	8	1 GPMG or 7.62 NATO Bren, 7 SLR's, some of which can be replaced by SMG's.
Japan	11	1 Type 62 MG with tripod, 2 Type 62 MG's with bipods, 1 Type 64 rifle with scope sight, 7 standard type 64 rifles.
Korea—Army (South)	9	1 BAR, 2 M1's with GL's, 6 standard M1's.
Korea—Marines (South)	13	3 BAR's, 3 M1's with GL's, 7 standard M1's.
New Zealand	8	1 GPMG, 1 SMG, 2 SLR's with GL's, 4 standard SLR's.
Philippines	9	2 BAR's, 2 M1's with GL's, 5 standard M1's.
RVNAF—Fire Squads	8	1 BAR, 1 M1 carbine, 1 M1 SMG, 5 M1 rifles.
RVNAF—Maneuver Squad	8	2 M1 carbines, 1 M1 SMG, 5 M1 rifles.
Thailand—Army	9	1 BAR, 2 M1's with GL's, 6 standard M1's.
Thailand—Marines	13	3 BAR's, 3 M1's with GL's, 7 standard M1's.
U.S.—Army	10	2 M14 Modifieds, 6 M14's—sometimes now 8 M16's—2 M79 GL's, 2 1911A1 pistols.
USMC	14	3 M14 Modifieds, 10 M14's, 1 M79 GL, 1 1911A1 pistol.
U.S. Special Forces	8	1 BAR and 7 rifles or equivalent.
VC and PAVN		These units still appear to have an LMG squad associated with 2 or 3 rifle squads without a special bipod-mounted automatic weapon.

TABLE XIII: MILITARY AMMO DATA

NAME OF CARTRIDGE	BULLET WEIGHT (GR)	MUZZLE VELOCITY (FPS)	MUZZLE ENERGY (LB)	REMARKS
7.62 NATO	150	2800	2750	Full rifle power.
.30-'06	150	2800	2750	Full rifle power.
.303 British	180	2540	2580	Full rifle power.
7.62 Russian (Rimmed)	165	2750	2700	Full rifle power.
7.5 French	139	2700	2250	Full rifle power.
7.62 Intermediate	122	2400	1550	Intermediate rifle power.
5.56-mm .223-cal.	55	3300	1328	Intermediate rifle power.
7.62 Russian pistol	87	1400	375	For obsolescent Russian and Chinese SMG's. Also pistols.
.30-cal. carbine	110	1970	948	For M1 and M2 carbines.
9-mm Parabellum	115	1140	332	For French and other SMG's. Also pistols.
.45 ACP	230	830	340	For M1 and M3 SMG's. Also pistols.

NOTE: Ballistic details can vary widely, even in a Western country. Further, combat units in Southeast Asia now use a bewildering number of other ammos, some loaded under primitive conditions.

Bibliography

IIIIIIIIIIIIIIIIIIIIIIIIIIIIIIIIIIIIIIIIIIIIIIIIIIIIIIIIIIIIIIIIIIIIIIIIIIIIIIIIIIIIIIIIIIIII

Source and reference material for this book has been far less important than for a study in military history. I have needed general knowledge such as is contained in *Whitaker's Almanac* and the *Encyclopædia Britannica*. Specific military details given in *The Military Balance, 1965–66*, put out by The Institute for Strategic Studies in London, and *Strategic Briefs*, compiled by the U.S. Air Force University, have also been useful.

A more important type of printed material includes training manuals, Fort Benning and other course brochures, and similar books and booklets. These are of extreme importance in connection with organization, weapons, and tactics in the various armies. So are organization charts and photographs obtained from Public Information offices. But since these are not generally available, a detailed enumeration of them would serve no useful purpose.

Two valuable available books are *Small Arms of the World* by the two Smiths and *Weapons and Tactics* by the author. The former is always useful for specific information about almost all military weapons, from medium machine guns down. The latter book is in part a study similar to this one, but the subject is West Europe rather than the Far East. Much of the material mentioned in the bibliography of my earlier book has been of some value in the preparation of this one.

The actual observation of small units of the armies discussed in their training and combat areas is more important than anything that can be found in print. Photographs taken by an author are much more useful to him in later writing than those supplied by others. In the 45,000 miles I traveled, I took sixty-three rolls of 36-

exposure film; these ranged from photographs of documents to tele-photo views of distant military installations, all of course with the permission of my escort officer.

I have also benefited from a general knowledge of weapons, visits to arms manufacturers, and tours of testing centers both in the United States and abroad. Descriptive writing has not yet progressed sufficiently so that most people can know much about a complicated machine without actually operating it themselves. Neither a turret lathe nor a light machine gun can be made meaningful to me by words, diagrams, sketches, and the like. Ten minutes of operating either one is worth hours of reading and study. My own expand-ing weapons collection and actual firing of other arms has been of great value.

From the above, it will seem that the Bibliography below is not a complete description of all facts and figures that have gone into this book. There remains, however, a large amount of printed study ma-terial which has been important. It falls into two categories: first, military periodicals published mainly in the U.S. and Britain; and second, books on guerrilla war, some of them dealing specifically with Southeast Asia. Anyone studying in this field will find the writ-ings of Bernard B. Fall of considerable importance. Carefully se-lected clippings from *The New York Times* and *Newsweek* will also be of value.

This abbreviated Bibliography is divided into three parts. First, books of general interest and usefulness have been listed. Second, the military periodicals with which I have kept in constant touch are included; there are others of almost equal value. Finally, I have se-lected a fairly large group of books on guerrilla warfare; this cat-egory is expanding fast.

Part I: GENERAL KNOWLEDGE AND WEAPONS AND TACTICS

Encyclopedia Britannica. Chicago, 1965.

Events of 1965. Encyclopedia Britannica, Chicago, 1965.

The Military Balance, 1965–66. Institute for Strategic Studies, Lon-don, 1965.

Pictorial Atlas of the World. Time, Inc., New York, 1961.

Strategic Briefs. U.S. Air Force University, Maxwell Air Force Base, Ala., 1964.

Whitaker's Almanac for 1966. London, 1965.

The World Almanac, 1966. New York, 1965.

Smith, W. H. B., and Smith, Joseph E. *Small Arms of the World.* 7th ed. Harrisburg, Pa., 1964.

Weller, Jac. *Weapons and Tactics: Hastings to Berlin.* New York, 1966.

Part II: VALUABLE CURRENT MILITARY PERIODICALS

Armor. Washington, D.C.

Army. Washington, D.C.

The Army Quarterly and Defence Journal. London.

Au Cosantoir. Dublin.

Globe and Laurel (Royal Marines). Portsmouth, Eng.

Infantry. Fort Benning, Ga.

Marine Corps Gazette. Quantico, Va.

Military Engineer. Washington, D.C.

Military Review. Fort Leavenworth, Kans.

Ordnance. Washington, D.C.

Royal Engineers Journal. Chatham, Kent, Eng.

Royal United Service Institution Journal. London.

Part III: BARGAIN-BASEMENT WAR AND SOUTHEAST ASIA

Browne, Malcolm W. *The New Face of War.* Indianapolis, Ind., 1965.

Burchett, Wilfred G. *Vietnam.* New York, 1965.

Cross, James Eliot. *Conflict in the Shadows.* New York, 1963.

Crozier, Brian. *The Rebels.* Boston, 1960.

Dixon, C. Aubrey, and Heilbrunn, Otto. *Communist Guerrilla Warfare.* New York, 1954.

Dommen, Arthur J. *Conflict in Laos.* New York, 1964.

Draper, Theodore. *Castro's Revolution.* New York, 1962.

Dyer, Murray. *The Weapon on the Wall.* Baltimore, Md., 1959.

Fall, Bernard B. *Street Without Joy.* Harrisburg, Pa., 1965.

————*The Two Vietnams.* New York, 1965.

Forbes, Duncan. *Johnny Gurkha.* London, 1965.

Galula, David. *Counterinsurgency Warfare.* New York, 1965.

Guevara, Che. *Guerrilla Warfare.* New York, 1961.

Halberstam, David. *The Making of a Quagmire.* New York, 1965.
Heilbrunn, Otto. *Partisan Warfare.* New York, 1962.
Heymont, Irving. *Combat Intelligence in Modern Warfare.* Harrisburg, Pa., 1960.
James, Harold, and Sheil-Small, Denis. *The Gurkhas.* London, 1965.
Johnson, John J. *The Role of the Military in Underdeveloped Countries.* Princeton, N.J., 1962.
Keats, John. *They Fought Alone.* New York, 1965.
Laffin, John. *The Face of War.* London, 1963.
Levy, Bert. *Guerrilla Warfare.* Boulder, Colo., 1964.
Mao Tse-tung. *On Guerrilla Warfare.* New York, 1961.
Mecklin, John. *Mission in Torment.* New York, 1965.
Moore, Robin. *The Green Berets.* New York, 1965.
Nasution, Abdul Haris. *Fundamentals of Guerrilla Warfare.* New York, 1965.
Ney, Virgil. *Notes on Guerrilla War.* Washington, D.C., 1961.
Nuechterlein, Donald E. *Thailand and the Struggle for Southeast Asia.* Ithaca, N.Y., 1965.
Orlov, Alexander. *Handbook of Intelligence and Guerrilla Warfare.* Ann Arbor, Mich., 1965.
Overstreet, Harry and Bonaro. *What We Must Know About Communism.* New York, 1965.
Paret, Peter. *French Revolutionary Warfare From Indochina to Algeria.* New York, 1964.
————and Shy, John W. *Guerrillas in the 1960's.* New York, 1962.
Pustay, John S. *Counterinsurgency Warfare.* New York, 1965.
Raskin, Marcus G., and Fall, Bernard B. *The Vietnam Reader.* New York, 1965.
Rigg, Robert B. *Red China's Fighting Hordes.* Harrisburg, Pa., 1952.
Roy, Jules. *The Battle of Dien Bien Phu.* New York, 1965.
Tanham, George K. *Communist Revolutionary Warfare.* New York, 1961.
Teixeira, Bernardo. *The Fabric of Terror.* New York, 1965.
Thayer, Charles W. *Guerrilla.* New York, 1965.
Thompson, Sir Robert. *Defeating Communist Insurgency.* New York, 1966.
Tregaskis, Richard. *Vietnam Diary.* New York, 1963.
Tregonning, K. G. *Malaysia.* Vancouver, B.C., 1965.
Trinquier, Roger. *Modern Warfare.* New York, 1964.
Truong Chinh. *Primer for Revolt.* New York, 1963.
Tully, Andrew. *CIA: The Inside Story.* New York, 1962.

Valeriano, Napoleon D., and Bohannan, Charles T. R. *Counter Guerrilla Operations*. New York, 1962.
Vo Nguyen Giap. *People's War, People's Army*. New York, 1965.
Warner, Denis. *The Last Confucian*. New York, 1963.

Index

||||||||||||||||||||||||||||||||||||||||||||||||||||||||||||||||||||||||||||||||||||||